THE BEAT OF MY DRUM

Babatunde Olatunji

THE BEAT OF MY DRUM

An Autobiography

With **Robert Atkinson**

assisted by **Akinsola Akiwowo**

Foreword by **Joan Baez**

Introduction by **Eric Charry**

Temple University Press ⏢ Philadelphia

Babatunde Olatunji (1927–2003), internationally renowned musician, teacher, and humanitarian, was "teacher in residence" at the Esalen Institute at the time of his death.

Robert Atkinson is Director, Center for the Study of Lives at the University of Southern Maine.

Eric Charry is Associate Professor of Music at Wesleyan University and author of *Mande Music: Traditional and Modern Music of the Maninka and Mandinka of Western Africa.*

Temple University Press
1601 North Broad Street
Philadelphia PA 19122
www.temple.edu/tempress

Text design by: Kate Nichols

♾ The paper used in this publication meets the requirements of the American National Standard for Information Sciences—Permanence of Paper for Printed Library Materials, ANSI Z39.48-1992

Library of Congress Cataloging-in-Publication Data

Olatunji, Babatunde. The beat of my drum: an autobiography / Babatunde Olatunji, with Robert Atkinson, assisted by Akinsola Akiwowo; foreword by Joan Baez; introduction by Eric Charry.
    p. cm.
Discography and videography: p.
Includes bibliographical references and index.
ISBN 1-59213-353-3 (cloth: alk. paper) — ISBN 1-59213-354-1 (pbk.: alk. paper)
1.Olatunji, Babatunde. 2. Drummers (Musicians)—Nigeria—Biography.
I. Atkinson, Robert. II. Title.
ML419.O385A3 2005
786.9'163'092—dc22   2004053726

2 4 6 8 9 7 5 3 1

Contents

PART THREE Passing the Rhythm On

Photograph gallery follows page 122

Foreword

Joan Baez

Baba was my introduction to the world that lies where drumming and the spirit intersect. My son had inhabited that world for a few years, and it was Gabe's relationship with Baba that pulled me in—into the drum circle of healing.

I have danced my way back to health many times to Baba's tapes and CDs and as often as possible have gone to his concerts for the joy of being in his presence. When I jumped onto the stage to dance, he would come out from behind that huge drum and dance with me. He seemed to know who was who even when he was nearly blind.

I suppose everyone who was close to Baba felt that they were special to him. I think they were. So I am not alone when feeling him suddenly in the room when Gabe is playing djembe, or when I'm dancing or walking in the field breathing in the smell of new grass. They say that the spirit is timeless and can be many places at once. Baba must still have a full schedule.

Introduction

Eric Charry

Many, many people whose lives have been touched by the revered cultural ambassador, spiritual guide, and drummer Michael Babatunde Olatunji (1927–2003) have long been waiting for this book, his life story in his own words. Olatunji's monumental legacy spans half a century and has touched vast communities of Americans, whether or not they are aware of it. Well before Alex Haley's *Roots*, James Brown's "Say It Loud," and Stokely Carmichael's "Black Power," Olatunji sparked a deep sense of pride among African Americans by strongly promoting positive images of African culture in the United States. The currents he helped along and also set into motion have flowed in various and unexpected directions—and continue to do so—impacting Americans of all ethnic and racial backgrounds. And he did it through drumming.

In tune with the times, and a formative influence in shaping them, Olatunji's debut album *Drums of Passion* was recorded several months before, and released a few months after, the February 1960 black student sit-ins in Greensboro, North Carolina, which would transform the growing civil rights struggle into a national movement overnight. Both events—one cultural (the release of *Drums of Passion*) and one social (the rapid spread of sit-ins)—permanently changed the consciousness of many Americans and helped jump-start one of the most dynamic and volatile decades in American history. In an era marked by towering figures such as Nkrumah, Kennedy, King, and Malcolm X—not to mention musicians such as Coltrane, Roach, Blakey, Belafonte, and Dylan—Olatunji, who knew all of them, was there and in demand. Through his recording, performing, and teaching (at first with black youth throughout the urban Northeast; much later with more affluent white adults in idyllic retreats), Olatunji built bridges reconnecting, and connecting for the first time, Americans with a lost past, be it a fantastic imagined mythical ancient utopia or a more recent and tangible one violently interrupted over the past several centuries. That past was Africa, a symbol that represented an endless source of pride, roots, spiritual rejuvenation, and powerful healing forces in the face of an increasingly industrialized world.

Olatunji's rich legacy, from *Drums of Passion* to the hand drumming and drum circle movement that has spread around the world, embodies important issues concerning race and representation that may escape many. These issues revolve around the place of Africa in the United States, more specifically, the struggles of African immigrant artists to represent and maintain African culture in this country, the stereotypes that can become mutually reinforced in the process, the struggles of African Americans to incorporate recent African traditions into their lives, and the capacity of Americans to understand, interpret, appropriate, reinterpret, and romanticize images of Africa.

In this introduction, I will try to place Olatunji's career in historical context so that readers may better appreciate his enormous contributions and better understand some of the issues surrounding his legacy. I will also fill in some gaps in the narrative, in particular, those relating to his predecessors, colleagues, and students who have carried on the flame.

Overview of Olatunji's Career in the United States

Olatunji arrived in the United States from Nigeria as a student to attend historically black Morehouse College in Atlanta in 1950, before the era of the modern Civil Rights Movement. He immediately saw the need to address widespread ignorance of Africa, and he took it as his mission to expose and enlighten Americans to the wealth of African culture. His cultural knowledge—as much as could be expected from a 23-year-old groomed, not as a drummer (a skill that is usually kept within certain family lineages in the region where he grew up), but rather to follow in his father's footsteps as a village leader—primarily came from his own Yoruba and Christian upbringing. His leadership skills very quickly became apparent.

After graduating from Morehouse in 1954, he moved to New York to begin graduate school in public administration at New York University. Eventually he had to abandon that path due to lack of funding. By then, already pursuing his calling as a cultural ambassador, he had formed a drum and dance troupe, recruiting talented young African Americans thirsty for the then-rare taste of African culture. In the autumn of 1958 he landed a job where he was featured nightly with the Radio City Music Hall orchestra in a piece titled "African Fantasy." The following year he gained a coveted prize: a recording contract with Columbia Records. The result was five albums released between 1960 and 1966 (see discography). His career took off, and he toured extensively in the early 1960s, playing at clubs like the Village Gate in New York, where in 1961 he shared the bill with John Coltrane and Art Blakey, and performing at the New York World's Fair in 1964.

He realized one dream in 1967, when he opened the Olatunji Center of African Culture at 43 East 125th Street in Harlem. By then, calls for civil rights had shifted to those for black power. As the 1960s and 1970s wore on, he taught extensively in community schools, and he languished as interest in Africa began to fade. His particular conception of African culture was becoming less and less relevant in black communities, and his center eventually had to close in the early 1980s due to lack of financial support.

An encounter with drummer Mickey Hart led to Olatunji and his group opening for the Grateful Dead at a 1985 New Year's Eve concert in Oakland, California (see videography). Olatunji's fortunes changed, and his influence began to spread again as he reached new audiences. He became a venerated father figure and spiritual guru to a predominantly white hand-drumming and drum circle movement that has surged around the world. A 1992 Marin County, California drum circle—one of the largest ever, with about two thousand drummers—organized by Mickey Hart (see Dunham 1992), attested to Olatunji's impact on this recent generation of hand drummers. He lived out his last years (into his mid-seventies) struggling with diabetes and strapped financially, teaching at holistic retreats and institutes such as Omega (in upstate New York) and Esalen (in Big Sur, California), and lending his presence to a variety of events for world peace.

He remains a symbol of African pride in certain circles, as evidenced by his powerful contribution to a recent CD commemorating the life and poetry of the late Tupac Shakur (2000).

Drums of Passion

The impact of Olatunji's first LP, *Drums of Passion*, can hardly be overstated, yet much about it needs to be qualified. Misconceptions abound as to what exactly that album represents, because it is not easily categorized; it slips between the cracks and blurs simplistic us/them and here/there dichotomies. It introduced hundreds of thousands and perhaps millions of Americans to African drumming, yet all the other performers on the album were African Americans or Afro Caribbeans from the New York area. Its songs and rhythms point to Nigeria, yet the performances on it are a hybrid of styles played on hybrid combinations of drums, many from Ghana. It established Olatunji as Africa's most famous drummer, yet he was relatively unknown in his home country as a drummer. And the three other drummers on it, Chief Bey, Taiwo DuVall, and Montego Joe—the ones responsible for much of its percussive power—not to mention the other vocalists, all remain relatively unknown outside New York's African American community.

What was so special about *Drums of Passion*? In short, it was an extraordinary document made by extraordinary people at an extraordinary time. America in the 1950s was slowly being prepared for it, and by the end of the decade the times were ripe, bursting with a new kind of energy waiting to be channeled and unleashed.

As for the musical climate, a Cuban chachachá craze had swept the United States in the mid-1950s, right on the heels of the mambo boom. These styles brought with them Afro-Cuban percussion, which was not too far removed (at least to the American public at the time) from Olatunji's Nigerian sounds and rhythms, some of which had traveled centuries ago to Cuba, where they were fostered in local Yoruba-based drumming. Calypso was also given a big shot in the arm with the launch of Harry Belafonte's successful recording career in the mid-1950s. The Folkways label was issuing close to two dozen albums of music recorded in Africa, including Yoruba drumming from Nigeria. More and more African-based percussion albums (primarily Afro-Cuban) were being recorded in the United States. And in 1955, Ghanaian percussionist Guy Warren began recording a series of albums for major American labels. American appetites for things

Caribbean and African were primed. Regarding politics, the independence of Ghana in March 1957 spawned a tidal wave that resulted in the rapid decolonization of Africa; eighteen more African nations (including Nigeria) had achieved independence by the end of 1960. In social terms, African Americans were making their presence and sense of urgency for civil rights felt in unprecedented and increasingly public ways. There was a growing sense that somehow a lost history had to be restored in order to instill pride and self-worth. Olatunji provided a window onto that history, one that could be widely appreciated by many Americans.

Some records released immediately before *Drums of Passion* offer a taste of the rising musical tide. In the two-and-a-half years between February 1957 (just before Ghana's independence) and August 1959 (when Olatunji began recording *Drums of Passion*), the Blue Note, Columbia, Fantasy, and RCA record labels recorded percussion LPs by Art Blakey (1957a, 1957b, 1959), Tito Puente (1957), Louis "Sabu" Martínez (1957, 1958a, 1958b), Guy Warren (1958), and Mongo Santamaria (1959a, 1959b). Blakey, who around 1947 traveled to Nigeria and Ghana to study and live, was an important force in raising awareness of African-based percussion in the New York jazz scene (see Monson 2000). By the late 1950s, that awareness was blossoming. Ghanaian saxophonist and percussionist Saka Acquaye, who was studying art and leading an ensemble in Philadelphia, released an African highlife and percussion LP on the Elektra label in 1959, sometime before November, when it received a notice in the *New York Times* (Shelton 1959).

In the 1950s, other musicians besides percussionists were also responding to impulses from Africa—if not yet in their music, then in their song titles. Saxophonist Sonny Rollins recorded his composition "Airegin" (Nigeria spelled backwards) with Miles Davis (1954), as did saxophonist John Coltrane with Davis (1956). Pianist Randy Weston recorded his "Zulu" (1955) and "Bantu Suite" (1958). Both trumpeter Thad Jones and Coltrane made recordings of "Dakar" (composed by Teddy Charles) in early 1957. Coltrane also recorded Wilbur Harden and Oscar Cadena's "Dial Africa," and Curtis Fuller's "Gold Coast" and "Tanganyika Strut" in 1958. Keyboardist and bandleader Sun Ra recorded his "Africa" about 1958 or 1959. An African consciousness was on the horizon, starting first with nods to the existence of the continent.

Another reason for the success of *Drums of Passion* was that Olatunji had a cultural mission and knew how to communicate with Americans, both musically and verbally. He crafted a recording that could speak to the growing American thirst for Africa. The liner notes, written by his cousin Akinsola Akiwowo—a sociology professor who came with him as a student to the United States and who would teach at universities here and in Nigeria—invited readers into a new world, one in which Africans were articulate and drums were respected:

> The drum, like many exotic articles, is charged with evocative power. The drum is not only a musical instrument, it is also a sacred object and even the tangible form of divinity. It is endowed with a mysterious power, a sort of life-force, which however, has been incomprehensible to many missionaries and early travelers, who ordered its suppression and influence by forbidding its use. (liner notes to *Drums of Passion*)

Nowadays, with more information available about the wide variety of drums used in Africa (for example, Thieme [1969] describes dozens of drums used just by Yoruba), some might question the generalizing tendency reflected in the above extract. African drums each have their own unique names; they are used as markers of unique cultural identities; they have specific cultural and religious contexts; and various levels of status are attached to them. But in its time, this was perhaps the most effective course for introducing Americans to African drumming. In doing so, it also prepared the ground for Olatunji's universalist message, which became so important in his later years. So did Akiwowo's comments on African cultural traditions, arguing for their universal significance—a necessary step in the face of centuries of European and Euro-American racism. And along the way, he made a case for the importance of drumming, although its links with the term "primitive" (no doubt reflecting contemporaneous thought) would play out differently in black and white communities, as we will see below.

> Babatunde has lit the flood-light upon the universally human significance of primitive mores and customs, of which drumming, singing, and dancing are significant parts. (liner notes to *Drums of Passion*)

Olatunji's vision for *Drums of Passion* included arranging the music for the relatively new LP format. With four pieces per side, each having a clear introduction and other internal sections, this was music crafted specifically for presentation on an album. It was African-based music composed and arranged for an American audience, and it worked. The music is, simply put, compelling. The combination of rhythms from Africa and the Caribbean (via his drummers), the original compositions, and the re-creations of songs Olatunji heard in his youth presented Africa as a living creative force. This was not an ethnographic document of Nigerian drumming traditions, but rather Olatunji as composer and arranger within a broad-based African-oriented drum ensemble with excellent players supporting him.

It also helped that the album was released by Columbia, one of the largest record labels in the world at the time, home to Louis Armstrong, Dave Brubeck, Miles Davis, Duke Ellington, and, soon, a young Bob Dylan (you will read about Dylan's encounter with Olatunji at Columbia's offices). Columbia had the money and visibility to promote the album well, and their efforts paid off, at least at first. Olatunji's later Columbia albums met with much less commercial success, and he was eventually left without a record contract.

In late 1959, after *Drums of Passion* was recorded but before it was released, South African vocalist Miriam Makeba made her American debut, first on television and then with an extended stay at the New York club Village Vanguard. She recorded her first American album in May 1960 with RCA. Three years later, with her third album, she became the first African to break into a Billboard Top Pop Album chart. Not until 1967 would an African break into the Top 40 on Billboard's Pop Singles chart—again it would be Makeba, with "Pata Pata." Very few Africans have done that since, notably, South African Hugh Masekela ("Grazing in the Grass," 1968) and Cameroonian Manu Dibango ("Soul Makossa," 1973). The R&B charts have been only slightly more hospitable to African musicians.

Olatunji's early recording years in New York were spent largely with musicians expert in jazz, and the impact of *Drums of Passion* on them was immediate. The month after it was released, he began a short but intense period of recording as a guest percussionist, with the likes of Herbie Mann, Max Roach, Randy Weston, Kai Winding, and finally Cannonball Adderley (in February 1961). Then there was a drought. He would record more albums for Columbia before being dropped from the label about 1966, but he would rarely record as a guest for the next fifteen years.

African consciousness among musicians continued to rise. John Coltrane composed and recorded "Liberia" (October 1960), "Dahomey Dance" (May 1961), "Africa" for his debut album *Africa/Brass* on the new Impulse label (May and June 1961), and then in June 1962 a homage to his friend and inspiration, "Tunji." Pianist Randy Weston recorded "Uhuru Afrika/Freedom Afrika" (November 1960), vocalist Abbey Lincoln "African Lady" (February 1961), and saxophonist Cannonball Adderley "African Waltz" (February 1961). (See Weinstein [1993] for a study of references to Africa in jazz.)

But the most compelling document of this initial surge was Max Roach and Oscar Brown Jr.'s *We Insist! Freedom Now Suite* (recorded August and September 1960). With a cover photo of three African American men sitting at a restaurant counter, and pieces called "Driva' Man," "Freedom Day," "Prayer/Protest/Peace," "All Africa," and "Tears for Johannesburg," this was perhaps the strongest musical statement on civil rights of its time. Olatunji, along with Taiwo DuVall, played percussion on "All Africa" and "Tears for Johannesburg." Years later, Olatunji would be a guest on Brown's public television show *From Jumpstreet* in the episode "The Source of Soul" (see videography).

Olatunji's presence on *Freedom Now Suite* was indicative of his standing at the time. He did not just represent Africa, he *was* Africa:

ALL AFRICA connotes both the growing interest of American Negroes in the present and future of Africa and also their new pride in Africa's past and their own pre-American heritage. In this collaboration between American jazz drummer, Roach, Afro-Cuban players Mantillo and DuVall, and Nigerian Michael Olatunji, it was Olatunji who set the polyrhythmic directions. It is his voice answering Abbey Lincoln in the introduction. She chants the names of African tribes. In answer, Olatunji relates a saying of each tribe concerning freedom—generally in his own Yoruba dialect. (Nat Hentoff in liner notes to Roach 1961)

Drums of Passion reached a new generation in August 1969 when Santana, just after their triumphant Woodstock appearance, released their self-titled debut album, which included a cover version of Olatunji's "Jin-Go-Lo-Ba." The impact on the millions who bought that album is incalculable. Olatunji continues to reach new generations with *Drums of*

Passion; the original recording was recently released in an expanded CD edition on Columbia.

African Drumming and Dance in the United States

Compared to some Caribbean and South American countries such as Cuba, Haiti, and Brazil, which still have rich and continuous drumming traditions dating back several centuries, African-based drumming in the United States did not survive slavery to any appreciable extent (see Epstein 1977 and Southern 1997). But in the early and mid-twentieth century, two distinct yet interrelated streams met, laying the foundation for a renaissance in African drumming and dance: the immigration of drummers from the Caribbean (especially Cuba) and Africa; and the formation of professional African-based dance troupes beginning about the 1930s.

(There are a number of excellent surveys and detailed studies of the development of African dance on the twentieth-century American stage. See, for example, Emery 1988, Heard 1999, Perpener 2001, Heard and Mussa 2002, and the 2001 video series *Free to Dance*, which includes clips of Dafora, Primus, and Dunham, who are discussed later. There is relatively little, however, that provides comparable coverage for African drumming in the United States.)

In the 1930s, Asadata Dafora Horton (1890–1965), an immigrant from Sierra Leone, laid the foundations for professional African drum and dance troupes in the United States with the public performances of his ballets, including *Kykunkor* (Martin 1934, Long 1989: 48–9, Heard 1999). Dafora's troupe was among the first, if not *the* first, in the United States to feature staged African drumming and dancing, and he performed extensively across the country up through the 1950s. Dafora also prepared the ground for Olatunji's cultural efforts. In 1943 he helped found the African Academy of Arts and Research, whose mission was "to promote cultural bonds between Africa and the United States" (Anonymous 1943). Dafora directed the academy's inaugural event, an African Dance Festival at Carnegie Hall, which was attended by special guests Eleanor Roosevelt and Mary McLeod Bethune. It featured a corps of seven drummers and a young Pearl Primus, who "literally stopped the show" with her dancing (Martin 1943).

Katherine Dunham rose to prominence as a dancer around the same time as Dafora. Beginning in 1936, she traveled throughout the West Indies for a year and a half on a fellowship, preparing for the trip by studying with anthropologist Melville Herskovits. On her return, she began choreographing Afro-Caribbean dances for the stage. Soon after, she formed a dance company and then she opened a dance school in New York. Dunham has become one of the most influential figures in the field, straddling the boundaries between performer, choreographer, teacher, and ethnographer. Pearl Primus, born in Trinidad and raised in New York, made a name for herself as a dancer in the early 1940s. For a year beginning in late 1948, she studied dance traditions in Africa (on the same fellowship that Dunham had), traveling extensively in West and Central Africa. Like Dunham, she was highly influential in the development of African dance in the United States. She is noted for having popularized *Fanga*, which is based on a dance of welcome from Liberia or Sierra Leone. (Possibly, it may have been staged first by Dafora, with whom Primus danced early in her career; see Heard 1999: 181–92).

By the time Olatunji arrived in New York in 1954, Dafora, Dunham, and Primus had already developed an appreciation for staged African and Afro-Caribbean dance with African-based drumming accompaniment. Some of Olatunji's drummers and dancers had worked with Dafora and Primus, and carried with them material and expertise, on which Olatunji then built. For example, the Derby sisters, Merle ("Afuavi") and Joan ("Akwasiba"), contributed *Fanga*, which they had learned from Primus (Derby 1996).

The first American tour of Les Ballets Africains in February 1959 must have inspired Olatunji. So, too, that troupe's "superb" (Martin 1959) jembe (djembe) drummer, Ladji Camara (1923–2004), who would move to the United States in the early 1960s, play with Dunham, and father a jembe movement in New York. Camara would play an important part in Olatunji's fifth and last Columbia LP, *More Drums of Passion*. Les Ballets Africains, formed about 1949 in Paris, became the national ballet of Guinea (in West Africa) at the time of independence (late 1958). Probably, it was the first of the many national ballets and dance ensembles that would be formed throughout Africa in the postcolonial era; certainly, it was a model for other countries. By the time of their tour, Olatunji was enough of a celebrity that a photograph of him mingling at intermission was published in *Bingo*, an African cultural magazine (Anonymous 1959). The previous year, he had gained his first of many notices in the *New York Times* for what would be his calling in life—bringing his cultural message to Americans, in this case Harlem junior high school students (Anonymous 1958a).

The African-based dance troupes and their leader–choreographers were relatively well known; their drummer accompanists were not. Olatunji would change that. Probably the most immediate antecedent to Olatunji was Moses Mianns (also spelled Miannes), a drummer from Nigeria who immigrated to New York in the 1930s. Mianns did not leave much of a public trace outside New York's African drum and dance community, although he performed at the 1934 Chicago World's Fair and also with the Dafora and Primus troupes. His student, the Olatunji accompanist Taiwo DuVall (who has written a short, unpublished biography), credits Mianns with disseminating the ashiko drum, which along with the jembe has become one of the most popular African drums in the United States. Mianns evidently did not bring an ashiko from Nigeria; rather, he had one constructed to his specifications after he arrived in New York. (He can be seen playing ashiko for Primus in Thorpe [1990: 123], and he appears on at least one of the tracks on *The Long Road to Freedom* anthology [Belafonte and others 2001: CD 1]).

Olatunji's three Drums of Passion drummers merit special mention, not only because of their collaborative efforts in shaping his sound, but also because they are key figures in the modern history of African American hand drumming. Thomas "Taiwo" DuVall met Olatunji shortly after the latter's arrival in New York, and they began playing together informally. DuVall, whose grandparents were from Jamaica, had learned from Moses Mianns as well as Alphonse Cimber, a Haitian drummer who performed with Primus in the 1940s (see Long [1989: 92] for a photo of Cimber). An accomplished visual artist as well, DuVall played with Dafora and Primus and taught at Olatunji's Center before moving to Washington, D.C. in the early 1970s. (DuVall can be heard playing solo ashiko on Sule Greg Wilson's 1994 CD.) James Hawthorne "Chief" Bey (1913–2004) learned drumming from Isamae Andrews, who had danced with Dafora and formed her own troupe specializing in East African dances (see photos in Long [1989: 50–3], and Heard and Mussa [2001: 145]). Bey appeared in a Broadway production of *Porgy and Bess* about 1953 and performed for years at the African Room, a club in Manhattan. After *Drums of Passion*, he recorded with Herbie Mann, Art Blakey, and Pharoah Sanders; since the 1970s, he recorded with Hamiet Bluiett, the World Saxophone Quartet, and (most recently) Randy

Weston. He was a venerated elder of the New York African American drumming community (see Chief Bey [1997] for a recent recording, and Associated Press [2004] for his obituary). Roger "Montego Joe" Sanders, who came to New York from Jamaica in his youth, also studied with Mianns and Cimber and performed with the Dunham and Primus dance troupes. He recorded a lot in the 1960s with artists such as Art Blakey, Ted Curson, Roland Kirk, and George Benson, and he released two albums as a leader on the Prestige label (with a young Chick Corea on piano). Montego Joe continues to work at educating schoolchildren (his early work with teens is documented on The Har-You Percussion Group recording), and he hosts a radio show Sunday evenings on WYNE (91.5 FM) in Brooklyn.

Olatunji's Drums of Passion dancers and singers also merit special mention for their great dedication and sacrifice in support of African culture. As Taiwo DuVall recently noted (in a personal communication), the lifestyle of those pursuing African drumming and dance in the 1950s and 1960s was very difficult for all, but especially hard on the women:

They [our women performers] went so far as to wear their hair in a natural bush for performances and then to don a wig to get a job. Then they would be fired when discovered. They were in constant fear of not having a job, a major concern because some had children to feed. My own children were in Catholic School and were being chastised regularly for being the children of an Afro-Cuban drummer . . . There was very little money or no money for what those women had to do, being singers and dancers in our shows, but they kept going! . . . Please give those unsung women some praise.

The arrival of jembe drummer Ladji Camara in New York in the early 1960s, and the opening of Olatunji's Cultural Center in 1967 and Camara's school in the Bronx several years later, further stimulated interest in African culture. It should be noted, however, that for a long time neither Olatunji or Camara enjoyed widespread support outside the small community of culturally aware African Americans actively pursuing this part of their heritage. As Olatunji notes, the support of John Coltrane for his center was crucial. The void left by Coltrane's death just a few months after he inaugurated the second-floor concert space was incalculable. (This turned out to be Coltrane's last recorded concert, recently issued on CD.) Ladji Camara added a new element—jembe-based traditions from the previously underrepresented francophone countries of Guinea and Mali. The highly virtuosic solo jembe drumming and dancing are different from what is practiced in the anglophone countries of Nigeria, Ghana, and Liberia, which had received earlier exposure in the United States.

The generation of predominantly African American hand drummers that came up in the post-Olatunji era in the 1960s and 1970s, and that passed through Olatunji's and Camara's schools and troupes, moved deeper into African traditions. They focused their attention more on jembe-based traditions from Mali and Guinea, and on Senegambian drumming styles, and they formed their own troupes specializing in these repertories. In New York, important milestones were the founding of the Chuck Davis Dance Company in 1968; of the International Afrikan American Ballet, which gelled in the mid-1970s from various formations of students of Camara; and of the Maimouna Keita School of African Dance in 1983 by Senegalese Mari Basse-Wiles and New Yorker Olukose Wiles. Still another was the inauguration of the annual DanceAfrica festival by Chuck Davis in 1977. Other scenes in other cities, such as Washington, D.C. and Boston, were also developing, again stimulated in part by Olatunji's teaching. (See Wilson 1992 for a personal narrative of this era.)

In the post-Olatunji, post-Camara era, African musicians began arriving in the United States, where they established community drum and dance schools and taught at colleges. The pioneer in academia was Ghanaian musicologist J. H. Kwabena Nketia, who in 1958 received a one-year Rockefeller fellowship to study music composition and anthropology at the Julliard School, Columbia University, and Northwestern University. He began teaching summers at UCLA in 1963 and in 1968 he joined the faculty as a professor there (see Djedje and Carter 1989). In Nketia's wake followed a number of Ghanaian drummers, who established Ghanaian drumming at American universities. Among them were Kobla Ladzekpo (Columbia University, 1964; California Institute of the Arts, 1970; UCLA, 1976), Abraham Adzenyah (Wesleyan University, 1969), C. K. Ladzekpo (UC Berkeley, 1973), and Alfred Ladzekpo (California Institute of the Arts). A community of drummers and dancers in Philadelphia, stemming from Ghanaian Saka Acquaye and his student Robert Crowder in the 1950s, has also remained active. In Washington, D.C., Senegalese jeli/griot Djimo Kouyate (1946–2004), who established Memory of African Culture in 1983, trained generations of drummers and dancers. So has Ghanaian Yacub Addy, who established Odadaa! in 1982 (see videography).

Today, weekly or even daily African drumming and dance classes taught by Africans from all over the continent can be found in dozens, if not hundreds, of cities around the world (see webography for some listings). Study tours to Africa lasting several weeks are also quite common. Thousands, perhaps even tens of thousands of drums from Africa—especially the ubiquitous jembe—are exported around the world each year. And American drum manufacturers are selling similar numbers of African-style drums made from synthetic materials.

Part of Olatunji's great legacy is his work in stimulating African cultural awareness in the United States, work that belongs to these broader currents, which have been in motion since at least the 1930s.

Hand Drumming and Drum Circles

It is only in the past several decades that African-based hand drumming has separated from dance and taken on a life of its own in the form of drum circles—a uniquely American development, with little African precedent, wherein all present play some kind of percussion instrument. Olatunji had a major hand in this movement, indirectly at first through the influence of *Drums of Passion*, and more directly in his later years.

In the early 1980s, on his return to New York after a brief and disappointing foray into Nigerian politics, faced with financial difficulties and diminishing opportunities, Olatunji must have been strongly attracted to the West Coast drumming retreats and workshops to which his longtime student Gordy Ryan then introduced him. Olatunji thrived in this new setting in which he was accorded status as an elder statesman to a whole new constituency. Meeting Arthur Hull and Mickey Hart, who had been deeply affected by *Drums of Passion* and who were developing their own drum circle philosophies in Santa Cruz and the San Francisco Bay area, respectively, further opened the door to new opportunities to spread his message. A worldwide hand drumming and drum circle movement soon followed.

Aided by appearances with The Grateful Dead that enabled him to reach large numbers of young white Americans beginning in late 1985, Olatunji's drumming mission found a different kind of audience. Nurtured on a jam band aesthetic (and, as Hart suggests, on Dead Head parking lot percussion jam sessions stemming from the 1970s), this crowd was less interested in the cultural background of African drumming and more attracted to the euphoria of a group experience. In such an atmosphere, the uprooting of African-style drumming from its cultural grounding was inevitable.

Olatunji's developing doctrine of communal drumming, influenced in part by Americanized notions of peace, love, spiritual enlightenment, and social action, found resonance in the 1980s and 1990s among white youth and adults searching for alternative means of expression and spiritual fulfillment. It is ironic, though, that his teaching, rooted as it was in fostering appreciation for the beauty of African culture, would spawn the notion of non–"culturally specific," non–"ethnically specific" rhythms and drum circles (Hull 1998: 12, 25–26). Yet it is also not surprising, given that his own drumming drew from a variety of sources, the result of which was hybrid rhythms and techniques not steeped in any one tradition.

As defined by Mickey Hart (2004),

the Drum Circle is a huge jam session. The ultimate goal is not precise rhythmic articulation or perfection of patterned structure, but the ability to entrain and reach the state of a group mind. It is built on cooperation in the groove, but with little reference to any classic styles. So this is a work in constant progress, a phenomenon of the new rhythm culture emerging here in the West.

This path, explored and expanded from the beaches of California to large corporation team-building workshops by Arthur Hull and others, led to a commercialization of hand drumming that involved Remo Corporation, a California-based manufacturer of drum accessories. In the early 1990s, Remo expanded its world percussion line to include jembes, ashikos, and dunduns (or junjuns), three of the main drums used by Olatunji. Made of recycled wood-based shells and synthetic fiber heads, these drums were easy for amateurs to maintain and they stood up to changes in weather. They also appealed to environmentally conscious consumers, especially in light of the fragile ecosystem of the West African sahel and savanna, which could ill afford to supply America with drums. This development facilitated Olatunji's dream of a drum in every household, and he eventually endorsed Remo drums. Even so, he must have had mixed feelings about their synthetic, factory-produced nature; his philosophy of the healing power of drums was based on the trinity of spirits inherent in the tree and the animal skin that make up the drum and the human player who brings it to life (see Chapter 1).

This drum circle phenomenon is somewhat distant from the pursuits of many of the African American drummers associated with Olatunji, who use drumming to, among other things, instill self-respect, cultural pride, and discipline among youth. One early document of such activity is Montego Joe's recording of the New York African American and Puerto Rican teenagers he taught under the auspices of the antipoverty agency Harlem Youth Opportunities Act (Haryou Act; see Har-You Percussion Group in the discography). Some of Olatunji's Euro-American students have also pursued this path, working to curb urban violence through community drumming. Nonprofessional drumming resembling drum circles does have a history in predominantly black communities, however. For example, the Congo Square drummers have been playing in what is called Drummer's Grove in Prospect Park, Brooklyn, since the late 1960s (see Choi [2005] and webography). But in this and other similar cases, there is a spiritual undercurrent of paying homage to ancestors and restoring severed historical and cultural connections (with a Yoruba tinge). This is absent in the other varieties of drum circles.

The relationship between hand drumming in black communities and the more widespread drum circle movement is one of the more difficult aspects of Olatunji's career to understand, because there would appear to be an irreconcilable tension here. Drum circles are based on the partial appropriation and transformation (indeed, simplification) of African-based drumming, to the point of obscuring cultural or racial origins. Their appeal to such a broad, predominantly white, population relies on a mystical universal consciousness— or perhaps a belief in the drum circle's healing powers—based not in African experience but rather in American imaginings of a global utopia. The very nature of the drum circle's all-inclusive philosophy (anyone can do it) precludes getting too close to African rhythms, which are typically performed in Africa by highly trained individuals (not everyone can do it). To many Americans, the complexity of these rhythms would present an insurmountable barrier.

It should not be difficult to see how some African traditionalists (and their American students) would be concerned about appropriation of their rhythms and instruments, many of which have profound cultural and religious meaning. In certain contexts, the misuse of drums can have serious consequences. For example, in Nigeria,

> nearly every Yoruba Òrìsà [deity] also has its own special drum ensemble . . . Drums also provide the medium through which the

worshippers are in constant ecstatic communication and communion
with their Gods and gods . . . The devotees of the Òrìsà do not
use drums indiscriminately. Appropriate drums must be used for
particular Òrìsà, otherwise they will incur the wrath of their tutelary
[guardian] deity. (Adegbite 1988: 15, 16)

The rhythms must be played properly too, hence the need for extended
specialized training. (For insight into the great depth and meaning of one
widespread Yoruba drumming tradition, see Euba 1990.) Although some
drums, such as the jembe, have more secular associations, perceptions
of cultural appropriation can be just as serious. This is exacerbated by the
enormous disparities in economic and political power between Africa and
America. Although some Africans may feel pride in seeing their drums used
around the world, they may also object to the export and transformation of
their culture with no tangible benefit to them or their compatriots. Olatunji's
Voices of Africa project (see chapter 9) was directly aimed at addressing
this problem, and it must have been a great disappointment to him that he was
not able to realize such an ambitious and unprecedented project.

It must also have been a great dilemma for Olatunji in his later years
that the drum circle and hand drumming communities in which he moved
had other uses for the African culture that he represented. His work during
his first three decades in the United States was with predominantly black
communities interested not only in past connections, but also in forging
new ones firmly rooted in Africa. Witnessing lost traditions being rebuilt,
only to see them transformed by others (predominantly white) using a
rhetoric of universal rhythm and spirituality, one that was devoid of
meaningful connections to Africa, may not have sat very well with some of
Olatunji's early students and troupe members and colleagues, and perhaps
even with Olatunji himself in certain cases.

Not being born into a drumming lineage may have been an advantage
for Olatunji. Not being bound to the strictures of any one tradition, he
could shape a generic universal vision of African drumming for American
students and audiences, one based on a more secular notion of spirit rather
than on specific religious practices. This may help us understand critiques
by some Africans and Americans aimed at his background as a percussionist
and his role as popularizer of African drumming. A universal philosophy of
peace and love, rooted in Africa yet malleable enough to be shaped by
Americans for their own needs, was his solution.

Africans and Rhythm

The central place of rhythm and drumming in Olatunji's portrayal of African life merits some reflection because it ties into larger issues regarding representations of Africa. The view he presents in the first sentence of his first chapter ("I'm the drum, You're the drum, We're the drum") can be a double-edged sword. On the one hand, it can serve to forefront a unique artistic sensibility. The inventiveness with which Africans have put their minds to exploring and celebrating sound and movement in the form of music and dance, and their cultivation of the art of percussion, can be a source of wonder and awe for all the world to appreciate. Yet this view can also serve to stereotype and assign a limited essence to a large mass of humankind, one that has suffered greatly from such characterizations of their humanity.

European colonial-era writers, African anticolonialists (such as Léopold Senghor, a champion of the Négritude movement that began in the late 1930s), and African American writers (such as Langston Hughes, whose early writing inspired Senghor) have all referenced the primacy of drums, drumming, and dance in Africa, emphasizing the distinctiveness of Africans and their culture. In response to a dominant European philosophical tradition that privileges the mind over the body, African writers and others of African descent have valorized the visceral and emotional aspects of their cultures. But valorizing these aspects to the point of considering them as defining marks of African-ness—and yielding rational thought as a mark of European-ness—in effect endorses the mind/body dichotomy and reinforces racial stereotypes that deny the full range of human potentiality to all peoples. As Nigerian writer Wole Soyinka, a critic of negritude, has noted,

> To Descartes' 'I think, therefore, I am,' they [negritude writers] responded on behalf of the black man: 'I feel, therefore I am.' Rationalism is essentially European, they claimed; the black man is emotive and intuitive. He is not a man of technology, but a man of the dance, of rhythm and song.
>
> This simplified view of the black man's world did not pass without its challengers however, and even the early Negritudinists soon found themselves compelled to begin to modify their position. (Soyinka 1988: 180)

This Cartesian philosophical legacy, which also devalued bodily expression for people of European descent, is one reason why Euro-Americans are today so drawn to African drumming experiences. Assured of the capacity (as a group of people) for rational thought and reason, they can enter into African drumming from a position of privilege (self-deprecating comments about being rhythmically challenged notwithstanding). The stakes are higher, however, for people of African descent, whose intellectual capacities have a long history of being denied in the Eurocentric world. This may help explain the difficulties Olatunji encountered in garnering widespread support in black communities. His conception of rhythm in Africa may not have been able to combat the stigma attached to African drumming, except among those most culturally curious. At the same time, his later conception of a universal rhythmic impulse may have been too generic to interest those seeking historical connections with their past.

To be sure, Olatunji's message of universal rhythmic expression which can be tapped into by all was intended to foster the notion of a single family of humanity—a family not troubled by racial essentialisms. In a world marked by racism and gross inequities in access to economic and political resources, however, this is no mean feat. But perhaps this is his most enduring message.

Conclusion

Few involved with hand drumming in the United States have not been touched in some way by Baba, as he was called by those who knew him. He instilled pride in generations of African Americans; he stimulated a popular renaissance in African drumming and dance in the United States; he provided cultural education for black youth across the country; he introduced mainstream America to African drumming; and he spread worldwide messages of peace and love through drumming. These are just some of the more resounding aspects of Olatunji's legacy, which has touched so many of us.

Unfortunately, he was unable to see the publication of his autobiography. Baba Olatunji passed away on Sunday, April 6, 2003, at the age of seventy-six, in California, after a long battle with diabetes. His obituary notices were published in major newspapers around the world (for example, Pareles 2003; and National Public Radio took note with a special tribute [see Webography]). The testimonials of his students the world over speak to his lasting presence.

Acknowledgments

I have benefited greatly from speaking with the following people over the past several months about Olatunji and his legacy, and I would like to thank them here for their generosity: Akin Akiwowo, Ernest Brown, Neil Clarke, Taiwo DuVall, Mickey Hart, Arthur Hull, Fred Lieberman, Montego Joe, Gordy Ryan, and Sule Greg Wilson. Any shortcomings of interpretation are my own.

Bibliography

Adegbite, Ademola. 1988. "The Drum and Its Role in Yoruba Religion." *Journal of Religion in Africa* 18: 15–26.

Anonymous. 1943. "African Academy Set Up." *New York Times* (November 14): 15.

———. 1958a. "Jungle Drum Beats Out a Cultural Message for Pupils." *New York Times* (May 30): 9.

———. 1958b. "Nigerian Student Plays Drums Here. Ph.D. Candidate at N.Y.U. Brings African Folk Songs to Music Hall Stage." *New York Times* (October 19): 128.

———. 1959. "Triomphe à New York de Ballets Africains de Keita Fodeba." *Bingo* 77: 18–20.

Associated Press. 2004. "Chief Bey, 91, Jazz Drummer, Is Dead." *New York Times* (April 13, late edition): C15.

Choi, Yoonjah. 2005. *Understanding American Drumming Circles: Case Studies of Congo Square in New York and Earth Drum Council in Boston.* M.A. thesis, Wesleyan University.

Derby, Merle Afida. 1996. "Drumming It Up for Africa: Michael Babatunde Olatunji, The Drumming Virtuoso." *Traditions* 2(3): 10–11.

Dietz, Betty Warner, and Michael Babatunde Olatunji. 1965. *Musical Instruments of Africa: Their Nature, Use, and Place in the Life of a Deeply Musical People.* New York: John Day.

Djedje, Jacqueline Cogdell, and William G. Carter. 1989. "J.H. Kwabena Nketia: A Biobibliographical Portrait." In Cogdell and Carter (eds.), *African Musicology: Current Trends*, vol. 1. Los Angeles: African Studies Center, UCLA, 3–29.

Donaldson, Bill. 2002. "Chief Bey Interview." *Cadence* 28 (May): 18–21.

Dunham, Elisabeth. 1992. "Grateful Dead Drummer Brings Healing Beat to Elderly." *Los Angeles Daily News* (March 9, final edition): N3.

DuVall, Taiwo. N.d. "Ashiko Drumming in America." Unpublished article. Clinton, MD. (duvall@erols.com)

Emery, Lynne Fauley. 1988. *Black Dance: From 1619 to Today.* 2nd, rev. ed. Princeton: Princeton Book Company.

Epstein, Dena. 1977. *Sinful Tunes and Spirituals: Black Folk Music to the Civil War.* Urbana: University of Illinois Press.

Euba, Akin. 1990. *Yoruba Drumming: The Dùndún Tradition.* Bayreuth: E. Breitinger/ Bayreuth University.

Hart, Mickey. 1990. *Drumming at the Edge of Magic: A Journey into the Spirit of Percussion*. With Jay Stevens and Fredric Lieberman. San Francisco: Harper San Francisco.

———. 1991. "Transcript of Testimony before the U.S. Senate Committee on Aging." August. www.mickeyhart.net/Pages/senspeech.html.

———. 2004. "Drum Circles Defined: What Is a Drum Circle." www.remo.com/drumcircles.

Heard, Marcia E. 1999. *Asadata Dafora: African Concert Dance Traditions in American Concert Dance*. Ph.D. dissertation, New York University.

Heard, Marcia E., and Mansa K. Mussa. 2002. "African Dance in New York City." In Thomas F. DeFrantz (ed.), *Dancing Many Drums: Excavations in African American Dance*. Madison, WI: University of Wisconsin Press, 143–67.

Hull, Arthur. 1998. *Drum Circle Spirit: Facilitating Human Potential Through Rhythm*. Edited by Angela Marie. Reno, NV: White Cliffs Media.

———. 2003. "Babatunde Olatunji: Changing the World One Beat at a Time." *Drum!* 12(5) (August/September): 68, 70–71, 73, 75, 79, 81.

Long, Richard A. 1989. *The Black Tradition in American Dance*. Photographs selected and annotated by Joe Nash. New York: Rizzoli.

Martin, John. 1934. "Native Cast Gives an African 'Opera.'" *New York Times* (May 9): 23.

———. 1943. "African Dancers in Festival Here. Mrs. Roosevelt, a Sponsor, Speaks at Inauguration of Academy of Arts." *New York Times* (December 14): 30.

———. 1959. "Dance: Africana. Lively and Handsome 'Ballet' Arrives From the Dark Continent via Paris." *New York Times* (February 22): X10.

Monson, Ingrid. 2000. "Art Blakey's African Diaspora." In Monson (ed.), *The African Diaspora: A Musical Perspective*. New York: Garland, 329–52.

Olatunji, Babatunde, with Doug LeBow (transcriber and editor). 1993. *Drums of Passion Songbook: The Songs of Babatunde Olatunji*. New York: Olatunji Music.

Pareles, Jon. 2003. "Babatunde Olatunji, Drummer, 76, Dies; Brought Power of African Music to U.S." *New York Times* (April 9, late edition): D8.

Perpener, John O. 2001. *African-American Concert Dance: The Harlem Renaissance and Beyond*. Urbana: University of Illinois Press.

Shelton, Robert. 1959. "Shifting Tides in African Music: Disks Show the Way Tribal Styles are Changing in Modern Times." *New York Times* (November 1): X19.

Southern, Eileen. 1997. *The Music of Black Americans: A History*. 3rd ed. New York: Norton.

Soyinka, Wole. 1988. "Cross Currents: The 'New African' after Cultural Encounters." In Wole Soyinka, *Art, Dialogue, and Outrage: Essays on Literature and Culture*. New York: Pantheon, 179–89. Chapter originally published in 1982.

Stewart, Gary. 1992. *Breakout: Profiles in African Rhythm*. Chicago: University of Chicago Press.

Sunkett, Mark. 1995. *Mandiani Drum and Dance: Djimbe Performance and Black Aesthetics from Africa to the New World*. Tempe, AZ: White Cliffs Media.

Thieme, Darius. 1969. *A Descriptive Catalog of Yoruba Musical Instruments*. Ph.D. dissertation, Catholic University of America.

Thorpe, Edward. 1990. *Black Dance*. Woodstock, NY: Overlook Press.

US Committee for UNICEF. 1958? *Hi Neighbor: Fun and Folklore from Five Countries being assisted by the United Nations Children's Fund*. Book 3 (Nigeria, Ethiopia, Greece, Chile, Thailand). New York: United States Committee for UNICEF.

Warren, Guy. 1962. *I Have a Story to Tell*. Accra: Guinea Press.

Weinstein, Norman C. 1993. *A Night in Tunisia: Imaginings of Africa in Jazz*. New York: Limelight.

Williams, B. Michael. 2001. "2001 PAS Hall of Fame: Babatunde Olatunji." *Percussive Notes* 39(4): 14–15. www.pas.org/About/HOF/olatunji.cfm.

Wilson, Sule Greg. 1992. *The Drummer's Path: Moving the Spirit with Ritual and Traditional Drumming*. Rochester, VT: Destiny.

Discography/Videography/Webography

Discography

OLATUNJI AS LEADER

1960. *Drums of Passion*. Recorded August and October 1959; released April 1960. Columbia, CS 8210. Expanded edition, 2002, Columbia/Legacy CK 66011.

1961. *Zungo! Afro-percussion*. Recorded January and February 1961; released July 1961. Columbia, CS 8234.

1962. *Flaming Drums!* Recorded February and April 1962; released October 1962. Columbia, CS 8666.

1963. *High Life!* Recorded December 1962; released June 1963. Columbia, CS 8796.

1966. *More Drums of Passion*. Recorded February 1966; released 1966. Columbia, CS 9307.

1969? *Drums, Drums, Drums*. Roulette, SR-25274/RSD-407; SR 42063.

1973. *Soul Makossa*. Paramount, PAS 6061.

1986. *Dance to the Beat of My Drum*. Recorded January 1986. Blue Heron, BLU 706. Reissued 1989, as *Drums of Passion: The Beat*, Rykodisc, RCD 10107. ("Se Eni A Fe L'Amo-Kere Kere" reissued on Santana, 1995.)

1988. *Drums of Passion: The Invocation*. Recorded January 1986. Rykodisc, RCD 10102. ("Ajaja" reissued on *The Big Bang*, 1994; "Orere" reissued on *Mondo Beat*, 1999.)

1993. *Drums of Passion: Celebrate Freedom, Justice, and Peace*. Olatunji Music.

1994. *Drums of Passions and More*. 4 CDs. Bear Family Records, BCD 15 747. Reissue of 1960, 1961, 1962, 1963, and 1966.

1997. *Love Drum Talk*. Chesky, WO160.

2003. *Healing Session*. Recorded 1992. Narada, 93646.

OLATUNJI APPEARS ON

US Committee for UNICEF. 1960? *Hi Neighbor (record 3): Songs and Dances from Chile, Greece, Ethiopia, Nigeria, and Thailand*. With one song performed by Olatunji and Akiwowo recorded about 1958. US Committee for UNICEF.

Mann, Herbie. 1960a. *Flute, Brass, Vibes and Percussion*. Recorded May and July 1960. Verve, V6-8392.

————. 1960b. *The Common Ground*. Recorded August 1960. Atlantic, 1343.

Roach, Max. 1961. *We Insist! Freedom Now Suite*. Recorded September 1960. Candid, CJS9002.

Weston, Randy. 1961. *Uhuru Afrika/Freedom Africa*. Recorded November 1960. Roulette, R65001. Reissued 1994, on *Uhuru Afrika/Highlife*, Capitol Records/Roulette Jazz, CDP 7945102.

Winding, Kai. 1961. *The Incredible Kai Winding Trombones*. Recorded November 1960. Impulse, AS-3.

Jones, Quincy. 1961. *Around the World*. Recorded January and February 1961. Mercury, 2014.

Adderley, Cannonball (Julian). 1961. *African Waltz*. Recorded February 1961. Riverside, RLP 12-377.

Weston, Randy. 1963. *African Highlife and Music of the New African Nations*. Recorded April 1963. Colpix, CP-456. Reissued 1994, on *Uhuru Afrika/Highlife*, Capitol Records/Roulette Jazz, CDP 7945102.

Ellis, Pee Wee. 1977. *Home in the Country*. Savoy, SJL 3301.

Lyle, Bobby. 1977. *The Genie*. Capitol, ST11627.

Silver, Horace. 1978. *Silver 'n Percussion*. Blue Note, BN-LA-853.

Juvet, Patrick. 1978. *Patrick Juvet*. Casablanca, 7107.

White, Michael. 1978. *The X Factor*. Elektra, 138.

Havens, Richie. 1980. *Connections*. Elektra, 242.

Forman, Bruce. 1981. *River Journey*. Muse, MR5251.

Taj Mahal. 1986. *Taj*. Gramavision, 18-8611-2.

Stetasonic. 1987. *A.F.R.I.C.A.* With Jesse Jackson. Tommy Boy, TB 899. Reissued 1999 on *Chuck D Presents: Louder Than a Bomb*, Rhino, R2-75873.

Sears, Pete. 1988. *Watchfire*. Redwood, RRCD 8806.

Shades of Jade. 1989. *Afro-Latin Jazz and Salsa*. Absolute Pitch, CD 5545-2.

New York Voices. 1990. *Hearts of Fire*. GRP, GRD 9653.

Hart, Mickey. 1990. *At the Edge*. Recorded 1987–90. Rykodisc, RCD 10124.

In the Blood. 1990. *In the Blood* [soundtrack]. Rykodisc, 20174.

Cimorosi, Tony. 1990. *NY International*. Epoch Records.

Hart, Mickey, and others. 1991. *Planet Drum*. Recorded 1986 and 1991. Rykodisc, RCD 10206.

Wonder, Stevie. 1991. *Jungle Fever* [soundtrack]. Motown, 6291.

Lincoln, Abbey. 1992. *Devil's Got Your Tongue*. Verve, 314 513 574-2.

Moreira, Airto. 1992. *The Other Side of This*. Rykodisc, RCD 10207.

Various. 1993. *Peace Is the World Smiling: A Peace Anthology for Families*. Warner Bros., 42507.

Hayes, Bradford. 1994. *Our Fathers*. Intensity Records.

The Big Bang. 1994. *The Big Bang: In the Beginning Was the Drum*. 3 CDs. Produced by Angel Romero. Ellipsis Arts, ELLI CD 3400 (3401 to 03).

Santana, Carlos. 1995. *Dance of the Rainbow Serpent*. 3 CDs. Columbia Legacy, C3K 64605.

Hart, Mickey. 1996. *Mickey Hart's Mystery Box*. Rykodisc, RCD 10338.

Hart, Mickey, and Planet Drum. 1998. *Supralingua*. Rykodisc, RCD 10396.

Morley. 1998. *Sun Machine*. Sony, 68703.

Mondo Beat. 1998. *Mondo Beat: Masters of Percussion*. Narada, 72438-45788-2-4.

Claussell, Joe. 1999. *Language*. Ibadan, 023.

Shakur, Tupac. 2000. *The Rose That Grew from Concrete*. Volume 1. Amaru/ Interscope, 0694908132.

OTHER DISC REFERENCES

Acquaye, Saka. 1959. *Gold Coast Saturday Night*. Elektra, 7167. Reissued 1969 as *Voices of Africa: High-life and Other Popular Music*, Nonesuch, H72026, and 2002, Nonesuch 79701-2.

Bascom, William (recordings and notes). 1953. *Drums of the Yoruba of Nigeria*. Folkways, FE 4441.

Belafonte, Harry, David Belafonte, Albert C. Pryor, and Leonard de Paur (producers). 2001. *The Long Road to Freedom: An Anthology of Black Music*. Recorded between 1961–71. Buddah/BMG, 7446599756.

Bey, Chief. 1997. *Chief Bey and Ile Omo Olofi (Children of the House of God)*. Mapleshade, 5132.

Blakey, Art. 1957a. *Drum Suite*. Recorded February 1957. Columbia, COL 1002.

———. 1957b. *Orgy in Rhythm*. vols. 1 and 2. Recorded March 1957. Blue Note, BLP 1554 and 1555.

———. 1959. *Holiday for Skins*. vols. 1 and 2. Recorded November 1958. Blue Note, BLP 4004 and 4005.

———. 1962. *The African Beat*. Recorded January 1962. Blue Note, BST 84097.

Camara, Ladji. 1975. *Africa, New York*. Recorded 1975. Lyrichord, LYRCD 7345.

———. 197?. *Les ballets africains de Papa Ladji Camara*. Lyrichord, LYRCD 7419.

Coltrane, John. 2001. *The Olatunji Concert: The Last Live Recording*. Recorded April 1967 at the Olatunji Center of African Culture. Impulse, 314589120-2.

Har-You Percussion Group. 1995. *The Har-You Percussion Group*. Recorded 1969. Cubop, CBCD 002.

Makeba, Miriam. 1960. *Miriam Makeba*. Recorded May 1960. RCA Victor, LSP 2267.

———. 1963. *The World of Miriam Makeba*. RCA Victor, 2750.

Martínez, Louis "Sabu." 1957. *Palo Congo*. Recorded April 1957. Blue Note, BLP 1561.

———. 1958a. *Safari with Sabu*. Recorded June 1957. RCA, VIK LX-1122.

———. 1958b. *Sorcery!* Columbia, WL 101.

Montego Joe (Roger Sanders). 1964. *¡Arriba! Con Montego Joe*. Recorded May 1964. Prestige, 7336.

———. 1965. *Wild and Warm*. Recorded May 1965. Prestige, 7413.

Puente, Tito. 1957. *Top Percussion*. RCA, 3264.

Santamaria, Mongo. 1959a. *Yambu*. Recorded December 1958. Fantasy, 8012.

———. 1959b. *Mongo*. Recorded May 1959. Fantasy, 8032.

———. 1960a. *Our Man in Havana*. Recorded in Havana early 1960. Fantasy, 8045.

———. 1960b. *Bembé*. Recorded in Havana early 1960. Fantasy, 8055.

Santana. 1969. *Santana*. Columbia, 9781.

Warren, Guy. 1955. *Africa Speaks—America Answers!* (With the Red Saunders Orchestra under the direction of Gene Esposito.) Recorded early 1955. Decca, DL8446.

————. 1958. *Themes for African Drums*. (With Chief Bey.) Recorded May 1958; released March 1959. RCA Victor, LPS 1864.

————. 1962. *African Rhythms: The Exciting Soundz of Guy Warren and His Talking Drums*. Recorded October 1961. Decca, DL 4243.

Wilson, Sule Greg. 1994. *The Drummer's Path: African and Diaspora Percussive Music*. Destiny. ISBN 0-89281-502-7.

Videography

OLATUNJI AS LEADER

1986. *Olatunji and his Drums of Passion: The Dynamic Dance Music of Babatunde Olatunji, Recorded "Live" at the Oakland Coliseum on New Year's Eve, 1985*. Video Artists International, VAI 69046.

1993. *African Drumming*. Brattleboro, VT: Interworld Music Associates.

OLATUNJI WITH DALLIE

1990. *Africa Calls Its Drums & Musical Instruments*. New York: Carousel Film & Video.

OLATUNJI APPEARS IN

WKYC-TV (Cleveland). 1968. *Montage: Search for Blackness*. 4/27/1968. Produced and directed by Bill Leonard.

CBS-TV (New York). 1969. *Harlem Festival*. Produced and directed by Hal Tulchin.

Jackson, Billy (producer, director). 1971. *We Are Universal*. (Black leaders, including Olatunji, discuss the lack of recognition and the roles of Blacks in the areas of the arts.) Columbus, OH: National Black Programming Consortium. Nommo Productions.

WCAU-TV (Philadelphia). 1971. *African Religions and Ritual Dances*. Directed by Dick Oanjolele. Philadelphia: WCAU-TV, and New York: Carousel Films. Produced in cooperation with the University Museum, Philadelphia and the Olatunji Center of African Culture.

WETA-TV (Washington, DC). 1979. *From Jumpstreet, with Oscar Brown, Jr.: The Source of Soul*. Produced and directed by Robert Kaiser.

WNEW-TV (New York). 1981. *Black News*. Weekly broadcast for 1/17/81. Brief interview with Babatunde Olatunji. Produced by Robert E. Martin, directed by Chet Lishawa.

Across Borders Productions. 1997. *Spirit of the Drum*. San Diego, CA: Media Guild.

PBS/BET. 1997. *Denyce Graves: A Cathedral Christmas from Washington, D.C.* Carmen Productions with Black Entertainment Television, and PBS. Produced and directed by Bill Cosel. Alexandria, VA: PBS Home Video.

Meeske, Brent (director). 2000. *The End of the Road: The Final Tour*. The Grateful Dead's last tour in 1995. Slow Loris Films.

OTHER

Dornfeld, Barry, and Tom Rankin (directors and producers), and Yacub Addy (artistic director). 1985. *Dance Like a River. Odadaa! Drumming and Dancing in the U.S.* Washington, DC: Oboade Institute of African Culture.

Levy, Madison D., and Adam Zucker (producers, directors, writers). 2001. *Free to Dance*. 3 vols. National Black Programming Consortium; Corporation for Public Broadcasting; and WNET 13 New York.

Webography

www.olatunjimusic.com
www.babaolatunji.com
www.drums.org/djembefaq/baba_files.htm
www.npr.org/ (search for Olatunji, 4/9/03 and 4/12/03)
www.furious.com/perfect/olatunji.html (Interview with Jason Gross, 2000)
www.drumpath.net/tribute.html
www.dinizulu.org
www.maimounakeita.com
www.memoryofafricanculture.org
www.rpi.edu/~addyy
www.prospectpark.org (Congo Square drummers in Drummer's Grove in Prospect Park, Brooklyn)
www.remo.com/drumcircles (Drum Circles Defined)

PART ONE

Learning the Rhythm

The Spirit of Drumming

"I'm the drum, You're the drum, We're the drum."

Where I come from, we say that rhythm is the soul of life. The whole universe revolves in rhythm. When we get out of rhythm, that's when we get into trouble. We are in rhythm or we are not in rhythm—the rhythm of life, the rhythm of relationships. Because of its rhythmic nature, because it helps keep us in rhythm, the drum, next to the human voice, is our most important, most sacred instrument.

I've thought about the healing power of the drum for many years, and I have come to a philosophy of the drum that says it is a very special kind of trinity. First, the tree, which is used for the body of the drum, contains a living spirit. Great care is taken to make sure that the wood of the drum is alive. In many parts of the world, especially in Africa, prayers are said, songs are sung, rituals are performed before a tree is cut down. It is necessary to recognize that there is a spirit in the wood that makes the tree grow so deep, spreading its roots far and wide. Second, there is a spirit in the animal whose skin is used for the drum, be it that of a goat, a cow, a deer, or a buffalo. The skin contains a spirit that is still alive. And when you join these two spirits together with the spirit of the person playing the drum, the result is a trinity, an irresistible force, a balance that gives the drum its healing power.

Probably the most important aspect of the drum is its use as a healing instrument. But how do the spirit of the wood and the spirit of the skin plus the spirit of the person playing it make the healing process happen? The person playing the drum does everything he does in rhythm. Every cell in that person's body is in constant frequency, in constant rhythm, because there is not a single thing we do that we don't do in rhythm. If you are in rhythm, and if every cell of your body is in rhythm, the sound that hits that cell must be affected one way or another. It is a tantalizing rhythmic pattern, a sound that is evocative and powerful and vigorous. The sound becomes an energizer of all the cells in our body. It energizes our lungs, our heart, everything in our body.

The spirit of the drum lies in knowing how to play what can be evocative, what is powerful enough to make people stop and listen, to make people feel something that they cannot find the words to describe, but that they can experience.

This is what I began to learn when I listened to a lot of the master drummers when I was growing up. This is what I was able to capture along the way to become what I have become today. I remember that certain drummers got across a message, a sound, a feeling, that others didn't. I could see it in their faces, and I could feel it in their reactions, in their involvement with the audience while they played. I noticed that in that particular moment in time, they were completely immersed in what they were doing. They saw you, but they didn't see you. The master drummers are those drummers who have made it their life work to become the best drummer possible. They have learned all the drumming traditions from other master drummers before them, and they have accepted the responsibility to pass on their knowledge of drumming to those who come after them.

In Yoruba culture, music permeates every aspect of our lives. I heard the drum while I was in my mother's womb. I woke up every day to the beat of the drum. I grew up hearing the drummers heralding the dawn of each day in front of the chief's compound, serenading shoppers in the marketplace, playing at name-giving ceremonies.

Drumming, dancing, and singing were all part of life. I listened as the beat of the drum announced every celebration, from the birth of a new baby, to the rite-of-passage ceremonies of the young men and young women of the village, to the engagement of a young and beautiful girl in the neighborhood, to, finally, the celebration of the ones who had joined the great majority, thus becoming spirits of the ancestors. To wake up in the morning and watch drummers leaving their homes, heading for the marketplace, taking time to dance to the beat of the drum along the way, and performing while the market people exchanged goods, was very natural for me. This kind of scene was very familiar to me, and very attractive to the people who went to the market every day to buy food or whatever they needed.

As a little boy, when I was two or three years old, I would walk over and watch—the drummers in particular. Sometimes the master drummers would let me carry their drums, and in return they'd give me a lesson. But my very first reaction when I heard the master drummer playing was to go after that drum and take over from him, to play it like the master drummer played it. It was quite a feeling! I would say, "I can do what you are doing." That feeling has always remained with me.

Sometimes I was asked to move out a little bit and not be so aggressive. That's because I was not standing where the audience usually was. I'd always be on the side where the drummers were. I never was just an onlooker. I wanted to be where the drummers and singers were. I was always standing behind the master drummers, trying to play with them, trying to listen to what they were playing. That's really how I received my traditional education about drumming.

There was no school for drumming. Every child in the village is exposed to drums, and dances and sings. It's like in the United States where there's a playground on every corner, and the little boys and girls play basketball or baseball. In my village there was always music and everyone would grab something to play. But I went beyond that. I would follow the drummers everywhere. They would go from market to market, from village to village, and I would follow. The master drummers would all say, "Are you here again?" And I would say, "Yeah." Those of us who became drummers were the ones who went beyond that common exposure and learned the craft.

I tried very hard, and finally they allowed me to participate. At first, they said, "Here's the bell."

I said, "I want to play the drum."

They said, "No, you've got to play the bell first. You have to learn how to keep the beat. You have to maintain the tempo. When you pick it up, you have to pick it up and stay there."

I learned that early. And that's very important to learn. So my first instrument was a cowbell. The first rhythm I learned was what we call *conconcolokonkolo*, which is a very simple rhythm but difficult to hold. The first few times I played with the master drummers, they usually said, "Grab the bell and let's hear you play *conconcolokonkolo*." Sometimes I had to hold the *conconcolokonkolo* beat for hours.

The next few times they let me play with them, they said, "Take the bell again." Only after many times like this would they let me play the shaker, and then finally the drum.

The first drum I had made for me was called *apesi*. The *apesi* is a clay drum, shaped like an hourglass, which is covered with woven cane for protection. My mother was a potter, so she made me my first one. With its woven cane covering, the *apesi* is a beautiful drum, but you only have to drop it once.

So I went around, and followed the drummers everywhere. I stayed behind them. I listened. I participated. And when I was alone, I made sure that I played every day. It takes years to become a master drummer. You have to know not only the rhythms but the dances as well. As a drummer, you have to be able to dance. You have to know all the songs and all the dances that go with them. Once you know all the parts of all the dances, you will be given the opportunity to lead the band.

But there was an urge in me. I was driven by curiosity and by the devotion of those master drummers in my village and the surrounding villages, who at a given time or place filled the air with vibrant rhythms that propelled their audiences to high-spirited movements and expressions of joy, celebration, and thanksgiving.

I could always feel the exuberance of the master drummers and see the expressions of love, satisfaction, and pleasure on their faces while they did what they knew how to do best. Those dedicated preservers of Yoruba culture and its traditions shaped and molded the life of the villagers. They were never adequately compensated for their contribution, but they remained loyal and true to their profession. They were the heartbeat of the village.

I learned a lot spending time behind the stage with them at all the places they played. Pretty soon, I was no longer a stranger or an intruder. I was always placing my hands on the drum, trying to see if I could repeat what I heard and what I saw. By the time I was seven or eight, I enjoyed the privileges and advantages of a fully committed apprentice. I became a disciple, the heir apparent to the keeper of the rhythms.

Here in the Western world, when we say apprentice it really means that you are going to classes and they are showing you things. I became an apprentice just by continually going to the rituals and festivals, then playing. One day one of the master drummers got me a drum, after asking me to play the bells so many times. Then he showed me: "Put your hands like this." And I was on my way.

The master drummers in the village don't say, "Here all you students, come to my village to learn." You go to them, after they play; you help them carry the drums. They might get home and play again for the community to dance. You participate there again, and they show you a few things. That is what they do all their life, what they do for a living. They are born into it. As someone born into a family of talking-drum players, you learn how to make the best talking drum, how to repair it, and how to play it.

I had no idea whatsoever where all of this was going to take me. But I remember very well that many times when I was growing up, I was always the one who would get up on a little box to talk to my peers. I did not know that I was actually preparing myself for the future. I couldn't explain it, but I saw myself benefiting from it one way or the other. I just couldn't put my finger on it. Whatever I was going to be doing, it was going to be something very important. But I had no idea I would be doing what I am doing today.

So drumming became the focus of my life very early on. I would spend all the time I could with the master drummers, learning the rhythms and when they are played. Many of the rhythms are only played at specific times, during the festival for a house raising, for example. Or when a drought occurs, we have a rhythm for that, a dance that is done only at that time.

But the most important Yoruba rhythms are the ones that communicate with the Òrìsàs, the spirits of the ancestors. Òrìsà really means "he whom Ori has picked out for distinction." There are many Òrìsàs, so many that no one can name them all at once. The Yoruba say that anyone who does something so great that he or she can never be forgotten has become an Òrìsà. There are several ways of celebrating these Òrìsàs. Sometimes we make sacrifices at the shrines of Òrìsàs and offer them gifts. Or else we have a feast with drumming and dancing, and as we chant and dance, the master drummers play an ancient trance rhythm that calls the Òrìsàs down into the bodies of the dancers, and some of the people become possessed by the spirit of maybe Ogun or Shango, and are raised to a higher spiritual level.

The master drummers—the ones in their sixties, the old men—can play these possession trance rhythms anytime, so that the dancers will become possessed and go into a trance. Some dancers who know that, when they are taking their solo, won't want to go in front of this drummer. I have a dancer in my company who won't let me play for her when she is taking her solo because, as she tells me, when she comes in front of me to dance, whatever I play throws her off, and she would end up on the ground, and it would take an hour to revive her. I am not doing it purposely. She just says that when I play, that's how it affects her. It is not going to hurt her. But in performing, she wants to be able to control herself. What happens to her when she becomes possessed is that she is so free, in a good way, that she takes absolutely everything in, the rhythm, the feeling of the music, everything. It just takes over her whole being. She is just totally focused. All of her attention and energy is focused on maintaining the rhythm, and it transports her to another level, another state of consciousness. She truly becomes transformed.

I think psychiatrists have a term they use for this kind of thing. When a psychiatrist is interviewing a patient, if the patient doesn't come and pour out his or her feelings, the psychiatrist is not going to be able to pinpoint exactly what the problem is. You really have to tell it all. Then he can say, "Oh yes, I see now. From what you said, this is what is happening to you." That is why psychiatrists are trained to listen carefully and let the patient do all the talking.

The dancer knows—and I know too, even when I am playing by myself—that sometimes I get so intrigued and so captivated by what I am doing and feeling that I begin to lose myself somehow. But I can't let myself go all the way. I have to stop myself and say "No." I can do that only because I am still in control of my feelings and all my senses.

If people follow the feeling of the moment, they can get themselves into a state where they lose their whole ego, and lose control over themselves. Before they know it, they just don't know when—or how—to stop. They'll be dancing, they'll be kicking, and all of a sudden, the music stops, and it's time to stop dancing. But it will take a few minutes to get them to stop doing movements. They are already entranced.

In the African Pavilion at the 1965 World's Fair, many of my dancers found themselves in the pool in front of the stage, but they didn't know how they got there. They were falling into the pool during the performance, without hurting one another. They would get possessed several times a week.

It happened one time to a whole dance company from Jamaica that came to perform with us. This was at the theater in Woodstock—the entire dance company got possessed on me, right on stage, one right after the other. We had to stop the show. While we tried to get one off the stage, one who was trying to help us was getting into the spirit. We had to take them backstage to revive them. They were possessed, rolling on the floor, shouting. Some of them were just laughing, some were clapping, just out of it. The whole dance company. It was quite an experience. I had to stop my drumming and call for an intermission. That was around 1986. When this happens I stop playing and give the dancers a wet towel to wipe their faces. I sprinkle water on them, read some incantations.

In Richmond, Virginia, last year when we performed there, one of the dancers from another dance company that performed with us got possessed in the middle of her solo. They had to carry her out and it took an hour to revive her. She just wanted to continue dancing, didn't want to stop. She had so much energy we actually had to hold her down. It took about four to six men. She became very powerful. No matter how strong you are, you cannot handle a person who gets possessed like that by yourself. You have to have at least two people if you don't want to hurt them, or yourself, because if you hold them by the hands they will kick. They will shout, "Get away from me!" You need more than one person, two or three, to hold them. That strength comes from somewhere. We are trying to find out more about that.

In the village, it is a different situation. The dancers are surrounded, and people have prepared native medicines, some herbs shredded in cold water, and sprinkle the water over them. It is like when you give smelling salts to somebody who faints, something to get their breath back. Something cool to get them out of that state.

Drummers can create that mood; drummers know they are very important. It all has to do with the music, the rhythm you are playing, and the state of mind of the dancer. You have to know what the occasion is about, the mood that you want to set. If it is a mood of meditation, you won't play the kind of music where people are jumping for joy. But if it is a different kind of gathering, the drummer can add more fuel to it just by increasing the tempo of the music, or changing its texture, and all of a sudden you send people to a different level. You completely lift them up, and they will be on a much higher plane than they were before. A mind that is at peace with itself, that is in tune with its environment, can be easily touched.

That is why, in the process of traditional African healing that we use, the way in which the rhythm is put together and played, as well as the environment in which we are playing, has an impact on the dancer. When people, as we say in modern times, are losing their minds and you can't make sense of what they are saying, it is possible for us to get them into a situation where we start playing and they will recover and find themselves again. Then you can record their conversations and find out that those are different from what they were saying two or three days before. In this situation they are probably able to tell you what their problems are, have been, or what happened to them. We can use drumming to do that. That is how far the spirit of the drum can lead, if you know how to play, what to play, and when to play it.

This is something I learned as time went on. I discovered it by myself. It is not written in a textbook. It took me years to know how to do that. It has finally gotten to the point now that I know what to play, how to do certain things to make that happen. It is not easy to understand, though. It really is a mystery.

Usually what is happening there is that you start out with a very simple rhythmic pattern of drumming and build it up to a polyrhythmic pattern. The same kind of thing will happen for just about anybody. Someone might be depressed, and somebody else not. They begin to hear it, sitting down, and probably don't make any movement, or don't say anything. All of a sudden you might see the person throwing his or her hands up, beginning to react—not wildly, but actually doing it in rhythm according to what is being played. He or she may stand up and give you a smile. The whole facial expression changes. You can observe it. Whoever is conducting it can take advantage of that, can change the whole feeling. Then, all of a sudden, he or she gets up, makes more movements, and people are dancing by themselves, beginning to do what we call normal reactions. This could even be somebody you couldn't get a word out of. Of course, it also depends on who is doing the drumming, and whether they know what they are doing. But you can get the same response from anyone—expressions of fulfillment, excitement, renewed positive energy, or a joyful experience of who they are. Remember now, every cell in the body is in constant rhythm, or as one of my more scientific students describes it, "frequency." That is how it becomes very effective. But the compelling factor is what is being given, what is being played. The drummer sets people's mood. I have been trying to find out what Shakespeare was dealing with when he wrote in *As You Like It*, "If music be the food of love, play on, give me the excess of it."

The spirit of drumming is in the circle, too. The circle is a sacred whole. When drumming is done in a circle, there is a great power there. So when you put a person in the circle, all the energies of all the people who are rounded up, drumming together, converge on that person. That person is bound to be affected by that energy. Whoever is standing in the middle of the circle feels the power of that sound, that healing energy, in his or her body.

If there are a hundred people, that is the energy of a hundred people. That's powerful. They express complete satisfaction and cannot describe how they were feeling at that particular time, but they know they feel something completely different from what they were feeling before they got into that particular circle. They feel completely relaxed. They are in tune with themselves. They become very expressive and very determined to go forward. "Now I know what I can do. Now I know I can do it. Now I know there is nothing I can't do if I put my will to it."

This can be proven. We have individual witnesses who may not be able to tell you exactly how it happened, but who will tell you they experienced it. Science is just beginning to recognize that there are certain things that cannot be fully explained by scientific experiments. Some things just happen, that is all. You cannot find words to adequately explain everything that does happen, but it still happens. This means we need to investigate these questions further, until we find out. The answer might be a very simple one. I think we are just now beginning to develop this higher plane of thinking. The spiritual way of discovery is not the same as the scientific way. I firmly believe it is in all the religious writings ever revealed. "Know thyself." We don't know ourselves yet. That is what keeps me going. I really don't know myself. I don't know how powerful I am. I have to discover that.

No matter how threatening, no matter how powerful the situation, the mind always finds a solution, if it can just be attentive and listen to the inner self. We have a great accumulation of knowledge that we don't understand yet. Self-discovery can go on forever. There is something about human beings that is more than their human nature, that is on the divine level. That is where we are going now.

There is great wisdom in the way the drum evolved in our communities. In Yorubaland, the villages are near one another, and there is a festival about something in each village almost every other week, so we hear the drum for one thing or another every day. They say there is a ritual to be performed every day except one day out of the whole year. This one day you will not know unless you become a chief. I don't know it because I did not become a chief. Only the one who becomes the chief will know it, and he will have to die with that knowledge.

There is a special rhythm that is played when a chief, or a king, whom we call *oba*, is installed. You hear that rhythm once in your life. When that rhythm is played again—that is, when you have joined the great majority— you won't hear it. It is your successor who will hear it.

Communities all over Africa have realized that they can all come together when things are not going well. When everybody recognizes that things are not going well, and that they are all in the same boat, the head of the village, the chief, brings everybody in the village together to participate in a ritual, which may involve the sacrifice of goats and chickens, or a feast and prayer—but it will be some kind of a celebration that features drumming and dancing. They address the particular problem that is facing the community through rhythm and music. They look for solutions, and they always find them in the special songs and dances they perform. Drumming, music, singing, and dancing have always played a significant role in our village life. When a child is born there is a celebration to welcome this child into the world, and especially into the community. The community participates in the christening of the child. When there is a significant project in the community, there is music and dance and singing to get people in the mood. When a young man and a young woman reach the age of puberty, there is a celebration of the changing of their lives. When one takes the giant step of getting married, there is drumming and dancing and singing beginning from the time of engagement until the culmination of the union, which is considered not a union between two people, but a union usually between two villages and always between two families.

Likewise, if a roof is blown away by a storm, the community shares in the labor of repair. This is generally done with drumming and music in the background while people go into the woods to get all the material they need to do the repairs. All these events take place with the beat of the drum setting the mood. When community work has to be done, it is not necessary to make any special announcement for it to begin. People know that to get people interested in such a project, there will have to be something to energize them. It is automatic. Drummers and musicians start the whole process by providing something that will make the job much easier for those who are really going to be doing the work.

The drum plays a central role in the life of the community. It is one of the first things that all children in the village learn about. They, too, in their own little world, beat on pots and pans, beginning their musical career just like that, by mimicking what they have seen adults do.

The story of a village, over a period of twenty-five to fifty years, is recorded through songs that tell about past events. Those who played important roles in events are mentioned in the songs. This is how young people remember those who were active in and useful to their community. In this way, music and rhythm keep the community together. Setting important events to music recognizes how valuable everybody is in the village.

Traditionally, drumming was something that master drummers did. It was both their living and their life. The master drummers were also the griots, or historians, the ones who told the stories about what happened in society—what we would call *opican* in Yoruba. They would tell you about the founding fathers of the village, who they were and what they should be remembered for.

They were more than musicians and storytellers. They had their own little farms where they grew things to eat. And they were the ones who brought the children together to tell them about the culture. These master drummers lived their lives according to the fundamental principles that make village life what it is. They kept the traditions, and they kept the community together through their performances and their stories.

People would pay the master drummers for what they did. They were never in want. Whatever they needed to survive, they got from the people, who regarded them as living treasures. They were usually just given whatever they needed. People would bequeath land to them, or part of their wealth to them. They were taken care of, because it was they who maintained the purpose of life. They were always there for a child's christening and for every other rite of passage. They were always gainfully employed.

We actually had categories of musicians. Some were comedians, or jesters. They would come in and brighten the day of the chief when he was facing too many problems and just needed to relax. The jesters would come and tell stories just to make him laugh and forget about his troubles.

Then there were the master drummers, who reminded us about our relationships not only among ourselves but also with the Creator. They made sure the community was linked with those fundamental principles that remind us who we are. These master musicians had gone beyond their general knowledge of music, dance, and art and to become spiritual leaders.

One of the griots I admired most was Denge, a very remarkable man. He knew the history of many important people, and he would dig out stories about them. He would tell you about your great-grandparents, and remind you of who they were, where they came from, and what their contributions were to the development of the village, and remind you that your name is a very important name that you need to protect. A good name is better than silver or gold, so you have to live up to the reputation of your parents.

Denge went around talking about kings, queens, and princesses. He sang songs about the changes in society, about what happens when young men go out into the world and forget their responsibilities. He reminded people of the days when things were not like this. He was a historian who noticed the changes in society, and he reminded people of the traditional way, and that you have to prepare to become responsible men and women.

He was a fantastic griot. He would go around and play a hand drum, and he had an accompanist with the two-string guitar. He sang a lot of songs that reminded you of great men and women in society. He was one of my favorites. I went around everywhere he was, from one village to another, I was always there to listen to him. He always had one or two songs that told significant stories about our ancestors, or stories with moral messages to remind you how important your character is. Character is the quality in man that lasts forever. His songs told stories about what happened in society. They were full of encouragement, and they instilled confidence in people. His songs brightened the day for those who listened to them. He was the man who, through his songs and performances, influenced me the most in that way.

I grew up with a passion for drums. The whole village vibrated with wonderful sounds of music because music was there for all the passages of life. You woke up in the morning, and it was music you woke up to. It was the drummers who made things lively in the marketplace. It was the drummers who made the market women leave their wares, even with a customer trying to buy something, and dance to the beat of the drum. The day would be incomplete without this happening.

This was the beginning of what helped me emerge as probably a *griot*. I remember all of these songs of the different deities. I attended many of the celebrations, and participated in many of the rituals, traditional and contemporary. I was really blessed to be where I could experience all this, and I am proud today of what I have become because of this.

My passion for the drums is beyond description, it is beyond comprehension to anyone who does not know my background. Only those who really observed me growing up know what I mean.

One of the most enduring gifts for anyone who plays the drums is the realization that drums are powerful instruments for unity, for bringing people of all levels, of all cultures, together through their *equal* contributions. No one person's contribution is greater than anyone else's. The drum is the great equalizer. When you play your part, and I play my part, it means the kind of collaboration that allows your light to shine as well as mine, because we both stay in rhythm and the whole effect is powerful.

Another gift of the drum, in learning to play it and appreciate it, is that it brings you peace. When you play the drum, you take your frustrations out on the drum itself, instead of on people. The energy you put into drumming is the kind of energy that will change your mood. When you are drumming, you really forget yourself, and probably certain aggravations, too, things that might trouble the mind. You may even find solutions to problems while you are playing. You may become resigned to certain things that would otherwise be bothersome. Drumming helps you re-establish your faith in yourself and your abilities. Drumming just does so much for you, especially if you are enjoying what you are playing. You become tuned into so many positive ideas that you forget the negative. Drumming can be the beginning of a healing process for what is troubling your soul. You can learn to say, "Look, things will change if I just exercise a little patience and forbearance."

Drumming will do a lot of wonderful things, if you can just play and let your ego get out of the way. Some drummers play because they want somebody to hear them. The important thing is not to play for anybody's satisfaction but your own. You are the one that has to feel good, to feel happy, to be in a good mood. Then you can inspire others. You have to feel good about yourself first. That is why I advise drummers to never be in competition with anybody. Enjoy what you play. Feel great about it. When you can feel that, you know somebody is going to be moved by your playing.

When I think of the brotherhood of the drum, I realize that the drum is the instrument that can bring people from all walks of life, all age groups, all nationalities, together. Different kinds of people doing the same thing at the same time together—that's a very powerful thing. It is more powerful than people pledging allegiance to a flag of any nation. It is like people working in unity toward a common goal. It is a gathering that has a divine origin. That is how I would put it. It is so powerful that, sometimes, I say to myself, "How and when will the leaders of the world in every continent realize this? God, why don't you give me what is needed to do the job, so I can go all around and do this in communities, in schools, all over the world?

Why is it that those who have the means will not support this kind of effort? What is it that has to be done to change the attitude toward the idea of bringing people together? What has to be done?" I am still asking the question. I haven't gotten the answer yet.

The brotherhood of mankind, of men, women, and children, young and old, is so strong, so real, and so right. If this were something that was promoted, encouraged, introduced into our educational system beginning from kindergarten or even preschool, this would be a wonderful world to live in. I don't know about on Mars, but on this planet it would be so peaceful, so safe. People would be so happy. People would be able to realize their inner strengths and really fulfill the purposes for which we were created.

If I have brought anything to drumming, I think it might be that I brought my generation—a generation that has gone through a gradual process of peaceful indoctrination into Western ways over the years—to the recognition that there is a cultural basis for our unity. One of the things we can use to bring people together is drumming. The recognition of our unity is one of the things we need to preserve for posterity. This has been one of the reasons why I am doing what I am doing now.

What I have been able to develop in drumming goes back to what I saw and grew up with in my village. Drumming is central to our lives, and the spirit of the person playing the drum, along with the spirit of the skin of the drum and the spirit in the wood, these are what matter the most. Together, they make up the spirit of the drum, an irresistible, powerful force.

As drums are used more to celebrate life, as well as to heal, we will see a tremendous affinity developing between people all around the world, because the drum will help bring people together. Children will be playing with children, brothers will be playing with sisters, mothers and fathers will be playing with children; the community will be drumming together and eventually people will dissolve their frustrations on the drums instead of on one another. The drum is going to become an important instrument in every household, just like the piano. I believe this is going to happen.

2 | Yorubaland

In Africa, we say it takes a whole village to raise a child. I know this from my own experience. The whole village raised me! I was taught the traditional ways of my people by all the people in the village. I am very grateful that I grew up in the village, and especially that I am from the good stock of the Yoruba people. I am very proud of being the descendant of a great people, with a great history and a rich cultural heritage. And I am so thankful that we have been endowed with so much. As the seed is sown, so shall it germinate. I am convinced of this. What I was taught eventually ripened into good habits.

I was born in Ajido, a small fishing and farming village on the coast of Nigeria, in West Africa. As a boy, going to and from the nearby villages, I discovered the richness of the Yoruba culture in the worlds of art, music, and dance. Sometimes I have to hide the joy that fills my heart—that gladness of heart when you know who you are, when you know you are connected with a tradition that is so powerful.

The Yoruba give so much life and meaning to whatever we see and touch. It was Yoruba art that influenced Picasso. And our language has such rhythm in the words. When we speak, instead of answering questions, we speak in parables. We have a way of explaining whatever situations we find ourselves in by giving comparisons. We try to make others understand through our experiences.

In our language, the whole concept of time is understood through the *feeling* of what we observe. What comes before morning? It is *idaji*, the dawn of the day. We say, "The dawn of the day is when you see what you don't see clearly." At the dawn of the day, you greet people in a soothing way. You don't raise your voice. Not the way you greet them when the sun is up and everything is bright and everything is moving. You kind of whisper and say, "Good morning. How do you do? How is everybody?"

And when you can see clearly—say, at seven o'clock—you say, "Hello! How are you? How is everybody? Good." Then, from there, it becomes *osan*, noon. Then you say, *osangangan*, high noon. That's when the sun is almost touching the center of your forehead, and you must get under the shade at that time, because the sun is devastating. One understands that.

Then, from there, you go to *irole*, evening. Things are cooling down. Then from evening you come to *oru*, nightfall. And as you do, you start preparing to fulfill the golden rule. Rest after labor is the fundamental principle in human physiology. You're getting ready to go and lay your body down and rest it up. And you are in bed before it becomes *oru*. You have no business being out, unless it's an emergency. Because the Yoruba believe that the night belongs to spirits.

So the Yoruba are philosophers. And our language is a very deep language. It is a language that I believe should not be forgotten. It is such a dynamic language that with one sentence, even one word, you can tell a whole story, or answer the whole question.

I discovered that in many ways the Yoruba are always the envy of other people, for one reason or another. One of the most important characteristics of the Yoruba is that they have learned—and they enjoy—the art of giving. Giving is an art. And many religious writings, not only in Christendom, but in Islamic writings and Oriental philosophy, agree that it is in giving that we receive.

Home is the place where you receive traditional education about life, how to survive it, how to be happy in it—it's all taught right there. Much of the moral code that has become part of the golden rule, we learned at home, even before the Ten Commandments came into being.

The Yoruba have a saying: *Afi Olorun, afi enia.* "Only God, then people." That was before the bible. So we learned, first of all, an ageless understanding that came from the traditional stories. When the moon is shining at night, that's when the elders in the village—people who have gone through so much in life, and have survived—tell you about life. They tell you true stories about how powerful God is. Because, you see, God is first. To know who God is—where He is, where He or She or It is—is most important. Nothing before God. Everything follows God.

We miss no opportunity to hear God. We understand God by observing the natural phenomena around us—the moon and the stars, the mighty ocean and all that dwells in the mountains and hills, and the changing of the seasons. The elders tell the story about our ancestors who lived so close to nature, observing year after year how the moon affected the rise and fall of the tides, that they could predict which direction a particular school of fish would be swimming at a particular time. There is nothing magical about it. When the tide changes and it is high, certain fish swim in shoals toward the east or the west. The only explanation given by the elders who have tried to answer many questions about this phenomenon is that when man lives close to nature, he becomes a student of nature and learns so much from it. If you live close to nature, you will learn more about nature and about yourself, too.

That's why it was very easy for the Yoruba to understand what Christianity is all about. That's why many of our people converted to Christianity—because of our belief in the existence of God, who is called by so many names. The Yoruba can understand God, or reach God, by observing natural phenomena.

But at first it wasn't easy to convert people to Christianity. It took some time before people really became believers. One of the problems was the way Christianity was sold to our people. It could have been easy to convert people from traditional religion to Christianity, but to come right out and say, "Only Christians are going to heaven, whoever watches God in another way, is not going to go to heaven" . . . It just didn't sound right to many of our people. The Yoruba said, "That kind of God cannot be."

They said, "The concept of God is like a triangle." At the apex of the triangle is Olodumare the creator. God is called so many names—he is called Olorun the owner of heaven. He's also called Oluwa, the Lord. And he is called Oyigiyigi. That's my favorite name. It means that God is something, somebody, that when you turn right, left, front, back, He's there. He's always there. No matter where you turn, God is there. I think that's a tremendous idea.

The Yoruba say that on both sides of the triangle, A–B and A–C, are the moon and the stars, the mountains, the mighty ocean, and all that dwells therein. We say that at the base of the triangle, B–C, is Mother Earth, on which we all stand and to which we will eventually return. And where is man? We say man is in the middle of this triangle, being supported by Mother Earth and looked down on by Olodumare, the creator, Oluwa, the Lord, and Oyigiyigi, the one that is everywhere. This is a very convincing concept about how we are related to all our surroundings and the Almighty God.

That is how we have an understanding of what God is. The way the - missionaries presented it to us was not the best approach. They condemned what we had before they came, called it paganism, and said that unless you are Christian you are not going to heaven.

We Yoruba say we know God, that we are created in His image. That is why many people did not accept Christianity as they should have. It took a long time before Christianity enjoyed a very strong following, in my part of the country. The Yoruba already had an understanding of God, they could not be called pagans. But the people were not taught how to even use the bible. And then, misinterpretation of the bible itself was a problem. The bible is more than literature.

Traditional stories and songs have always been a central part of our life, conveying what is most important to our people. Over the years, I have accumulated a tremendous body of knowledge of songs for different ceremonies, different deities. Most of my colleagues today wonder how I remember all those songs. That's the way it happened. Over the years, all the folk songs, all the lullabies that mothers sing to their children when they are nursing, trying to lull a baby to sleep, all those songs became indelible in my memory.

The songs that I heard—songs that had been passed from generation to generation, as well as new songs composed by talented songwriters—told the history of the whole village. There was a song to represent every event. If there was a benevolent chief, there would be a song about him. If there was a notorious gangster, there would be a song about him. There were songs about anything that had to do with people's character, or their way of life. There was a song about the philanthropist, to say that no one else was like him or her, as far as helping others was concerned.

Through songs we wrote the history of the community. I remember songs about when the first train came to Nigeria, and that's where the story of Akiwowo came from. I remember the song of the first strike in Nigeria, the first

organization, the song that came about when the fight for freedom, for independence began. There were songs about skirmishes between villages, and
who started them, and who was responsible for the skirmishes continuing as
long as they did. Through these songs you could tell who were the perpetrators.

You learned about distinguished families through songs. They were
passed from generation to generation. Songwriters were historians. Their
songs told stories about the community and all its people. Even the songs
that I have written myself tell stories.

But the story must be alive. It can't be a dead story. What makes a story
powerful is the way the storyteller tells it, whether it is about an experience
that is universal, and whether you can actually feel the event happening
right now. A story that is alive is universal, it is about something that can
happen anywhere in the world. So you have to look at stories like that. A
universal character is a character that could exist anywhere in the world.

One of the stories is in the form of a saying: *Enia ni o nko ni ki a kuru;
enia lo nko ni ki a gun.* "It is people who will teach you how to be short, and
it is the same people who can teach you how to be tall." In other words,
sometimes a person will be honorable, and other times that same person
may not be; or, actions speak louder than words. Songs also remind you that
the shortest road has a turn, and the longest journey has an end.

There was one storyteller in the village, named Alose, who always sang
about the most notorious gangster that ever invaded all our villages. He was
called Ogbenu, and the song, "Ogbenu Jewe" went this way:

Ogbenu Jewe	Ogbenu, it's you,
Jewe, Jewe, Jewe	It's you, it's you, it's you . . .
Menu die, Jewe lo	Who is this, it's you,
Ogbenu, Jewe	Ogbenu, it's you.

They say that Ogbenu was so notorious, so powerful, with his organized
group of gangsters, that he would send messages to people in the
surrounding villages, saying, "I'm coming to rob you people next week,
Thursday at five P.M."

They thought he was kidding. They would say, "How can he be so
ridiculous? Forget it. He would have to be crazy to do that."

Then they discovered that he would actually come. They would be
unprepared, and he'd rob them blind, and leave. He would go from village
to village, doing the same thing. But one day he got caught.

Then you remember the story that God always answers everybody's prayers, including the thief's. Even a thief prays to God. The thief wakes up and says, "God, please don't let them catch me today." So God says, "Okay, they won't catch you today." He goes ahead and robs them and doesn't get caught. The next day he says, "God, don't let them catch me today." God answers the thief's prayer again. Then he goes back again. "God, don't let them catch me this week." God says, "Look. They didn't catch you the other times, but one day they are going to catch you and I will do nothing to save you."

In other words, the storyteller was saying, when you are doing bad, when you are doing good, God has nothing to do with it. The law is there. When you do good, you get good in return. When you do bad, you will reap what you sow. If you go around robbing people, you are going to be caught one day. God has nothing to do with it.

So when Ogbenu got caught, they paraded him everywhere, through all the villages. The day of reckoning had come.

They would say, "Who is this? It's you! You are the same person! It's you, going from village to village. It's you. We finally see you face to face. You should be ashamed of yourself."

What do you do with a person like that? How does a person like that feel? How would you feel? I don't want to be like that: "It's *you* . . ." All the kids see him mess up the city. This is what they're going to do to you. They're not going to put you in jail right away. They're going to parade you in all the villages, if it takes a month. They will feed you and make sure you are strong enough to be able to walk from one village to the next. Kids and everybody pulling on you. You go through the marketplace in one village, and then on to the next. So they tell you in this way, and give you examples of what happened.

Then they tell you stories about life itself, such as how the animals in the jungle got together. The animals know that they all live in the same natural habitat, so they say, "Look, this is where we all live. We must know our 'do's and don'ts.' So many of us are represented here. The big one. The fast one. The slow ones. The fiercest ones."

The lion says, "I am the king and the fiercest among you."

The elephant says, "I am the biggest. No animal in this jungle is as big as I. You see how long it takes me to lift up even one leg just to walk?"

And the cobra says, "I'm coming to represent everything that sneaks around."

So they get together at a meeting. The lion says, "I'm the king of the jungle. I want to tell you my 'do's and don'ts.' You can look at me, but don't look at me straight in the eye. I can't stand it, I am not a mind reader. Take your eyes off me. If you do that, no bother. But if any of you look at me steadily for too long a time, I'll do a job on you!"

And the elephant says, "I am the biggest thing here. I weigh so much, I can hardly lift my leg." He says, "Look, I'm not a cow. I ain't got a tail. So all you flies and bugs get off my back. If not, I will splatter you with my trunk, or roll over on you!"

The turtle says, "Look, I have tiny little beady eyes, and a tiny little coconut head. And I'm a navigator. Once in a while I stick my neck out. And I can navigate up to ten miles where I'm going. I follow my path, without falling into a hole. So, all you giraffes—you long-legged animals—who's chasing you? Take it easy. Don't put sand in my little eyes. I can't see if you do that. I will go blind. Take it easy. Don't be running around like jackasses. That's my 'do's and don'ts.'"

The cobra says, "There is no beginning and there is no end with me. I can wrap myself around so you don't see my tail or my head. When I spit, I spit fire. And I can blind you just like that. When you see me all wrapped up around myself, the reason is that I only have enough for me to eat. Don't come near because you'll be blinded."

And so they each told each other their 'do's and don'ts.' And that's how they all live together in peace since the creation of the jungle.

I always tell children that story when I give children's programs. I say, "Okay? You hear that?"

Someone will say, "Stop pulling my hair. What are you doing? You're scratching me." I'll say, "Remember the 'do's and 'don'ts.' The 'do's and don'ts' in this class is that if you have a question, you raise your hand."

And from that kind of story, I ask them questions. I say, "Can anybody tell me a story?" They say, "No, I don't know any stories."

I'll say, "You can't even make one up?" They'll say, "No."

So that's when I say, "I'll tell you a story." So I tell them.

"Oh, I can make up a story," they finally say. "You see, my sister—she is just always doing so-and-so and so-and-so. And one day I told her enough is enough is enough is enough."

Everybody can tell a story. Those who had not been talking in class, pretty soon they are talking and don't want to stop. But in the beginning, they are so shy. Now I have opened them up, by telling those stories. I have lots of stories like that.

In my village, Ajido, and the surrounding villages, because stories played such a central role in our lives, good and bad news spread like wildfire by word of mouth. Ajido is one of four villages along the coast east of Lagos. Meke, Latho, and Agbadarigi—later called Badagry by early English missionaries, who probably found it too difficult to say *Ah-gba-da-ri-gi*—are the three other villages close by. From the accounts of the elders, Badagry was supposed to be the capital of Nigeria. It grew in size and population, and became famous as the port where slave traders selected and abducted young African men and women to be shipped overseas. Many young people of my age group always feel very funny and skeptical about the early accounts of how the slave masters managed to select the most handsome and strong men and the most beautiful and promising damsels.

Village life was the most important experience for me as a child. Every adult in the village, related or not, was considered an elder, whose responsibility, among other things, was to share in the development of every child in that village. That is what communal living is really all about.

All the children growing up in the village soon realize that every adult in the village old enough to be a parent will contribute something to their development, one way or another, and will give a pat on the back when necessary, or a smack on the bottom when deserved . This probably does not happen by any stated agreement among the parents in the village. It is just understood as a mild form of discipline that has been passed on from generation to generation.

The birth of a child is celebrated by everybody in the village. Nobody needs an invitation to come to the naming of the child. Everybody in the village comes to rejoice at the birth, saying to himself or herself, "Who knows what this child will become tomorrow? Who knows what contribution this child will make to the future of this village?" And then we see to it that what the Creator has planned for this child will come to pass. And this child will come to understand that he or she will have to carry on this tradition. There is never any doubt in the mind of the parents that they will have all the help that is needed to raise the child, because the community is made up of people who believe that it is one of their responsibilities to help the child grow into proper adulthood. As I learned later in my village, one of the most important reasons to get married is to leave the world a copy of yourself. I learned from my mother, and from my paternal aunt, the meaning of the oft-repeated proverb: *Omo-lere Aye*. "Children are the crown and the glory of life." Tradition says that when people see you, they do not ask,

"How are your clothes? How is your money?" They ask you, "How are your children? How is your wife?" In this way, they express their conviction that children are the crown and the glory of life. I grew up in such an environment. I had a wonderful childhood.

When I was growing up, Ajido was a small fishing village, with a little bit of agriculture. The buildings, in those days, were made of mud blocks, because it was so hot. They had a cooling effect. Most of the roofs were made of thatched leaves, to fit with the climate. Some had roofs of corrugated metal sheets. If you had one of those, you really were in the upper class.

We have three seasons, the dry season, the rainy season, and *hammattan*, which is a dry, cold wind that blows from the Mediterranean Sea, across the Sahara Desert, to the rainforest below at the equator. It is very dry, and it brings dust with it, and is like spring but not spring entirely.

During *hammattan*, which is October, November, and through to the end of January, the air is so dry that if you have a cut, it just dries it up, it heals it right up. When you take a bath and you don't rub any oil on yourself, your skin looks ashen and your lips crack. You look like somebody who hasn't taken a bath for days. But it's cold, dry, very nice weather, actually. If you have a little cup filled with water, the *hammattan* will evaporate it. It looks very foggy in the morning, and then it clears up as the sun rises.

After *hammattan*, we have the dry season, when it does not rain. After a long period of drought, there are songs and dances performed. There are rituals to make sure the rain will fall in season. Even then, during the harvesting of the crops, dancing is performed. Farmers bring their harvest from their farms to a particular place in the village where people gather. They bring gifts for thanksgiving. Thanksgiving in the United States only lasts one day; that is not the way it is back home. The whole community gets together. Everybody brings some part of the harvest, and dances are performed, and praying is done through the movements of the dance and the music. Praying that the rain will continue to fall in season, not out of season, so that the crops will be better the following year.

The rainy season starts at the end of April and goes through May, June, July. There is heavy rainfall in June. Sometimes it rains for seven days and seven nights straight. So nature provides us with wonderful vegetation. Our crops grow so fast that in the western part of Nigeria, you see pineapples growing next to tomatoes and bananas and peppers. Anything you put in the soil will just grow. During the rainy season, most of the thatched roofs on the houses get blown off, but let me tell you, they are all replaced within forty-eight hours, because all the men in the village stop going to their fields, everybody stops fishing, and we go and get the materials to build them back. We all come together, it's a community responsibility.

In my village, everybody earned a living either fishing or farming. Those who could, did crafts. My mother was a potter. In those days, Ajido had fewer than two thousand people. Today, it has grown tremendously, to probably five to six thousand, but many people have left the village to find good jobs in the cities.

The exodus of people leaving villages for the cities has had a tremendous negative impact on many parts of Nigeria. People who live in farming areas come to the big cities to shop. Sooner or later, they stop farming. They have come to depend on imported foods that we should be growing ourselves. There's no reason for us to have to import these things.

Tomatoes grow in your backyard. You can grow enough to feed not just yourself, but almost everybody in your neighborhood. Tomatoes, peppers, greens, you can just grow them in your backyard. You raise hens. If you feel like having chicken for dinner, you go to the yard and pick one and prepare it. If you want to have a big feast, your yard is so big you raise goats, or pigs. The number of people and how important the guest is determines whether you roast a pig for a visitor. You don't have to go to the market to buy this. You just go to your backyard. I grew up in that kind of place.

What you don't have in your village, you can find in the surrounding villages. They all have different market days. Wednesday is our market day in Ajido, so people come from the other villages to shop there. Thursday or Friday is the market day in the next town to here. People go there to see what the farmers bring there. What you don't find in this market, you find in the other markets.

When I was growing up, people walked to the markets, anywhere from a few miles to ten or twenty miles. If you had a bicycle, you were considered very rich. The village had a facility that we might call today a day care center. But it really wasn't the kind of day care center we think of now. This whole idea of having a babysitter is very simple. One particular mother can be taking care of five to ten children. The women take turns doing that. They volunteer. The mother will say, "You are going to so-and-so's house until I come back from the market. When I come back, I'll pick you up." The mother and the father know that their child will be well fed, that when the children in that household eat, their child will eat, too. All the families are very close. They have to be if all the children are to be taken care of. It doesn't even have to be a child from this village. It might be another child coming to visit a friend in this village.

The naming ceremony is an important part of village life, too. It's important what you name your children. Babatunde means father. It means "the great man who died has come back in your person." Olatunji means "honor and wealth have been revived in the family."

I was named Babatunde for my father, who passed away two months before my birth. According to those who live in the village, my father was one of the most powerful young men in the village. He was looked on as heir apparent to the chief. He was a leader. He was respected as a promising young man who would do so much. He was one of the most popular and beloved people in the village and the surrounding villages as well.

But my father died just before I was born. They were in mourning when the news of my birth spread. Zannu was my father's first name. They called him Zannu Lofinda, which means "he is such a sweet person," "like a sweet-smelling perfume of persuasion."

The passing away of my father coincided with the passing away of one of the chiefs in the village. I am told that people in the market were whispering, "Zannu has returned." I know that I am my father reincarnated. That's what my name means.

He was a very successful fisherman. He was known as the fisherman's fisherman. He was the most famous of all the fishermen in the village. He always managed to come home with the biggest catch of the day. The stories told about him as a fisherman are incredible. One was that when everybody went fishing and came back only a few people were fed, but when my father went fishing the whole village would be fed. He would come back with enough to feed the entire village and have plenty left to sell. This would happen many times a week, even though he spent less time throwing his nets than the other fishermen.

Stories were told that he would suddenly decide it was time to leave a gathering and head home to go fishing for a few hours and would return with a big catch. Somehow he knew when to leave and where to go fishing. When he decided to go fishing, that's when people would say, "Well, I'd better go too. Maybe I'll get lucky like he does." They figured that he had something special, something that might be called luck. He always had a contingent of men who went fishing when he went fishing, and dared not go when he was not fishing. This earned him his reputation among all the fishermen in the village.

He was only following the practice of our people of looking at the stars in the sky, or observing the rise and fall of the tides, in order to tell where the school of fish would be swimming at that moment. He was the one who learned the most from being so close to nature. And when he came back with a big catch, there would be a big celebration at the fishermen's wharf. Because of the close-knit family structure and community organization, people in the village were always the beneficiaries of his big catch before anything was taken to the market to be sold. All the children in the village participated in the celebration after the big catch, too. I remember very well my first taste of the delicious egg of a sea turtle. It was such a memorable event that we all looked forward to the next celebration, hoping that the big catch would include a sea turtle. That happened only once in awhile.

My father was like magician. But he was also known for his kindness and his gentle character. He was a jovial, amiable fellow. My father never became chief because of his early and unexpected death. His sudden death without being sick was a shock that ran through the village as well as the surrounding villages.

So I was groomed to become chief of the village. This notion came from my family on my father's side, not on my mother's side. According to tradition, if you are from the family from which chiefs are always selected, you are prepared for that from birth. Great care is taken to make sure you are brought up to know all the customs, traditions, and values, all the rules and regulations. It is of utmost importance for you to go through a very exacting upbringing. There is so much love and care, but also strict discipline.

There are so many do's and don'ts to learn that you might ask, "Is it worth it?" You are told to respect the rights of others, you are asked to look at the other side of the coin, you are invited to attend meetings even though you may not have anything to say. You are expected to observe quietly how judgments are arrived at, without interrupting or contributing. You are expected to just sit back and watch what is going on. But you find yourself wondering, "How can I just sit back and not have anything to say?"

The most difficult virtue to acquire is *suru*, which means patience. I had to be patient, and understand that my time would come. I had to learn how to sit down and listen to others before passing judgment. That is why we say, "Sit down and observe. Have your ears and eyes wide open but keep your mouth shut." It was so grueling, there was so much I had to learn, so much

I had to take in. I just about lost myself in the whole process. This went on every day, dealing with people who were strangers, people in my family. I learned how to deal with males and how it is different from dealing with females. I learned how to regard every woman as a mother, no matter how young. There is a great deal of pomp and power that goes into becoming a chief.

All the important people in your life that you have known come to visit you when you go through the ritual of becoming a chief, and they talk to you, ask you questions, some of them very annoying. They do things to aggravate you, they want to test your patience, your tenacity. They want to know how you react under pressure: Can you stand it? Can you stand criticism, or somebody calling you names? "You foolish so-and-so. You want to be a king? Who said you ought to be?" They say things to make you angry.

In some places, the chieftaincy is limited to two or three families, and the diviners will declare: "Okay, this is the man who ought to be chief." Another way is if he is the first-born of the present chief, he is considered. But sometimes the diviners will say: "No, it's his brother, his junior brother. Not necessarily the firstborn." It has happened many times, but by the traditional process it should be the first-born who should replace the father. In my case, it became so intense that up till I was nine, my grandmother always cooked separate food for me.

But I came to realize that once I was in a position of such prominence, my life would never be my own. The pressure would become intense and I might not be able to cope with certain situations, or make decisions. Different groups might pressure me, and at the same time I'd realize that I must be scrupulously just and cautious. Many in the community would want to test my patience. That frightened me.

I began to understand the meaning of the saying, "Uneasy lies the head that wears the crown." It means that even though you are in a position of power, you have certain responsibilities and what is expected of you is beyond your own personal comprehension.

I started thinking this way when I was twelve or thirteen. I was saying to myself, "I really don't want this kind of power, or to be the center of attention where I cannot express myself truly. When I'm angry, I want to really let people know that I'm angry. When I'm dissatisfied with a situation, I want to tell whoever it is. But by tradition, if they are older people, I cannot really express myself." I was beginning to feel very sorry for any chief who was in that position.

At the same time, I thought about all of the wonderful things that would go with the position—the authority it would offer me, the power I could wield, the influence I would have beyond the boundaries of the village. Those were things to think about. But they were also things I would pay a price for. So I wanted to find out about my other abilities. I wanted to explore those and didn't want to be limited to village life. I wanted to learn about the rest of the world. I had a sense of that from childhood.

I have two older sisters. Ayo (whose name means "joy") is about five years older, and Suru ("patience") is about two years older. They are like elders to me because according to the law that pertains to family structure, I am not supposed to call them by their first names. If I want Suru, I have to say "My elder sister Suru." That is how it always was and will be, no matter what. For the rest of my life I cannot just say, "Joy"—I have to say, "My elder sister Joy." I have to qualify that name to show that she is older than I am. I have to give her that respect. That is required of me. I cannot get casual. She is not one of my peers, like "Hey, Nancy!" No way, I would be punished for that. The same thing would apply to my younger siblings, if I had any. They would have to call me "older brother Babatunde." You are not allowed to call your elder sisters by name without the qualifying adjective. You definitely would fall out of favor immediately with the rest of the family. Somebody in the family would say, "Who do you think you are, calling so and so by their first name? You must think that you are somebody. They were here before you came."

The same thing applies to twins. The Yoruba consider twins a miracle performed by the Creator. We say, *"Taiwo,"* for the first one, the one who came to have a look at the world first. Then, we say *"Kehinde,"* for the one who came last. We consider the one who came last as the oldest, because he or she stayed longer in their mother's womb than the first one. *Taiwo* cannot call *Kehinde* by their first name.

My two sisters were probably the most loving sisters any young man could have, and they too contributed to all that I am. They tried to spoil me, too. They have love and affection for me that is beyond description. They made sure they were not jealous of my position in the family. By being so nice to me, they gained the affection of everybody else in the family, until my eldest sister left the family to marry someone my family did not approve of. That created rumbles within the family, but it didn't last too long. Every family in the world will always have something to say about whom their child married. In our case, we must look into that family.

Who are they? What have they done? What are they doing now? What are they known for? Are they the kind of family that is always in trouble with the law? Are they the kind of family that is not respected in the community? You don't want to marry into that kind of family. They don't have to be a rich family, but they must be a family with a good name. A good name is better than silver and gold. You have to be able to connect yourself with a good name. A name is very important in the African tradition. Your name must mean something. It tells people who you are and how you are and what you probably will be.

The circumstances surrounding my birth and the fact that I was a boy shifted the spotlight to me. At my naming ceremony almost all the adults in the village came and gave me a name as well as their blessings. When I visit the village now and stop at each compound before reaching the family residence, a few surviving elders still call me by the name they gave me. It is considered arrogant and disrespectful to ignore the existence and the presence of those who knew you when you were young. Those who helped change your diapers and aided you on your way are always in the family circle.

They said I was the reincarnation of my father. In my district I would have been selected chief, since my father wasn't alive. Everything was done to make sure I was prepared for it. I had to be a responsible person, a loving person. I had to think about others. I had to have a feeling for people, try to make things happen, try to make people happy. I had to be able to listen to people. At the same time, everything I needed was provided for me— everything I needed was there. But what was I going to give in return? It was a very, very difficult process. I can understand now what the British Royal Family goes through. You are supposed to be open to people, but at the same time, you have to maintain your dignity. You have to let them know that when the time comes to make a decision, you are going to be fair to everybody. It is the toughest job.

As I grew older, and got to see more of the world, I reflected on all the positive aspects of this upbringing. The entire village was my territory. When I did something right I got praised by everybody. When I acted like a little boy I got smacked by everybody. But at the same time, they applied traditional rules. They say, if you spank a little boy or little girl with your right hand, what do you do with the left? You pull him toward you with the left hand. You still have to tell him, "I love you. I do not tolerate what you have just done, but I still love you, so you have to remember that." I had many fathers and I had many mothers. I didn't grow up to know my father, but I had many people who played that role so very well, and I will never forget their effect on me.

For me, if I were to sum it all up, I would say that when you are a chief, your life is never yours again: you become completely the servant of all the people. It is like all the religions say—the shepherd of the flock is always to be provided for, the flock will always take care of its shepherd, but the shepherd must lead to make sure that nothing disturbs the flock. If I had become chief, I would have been the busy one, dealing with people, always present at all the functions, all the pleasures of life. I would have enjoyed that. And I would have been able to bring about some changes that I would love to see in the village.

Our family was one of two or three land-owning families in the village. Our property was the piece of land between the ocean and the lagoon, where there was freshwater fishing. You had to cross our land to go sea - fishing. Our two families, my mother's and my father's, owned this enormous piece of land, over fifty miles long and ten miles wide. My aunt—the oldest on my father's side—made sure my name was put on the deed of this property because I was the only male. This is always done in the name of the male, because the woman will always get married and assume another family's name. So the property goes to the one who carries the family name. But the property does not belong to me, it still belongs to the whole family.

So I grew up in a small fishing village, but I grew up in style. I enjoyed my childhood. I played in the sand on the ocean side. I could have been completely spoiled.

My grandmother made sure I was taken care of in a lot of different ways. She would take me to the beach and sing songs of praise about great men in our history while carrying me on her back. And I would sleep calmly as she walked home. She supervised everything I ate and drank, where I ate, and where I went. I was followed and watched like a hawk. She insisted that my food be prepared in a separate pot, and that nobody else touch that pot, since I was being groomed to be chief of the village.

But before she knew it, there would be ten or fifteen people around, and we would eat it up.

She'd say, "What have you done? I cooked this whole thing this morning and it's gone already? You ate *all* of it?"

And I'd say, "These are my friends from the village. They came, and we ate it up."

She'd say, "Oh, I don't know what to do with you." So she'd have to cook it all again. She was always in the kitchen. Of course, it probably was a test to see what I would do. You learn how to share, to give and also to receive.

My grandfather didn't have much to do with me. Between my grandmother, my aunt, and my mother, nobody else had a ghost of a chance with me, really.

But my grandmother would spoil me. When I was twelve, she wanted to take me to the lagoon and give me a bath. I said, "I'm twelve years old."

She said, "Shut up. Come on." You know?

I said, "I'm twelve years old. I can give myself a bath!"

She said, "You're not going there yourself. I'm coming." My grandmother was just like a drill sergeant. She told everybody what to do.

My other grandmother, on my mother's side, was a priestess for the traditional religion. My mother's side are from Dahomey. Their language is derived from Yoruba, and I do speak that language. That's how I have been able to learn some of the old traditional songs they sang to the different deities—the God of Thunder, the God of Iron, the God of Creation, the Goddess of the River—it was because I heard them sung all the time in the village. I was lucky in the sense that I have had since childhood access to traditional African religion.

My great-grandmother was a priestess, too. A priestess is a woman who can become like Kori, the Goddess of Fertility. Say a young woman had just married but wasn't pregnant after a year. By praying to this goddess, or offering sacrifices to her, you would be helping her become pregnant.

If she wasn't an expectant mother, the people in the community would start getting worried. "Why aren't you? What are you waiting for?"

There was no family planning in those days. When you got married, they expected you to become a mother immediately. So all the women in the village were watching. I mean, this was fascinating. Gossip went around. "She's been married three months, six months now, and nothing." They'd start becoming very outspoken.

A year gone by, and they'd call on you: "Are you all right? You don't want to have a child now?"

"We wanted to start having a family after we both have a car in the garage, or we have our own house."

No way! That had nothing to do with raising a family. They'd reply, "Look, the Lord will take care of this child. The people of this community will take care of this child."

Today it's not the way it used to be. I grew up in a community where everybody took care of the children. Everybody contributed to the development of the child. Everybody knew that. Everybody was raised like that. It was passed on from generation to generation. It is no longer like that. Everybody looks out for themselves now.

But when I was growing up, the women in the village would call and say, "Tell us how we can help you." They'd ask, "Is it psychological? You are not really in tune with your husband? What is happening?"

They'd break the news to her. They'd say, "Look, we've been watching you a year now, and you have no child. What happened? Maybe you should consult the oracle. You might need to do the sacrifice to the Goddess of Fertility."

Then the priestess would say, "This is what you do. Call the rest of the women and say, 'A month from now we're going to lead her to the alter of the Goddess of Fertility.'"

So all the women in the village would prepare this young woman, and give her support. The priestess would say, "Well, you need to bring this or that. Twelve yards of white material, a goat, a rooster"—or whatever—"to do the sacrifice. And then we are going to cook a lot of food for people in the village."

We would get ready to slaughter a goat, serve it with rice and beans. It would be a big, day-long celebration. They would make this offering to the Goddess of Fertility, and make the woman sing and dance to her—"Give me a child to play with. Give me a child to dance with"—and she would become pregnant in no time.

That was the tradition: the priestess gave the young woman advice about how to be in tune with her own self, what her role was in the community, in the family. She'd say, "Look, this is what you're supposed to do. What do you do to get the attention of your husband?" Almost like a psychiatrist, who says, "Look, you have to change your ways with your husband. This is what you do to keep your husband."

This worked many times. People might say, "Oh, that's psychological." Whether it was psychological or not, it worked. Actually, you say, *Vox populi, vox dei*. "The voice of the people is the voice of God." As long as it works, who knows?

Two people can love each other, and they start living together. But they may not be in tune with each other. Love is a divine element. Two souls together meet, but they may not be firmly secure. They may not be relaxed with each other, psychologically. So they are not going to achieve anything that is expected. They know that.

So the priestess says, "Are you really relaxed with your husband? Do you share completely with each other? Why did you get married?" It comes back to the same point: to leave the world a copy of yourself. Remember that when fire dies, it leaves ashes. When the banana tree dies, it leaves its offspring. So we too must leave our offspring when we pass on.

So I enjoyed that period of my life. I don't think I was spoiled, but everybody showered their love on me. And this was true of all the other children in the village. This is what happened to a child, in a village so different from most of the world, in a place where the community accepted responsibility for bringing up those who would replace them. That was the kind of village life I enjoyed. You were praised when you did something worthy of praise, and you were immediately reprimanded when you fell out of rhythm. That's why I say that rhythm is the soul of life. Everything we do, we do it in rhythm. When we get out of rhythm, that's when we get in trouble or become diseased. We are not at ease anymore.

I grew up knowing very well that people cared about us and that we had to be on our best behavior all the time. You knew that if it was necessary you would get spanked on your way home from school, before you got home. If you said, "Please, don't let people at home know what I have done to deserve this," you would get punished a second time. Not beatings, though, not abuse. It wasn't the same as we experience today, where children are abused by adults. It was appropriate discipline—that's a necessity. If any kind of abuse was suspected, just suspected, that particular adult would no longer be respected in that community, and would have to leave that community because he or she would be ostracized by the whole community, no matter how rich and powerful they were. It was very severe, to have to leave the community.

One of the most fascinating characters in my family was one of my uncles. My father had three older brothers. The best-known one was the one who became a midwife, almost like an obstetrician. I believe this man had some kind of a traditional power, not magic. He had a tremendous knowledge of herbs. According to African tradition, men have always been the healers, the ones who know so much about the use of herbs. Generally, they are the ones who know how to prescribe medicines for expectant mothers, and how to help a woman deliver a baby without much pain. They know all the ingredients to put together.

I remember very well going with this uncle of mine to select the different herbs for the concoctions a pregnant woman could use to help the child develop fully at various stages of the pregnancy. He prepared various medicines for expectant mothers. Some herbs were put together and cooked fresh to be taken internally, and some were put together and broken into big pieces that the woman would use for taking a bath. At the beginning stages of the pregnancy he would let all the leaves dry on her, then maybe fifteen to thirty minutes later she would wash them off with water. This was to give the woman some kind of strength, according to him. The herbs taken internally were to hasten the normal development of the child. Then, at another stage of the pregnancy, maybe after three or four months, when the baby began to move in the mother's womb, he would change the herbs to other kinds.

So first he would prepare a special soap for the woman to take a bath with, then he would prepare a special oil for the woman to rub on herself, and he would also prepare a special medicine for the woman to take, and then another special one for the woman to take a bath in. A lot of different formulas were developed for the different stages of the pregnancy. Also, in my village after the birth of a child, the baby was not washed with ordinary water for the first three months. The baby was washed with a special herb treatment from the first day to strengthen the body. It is like an energizer, or like putting certain drops of vitamins in the water for you to take a bath in. I know for my first three months I was given that treatment. Then the baby had to be breast-fed by the mother. All this knowledge was all passed on from generation to generation.

It was the men mostly who knew the use of herbs. Men would pass the knowledge on to women who were inclined or interested—I know my uncle did that.That was part of your responsibility as the man of the house—to know what to do to take care of your family. As the man of the house, you had to know how to do everything.

I was four or five when I started following my uncle around. I was right there in the house helping him, passing him what he needed. He would make sure I didn't come in when women had to undress. He didn't allow me or any other younger person to be around. This was out of respect for the privacy of women. He would open the door and call me. He'd say, "Hand me so and so and so and so." And I'd hand it to him. Those are some of the rules you observed. You had to know your place as a child among the adults. He'd always say, "Babatunde, follow me." He wouldn't tell me where he was going. That's all he had to say. If I was doing anything when he said, "Follow me," I didn't say, "Where are you going?" I just followed.

When I was a child, he'd say, "Babatunde, take that small basket." He did it a couple of times, and I always knew where he was going. He was going into the woods to pick some leaves from different plants that he made medicine with. He pick the leaves and we'd put them in the basket. Then he'd go home and cook them.

He'd say, "This is what you're going to be drinking in the morning."

You wouldn't say, "Why?"

Some of it would be so bitter, you'd wrinkle your face in front of him.

He was great with delivering children. Whenever there was any difficulty in giving birth, he was usually the one who was called on. You might call him and say, "So-and-so, about a block away, has been delivering since last night."

He'd say, "Okay, I'm coming." He'd go to his room to pick up something he had already prepared, and then go there.

He knew exactly which treatment to use, and with the help of the other women, within an hour or two, the baby would be delivered.

He knew the use of herbs, and what to put together for other things, too, like what to give you when you have congestion. He knew what to give you when you had a stomachache. I learned some of this from him. Today, I can go into a tropical place and pick some leaves up, and cook them for anybody who has a stomachache. If you drink it, it will go away in one hour. I would recognize those leaves today if I saw them.

He would tell me, "Look at this plant. Uh-oh, I'm not going to touch it. This leaf you don't touch after sunset."

"Why?"

"Don't you see the way it is? The leaf closes after the sun sets. We'll come back tomorrow morning, and it will open when the sun comes up."

"Why don't you take it now?"

"You see, if you use it now, it will not be effective."

"How do you know that?"

"I've done it before. During the day, it is soaking up all the energy from the sun."

He taught me a lot of little things to do, to take care of yourself. He was really a character. He was very quiet, but when he said, "Come, let's go," he'd say it in such a way that you didn't question it. You'd just go. He was very precise, didn't say much. He didn't want to repeat himself. I got that from him. Today, when I tell people something, I say, "If you don't understand me, ask me again. I don't want to be repeating myself."

He became very well known for his use of herbs. But he did more than that. I believe he had the knowledge of how to make it rain. You know, like a conventional rainfall. I mean, this is a fantastic story. He could make rain in this area right here, and when we got to the next town it wouldn't be raining.

We had a big yard behind our house where he would gather fire-making materials to make a big fire, usually when some event was going on. According to stories told, a family would go to him and say, "Look, there's a fair going to happen here and another in the next town, twenty miles away. We want it to rain there but not here."

It would rain cats and dogs there, but not a drop here. But you see, around the time that he did what he did, he would send me to the market to buy things. I couldn't refuse. So I missed how he did it. I asked one of the others, "How does he do that?"

From what we know now, according to modern science, it's evaporation in the air, and heat. There is moisture in clouds. Somehow, through certain methods, you can make it rain in a particular place.

These are some of the things I didn't get to learn. There were certain things you found out only if you were a real apprentice, someone who stayed with him for years. You had to be there every day, you had to help him prepare everything. But I was going in and out, in and out, so he wouldn't show me everything. We've lost a lot of knowledge that way. The strict rule was that he could only pass on all his traditional knowledge to a dedicated apprentice. That apprentice would learn how to observe things, how each woman is different from the others, how to read the character of the person he was dealing with, how to approach somebody who is strong or somebody who is maybe emotionally unstable. He would have to learn how to prepare patients for the necessary treatment. He would have to learn all of that and more. Quite a few people became true apprentices of my uncle.

My uncle explained to me. "One of the most important reasons why tradition is not passed on is because the old ones believe that you have to pay your dues. You have to serve. You have to really sit with the master, day in and day out. They test you to see whether you have the patience, the character, and the understanding that only when it is necessary do you really exert the power you have. Only when they know this about you will you get to know everything they know. They don't want you to be able to use that power to hurt anybody, you see?"

I stayed with my uncle until I was about twelve. He would just call me, and I would follow him and do what he said. One of my biggest regrets is that I didn't learn more from him. I wasn't able to at the time, because you don't question your elders too much. I'm sorry that I didn't ask him all my questions. I was very careful not to offend him. I should have been able to play those childhood tricks and tried to see what he was doing. But I was taken away from the village at an early age to go to school in Lagos, about forty miles away. My only returns would be at the end of each month to spend a weekend in the village. I suspect that he didn't teach me everything for this reason. He was a very, very valuable member of my family.

I was educated first at home, then in the village. I was almost twelve when I entered school in Lagos. From the first grade, I was being taught at home because I was like a special child. I was the last-born of the family. I was the one who was being prepared to become chief of the village. I didn't know that at that time. I was just being taken care of by everybody.

Any village as unique as mine was, always has one or two unforgettable characters. In Ajido, no one will ever forget Gbemado, tall, handsome, almost a giant of a man, who didn't need to open his mouth to discipline you. Just standing and leaning toward his left or right with a stern look on his face, while you looked at him, was enough to convince you that you were doing something you were not supposed to be doing. He was a man of few words. He would tell you either "Keep going" or "Stop right there." He spoke in very short sentences and very, very directly. He was probably the most respected disciplinarian of the village children.

Gbemado was a boat builder, and he had a hand in practically every fishing boat that was built. He was very good at it. If you really wanted to be his friend, you had to show some kind of interest in what he was doing. Then you would find out that even though this man was so stern, so overpowering, so overwhelming in his physique and look, he could be as gentle as a puppy. He would tell you, "Let's have some smoked fish." That was one of his loves. He would smoke a whole trout for you to eat right there. Then you would wonder if this really was the same man who could just stand there and look at you and you would freeze just standing there. He didn't have to say any words. He could just put both his hands on his hips and look at you. But if you showed some kind of interest in his craft, and got a little closer, he was very gentle.

That was Gbemado. I was one of his favorites because I would be singing all the fishermen's songs. He would ask, "You remember that one?"

"Sure I remember!"

He would say, "Alright. Good! Good! Keep on singing," and go on with his work. Maybe I was entertaining him. Maybe that's where my whole entertaining and performance thing started, with Gbemado.

One of my most stirring memories is of a night when I was eleven or twelve. One beautiful evening, right after supper, the moon was shining brightly and all the stars were out. I had just gotten into bed and was dozing off. Suddenly I heard the captivating sound of tremendous, powerful voices, forty to fifty men beating their bare chests while they sang: *bo so yi je Meke, jewe . . . bo so yi je Ajido, jewe.* "From here to Meke, it's you . . . from here to Ajido, it's you."

I felt exhilarated. I was eager to see what those voices were all about. So I said to my mother, "I want to go outside and see who they are."

"No, you don't," she said. "Get back in bed. If you're at your best behavior, when you've come of age, you'll find out what it is all about. This is not the time to worry about that. You will be invited when the time is right."

I heard it once or twice a week. What was it? When was it going to be for me? I found out that it was one of the most important village rituals for men. It was the one you undergo in order to assume the responsibilities of a man. But I had to be on my best behavior. I had something to look forward to. In other words, if you are twelve, be twelve. Don't try to be fifteen, seventeen, or eighteen. So I had to wait.

Sure enough, the time came, and I was to be inducted into the cohort of young men in the village who took turns every night protecting the village while everyone else was asleep. This was my rite of passage. My uncle told me that some people wanted to talk to me.

I said, "Who are they?

"You'll see them when you meet them tonight."

"Okay."

So the people came, and said, "Look, how old are you now?"

"I'm twelve."

"Well, you are getting up there, you know? You are the son of Zannu."

Then they just looked at me, and talked about me, and where I came from, and everything.

They said, "Tonight meet us at twelve o'clock at such-and-such a place."

"Twelve o'clock? I will have gone to sleep."

"No," they said, "don't sleep."

And that's what I did. That night, I found so many men.

My friend said, "You're here, too? Great."

I said, "What's so good about it?"

As the evening progressed, they told me to get in the circle. They said, "These are your responsibilities. For the next month, you're going to come out every day at midnight and join the people here."

I said, "Oh, my God! Every day? I have to do that?"

One of the most important things I learned was that every young man had to serve the community in many ways. That's how I began to understand what I had been told as a child, that we had to be responsible to the village. I became part of the group that protected the village when everyone else was asleep. I had begun to pay back to the community what had been given to me while I was growing up.

That was how I learned to be a keeper of the village, a protector of the village, a member of the group that made sure that nothing went wrong, that no one came to rob the village while the people were asleep. It was through my rite of passage.

The responsibilities of any young man growing up in a village like mine are twofold—there is the responsibility to your family, and to the community. Once you come of age, you are reminded that you are no longer a child. Like I read in the bible, when I was a child, I spoke as a child, and when I became a man, I gave away childish things.

We could demonstrate our responsibility to the community in so many ways. For instance, coming out every night after we were inducted into the group of men meant that when the village was almost half-dead, when everybody was fast asleep, we were the policemen, we were the firemen. We were the men who made sure the village was protected. We were the ones who made sure there were no people coming to attack the village by night. We were the ones who put out fires. If people cried out for help, we were the ones who ran to make sure they got that help. We owed it to the village. We were constantly reminded that we owed it to the village.

That kind of responsibility is something you pass on to the generations after you. The training involved in assuming this responsibility was that we had to stay strong. And we were reminded that everything we did in life had to be done in moderation. If we drank in moderation, we would become adults. They told us about the taboos. We could not go after other people's women. We would all of us one day become fathers, and we had to be ready to assume that responsibility as well. They showed us things to do to maintain our strength. Among those people who showed us these things were the elders, whose knowledge we learned from as well. They told us what to put together once we started our families. If one of our children had a cold, we would need to go to *this* place and gather *this* and *this*. They showed us where we could go to get certain things if the community needed help. They'd been there before us.

So each of us took a vow, and we used our new knowledge accordingly, in the way it had been passed down from generation to generation. Any of us who broke that vow would have to pay the price. There was no getting away from it. They reminded us, "You remember so-and-so and so-and-so?"

"Yes."

"You know what happened to him?"

"Yes."

"He paid the price."

This is how we were taught about life itself, about how to deal with life's circumstances. We were told stories about how to deal with different situations, with family life, everything. Complete lessons about values in relation to people in the village, to our immediate families, to people in the other villages, to life in general. They showed us everything. They said, "Look, you know you have the power to kill, but you don't have the right."

It was completely spelled out what our rights and responsibilities were. We were constantly reminded of these by the ones who had been chosen to teach us. It was their duty to teach us. They strongly embraced their responsibility to convey that message to us in no uncertain terms. This initiation was an amazing experience. I realized that all children have a responsibility to make sure the village stays alive, to give of themselves and be of service. Loving is caring, and caring is loving. This has shaped my way of living to this day.

Living in the village, I was exposed to all that went on. There was no way I could escape what it all meant. I saw all the rituals, observed the naming ceremonies, learned firsthand the rite of passage when a young man or young woman has come of age, and learned exactly what is appropriate for each age.

A girl would see an expectant mother and all the stages of pregnancy. She would see what she would look like at three months, six months, nine months, if she did certain things. Some might call this scare tactics. They were saying to her that when you are thirteen, don't try to be twenty-one. As a child, you might be physically able, but you aren't emotionally able to cope with being a mother.

The elders, the women, would come to me and tell me, "You see where I am now? I am eighty years old. There are certain things I can do, there are certain things I have done. That is why I lived to be eighty years old. I don't cook for myself anymore, everybody cooks for me and serves me. Everybody brings things to me. Everybody cleans up for me. They don't let me do anything. Do you want to get to be this old? Do you want people to serve you like that? Then you serve people, so that other people will serve you."

It's the same thing for men. As a young man, you don't want to be a father. Once you become a father, you have to assume the responsibilities of a father. You cannot shirk those responsibilities. You meet fathers, people who do things with their children, and then the fathers bring their children with them in their arms. When the children run around, and the fathers discipline them, and the children obey them, you see that. All of this you observe, during the rite of passage before the final ceremony.

I was right there in the midst of all this in the village. It all made a strong impression on me. My greatest passion was being where the drummers were. I followed the drummers wherever they went to play their music. They would wake up every day and go to play for the chief. That was their first stop—to wake him up in the morning and pay homage to him. The chief would come out, like my grandfather used to do, and peek through the window, and salute them good morning and ask them if they would like to eat breakfast before they continued on their way. He would usually give them a gift, like a certain amount of money, whatever he could afford, because drumming was what they did for a living. Then the drummers would go on to different places. Some would go to the market and play, and enjoy the celebration of the day. Some market women would forget their customers standing there bargaining for their goods, and they would take a few minutes to dance. It was unbelievable!

The drummers would go throughout the market, just like people who go to work from eight to four. Then they'd go home and fix their drums. Maybe one or two drums would get broken during the day. I used to follow them all day. I observed everything, and when they had a minute, they'd show me how to treat the drums, how to play them, and even how to make one.

The other interesting thing about my life in the village is that as I got older there was a constant battle for my affection and for my care. It became a fierce struggle between my natural mother and my aunt on my father's side, who never did recover from my father's sudden death. She was more than happy that I was born a boy. She believed two things until her death. One, that I was her brother reincarnated. My father was her favorite among all five of her brothers and sisters. And two, because she didn't have any children of her own, she believed that I was her son.

My casual weekend trips to Lagos were my aunt's clever way of getting me out of the village and preparing me for school there. She was making sure that when the time came for me to leave the village, she would take over my training, my development as a young man. After a few months she had convinced everybody, including myself, that it would be better for me to live and go to school in Lagos.

There was no real school in Ajido. At the village church, a few teachers, people who graduated from high school in Lagos, had started teaching the children of the village how to read and write. It was just a primary school, up to second or third grade. It was more like a preschool. Later, they built another building for the school. Those who really demonstrated some kind of ability in reading and writing were usually sent to Lagos for school. When you went there for school, everybody looked up to you: "You've become *big time*." I remember very well that I was much older when I entered the fourth grade. I was about a year behind. I was so busy participating in the traditional things that my family was involved in.

So the time came when my aunt announced that I would be going to high school in Lagos. I was finished with the school in the village, and the only possible next step was Lagos, so I would have to move there. I could come back every weekend to the village, though. It took more than two years for my aunt to convince my mother that I needed to live with her while going to school in the city. But my aunt had planned it all out. She played her cards very well.

Adisatu, my aunt, was a big influence on my life. She was a society lady. Her husband, Joseph Adeyemi Vaughan, was an administrator at the Government Printing Press, which at that time was a very high position. She was tough, kind, determined, and clever; she was also a traditionalist and a preserver of the culture. She would fight tooth and nail for her rights.

I remember her as seven men rolled into one woman—that's how strong, possessive, and jealous she was. She would give her heart for my friends, and she would fight anyone who showed any signs of dislike for me. If you gave her any idea that you didn't like me, she was going to go to war on you.

"Anything you want to do to this boy here, you'd better do to me. You're not going to succeed in anything you plan that is not good for this guy here.

Forget it, it's you and me. You ready for war? I'll fight you. You want peace, we'll make peace. But don't you touch that child." It's unbelievable what she would say.

She was deeply moral. She was also deeply spiritual. She taught me respect for womanhood. I learned a tremendous lesson from her that is still with me today. She would point and say, "You see that little girl there? That's a mother, and you should respect that."

"She's just a little girl."

"She's a potential mother. She's going to bear a child someday. You may be the one responsible, but she's the one who will carry it. She's a mother, and you will recognize that *now*, and respect that."

She impressed that on me all the time. She would not let me get out of line. "You should be able to treat women right. A potential mother is a family builder, a country builder, the backbone, together with the man, in the house. She is the one who is the quiet storm. In everything you do, don't forget that. Every little girl you see, remember she's your mother."

Then she would sing a song for me: "Mother is a jewel, and father is a mirror." When you think about it, a jewel is really a very important thing with women. They have a special place where they keep their jewels. That's how important the mother is in the household. What about the father? The father is like a mirror, a reflection of the whole family. He can go out and mess up your name, and it will be a reflection on the whole family. The lesson is that it takes two of those people to make a family. Right from the beginning, we were taught this. It is a universal thing: honor your father and your mother, so that the days of your life will be prolonged. In other words, these are your best friends. They are the people who will stand by you.

My aunt was incredible. Because of her love for me, and her powerful character, she was probably overprotective sometimes. But she laid down the rules, the do's and don'ts, and I learned a lot from her. Her spirit follows me everywhere I go. She was my second mother.

My natural mother was the quiet invader. She was the third daughter in the house of chiefs from Porto-Novo, Dahomey. She was a petite and pretty woman. She was a great potter. She was soft-spoken, but she let you know her feelings through her facial expressions. She was never afraid of anything or anybody. She was the kind of person who will not let the sun set on her anger.

So I had two mothers, my biological mother and my aunt. My aunt made sure she would be the one to take care of the important things. She

That's why I'm so grateful to my aunt and my stepfather for exposing me to the different religious teachings. I discovered that all religions have the same principles. They all have rules of conduct, they all offer consolation in sorrow, and they all agree that no one really owns anything. All revolutions have been based on land. So I watched land issues tear families apart and turn intimate friends into enemies, and I told myself no, I don't want any part of it.

My decision didn't sit well with some people on my father's side of the family. I didn't want to be involved with anything that could lead to a land dispute. I mean, my family was supposed to be part owner of this huge parcel of land that stretched for more than fifty miles between the lagoon and the ocean—practically the whole village—but how did they own it? Who was there first? I didn't know, and I didn't want to have to answer that question, or questions about what they were going to do with it.

I wanted to be as free as possible, so I gave it up. I took my name off the legal list of part owners in 1963, while I was still in the United States. I believe that my father's side of the family has never forgiven me for it. I did not believe that one family or two families should own that much property. I have never revealed this before.

So I felt that I could become more valuable to the village outside of the village. Now, what I'd like to be able to do is establish something that will bring back all the things that made me who I am, that the village has given me. I still dream of helping create a Center of African Performing Arts there, where all the good things in the culture will come into focus, where people will always be able to come to learn about, preserve, and enjoy their culture.

3 | From Lagos to Atlanta

Village life gave me a wonderful foundation. It prepared me in many ways for going to Lagos, the capital. Lagos is the New York of Nigeria. First of all, it is a melting pot. Everybody from every part of Nigeria and the neighboring countries comes to Lagos. It has had songs composed about what it is and what it is not, just like you have songs about New York. It has Broadway, it has everything.

Lagos is the most important, the most dynamic, and the most populous city in West Africa. You can find almost all the different ethnic groups that you see on the west coast of Africa right there in Lagos. We had what Mayor Dinkins of New York called a mosaic. You have to be able to deal with culture shock.

Lagos is also the capital of Nigeria and where the headquarters of many banks and corporations are located. So there has been an exodus of people from all over Nigeria, a country about the size of California, New Jersey, and New York combined. Lagos has become so crowded. You know you are in the center of everything. You can tell that just by how people dress, act, and talk—there are all styles in Lagos.

There is a song about Lagos, "Eko akate ile ogbon Lagos." That means "the little house of wisdom." It tells you about *arodede ma ja*—"the city that swings back and forth but never breaks." *Ko si'lu ta o f'eko we*—no city can compare to Lagos. It is the house of wisdom. If you arrive from any part of Nigeria, and you don't wise up fast, you will always remain a dummy—you will never make it, you will never survive. Just forget it, you won't last a week. But if you can survive in Lagos, you can do that anywhere. I believe that.

That's why I love New York—it reminds me of Lagos. It is where you find people from every part of the world. It is also a place where you can get yourself into trouble, or allow other people to get you into trouble. You can be in New York for twenty years, and somebody you know is passing close by you, and you never see each other. It is also the kind of place where if you know the people you live among and the place where you have your bed, you never get in trouble. Yet it is also a city where the very day that you arrive, depending on the people you meet, you can be in big, big trouble, because everybody is there. It is a place where you learn how to live a simple life. And it is also a place where you can become extravagant, or very arrogant, or outrageously and unscrupulously unjust. It is a big city that will beat you with one hand and stroke you with the other. That's why they say New York is so great, yet so complex they had to name it twice. Lagos can be described the same way. It was full of excitement.

Village life and my visits with my aunt came in handy. All of that prepared me to deal with Lagos. The traditional education that I received at home, on how to take care of myself in many situations, came in handy too.

In Lagos, you are likely to get mixed up if you keep the wrong company. You know for sure that you don't want to be running around with just anyone. You pursue your goals, your objectives, with eagerness when you come to Lagos. When you do that, you will not get in trouble and you will succeed. Once you make it in Lagos, it's going to become known everywhere else in Nigeria and the neighboring countries.

I was ready to go there. I was filled with joy and excitement. I was prepared mentally, physically, and spiritually to go to Lagos and to live with my aunt and my uncle.

My uncle was a strict disciplinarian, and a devout Christian who insisted that in everything you do, you must put God first. He insisted that we all keep the Sabbath. That meant no cooking—only warming up the food from Saturday. There was no washing of any clothes, not even a handkerchief. He made sure I attended a prayer meeting every morning. I walked a mile to the church, every day, just for prayer meeting.

I'd say, "Why can't we pray at home?"

He'd say, "Don't even suggest that we should do the prayer at home."

Of course, we prayed at home, too. Remember, "When two or three gather together in my name . . ." But on Sunday there were no other activities. The prayer meeting was six o'clock every morning. On Sunday, we went there, then we came back home and then I went to Sunday school.

My uncle was one of the deacons at his African Methodist church. He led the prayers every morning. On Sundays we went to the morning prayer service. Then I went to Sunday school. And then we went back in the evening for another service. The Sabbath was the day we put aside to give thanks to the Creator for taking care of us through the week. So for me, this was like going through a whole process of religious training.

I remember what happened to me when I became the secretary of the local soccer club, Boons. It was very popular. I was the secretary. Our club reached the semifinals, and the captain called a very important meeting. It was on a Sunday. I attended the morning church service, but I did not go to Sunday school that afternoon. Instead, I went to the meeting, and then the evening service because I hadn't got to the afternoon Sunday school. Went I got home, all my school uniforms for the following week had been dumped into the water. They'd already been ironed and pressed. So that meant I had to go to school on Monday out of uniform, and the reason was that I hadn't put God first! That's how strict things were in my uncle's house.

I had left the village understanding the traditional religion as well, because I grew up around that. Every morning the drummers came to greet the chief, and people danced. I heard the chants. There were ceremonies I attended. I knew the chants and the music and the dances. But even though the fear of the Lord had been instilled in me, I had never been put through such a test until I got to Lagos.

My life was getting complicated as far as religion was concerned. First I got an understanding of the traditional way of life. Then I came to the city, where I was introduced to the African Methodist Church. When African people tried to take their drums to the Anglican churches, and praise the Lord with all their instruments, the Anglican priests would say, "No, you can't do that. You can't be bringing drums, and playing, and having people dancing. This is no place for that."

Then the Methodist churches came along, as we now know them, where we were allowed to use the drums and chant, and people could call out "Praise the Lord!" and clap their hands. People would see visions, or faint, or get possessed and speak in tongues. They would get all wrapped up in what they were doing, praising the Lord through their songs and celebrations while they interpreted the Bible. They would be praising the Lord with all their voices, their instruments, and their drums.

Finally, I was placed in the Baptist Academy, run by the Southern Baptist Convention. The principal of my school was from Atlanta, Georgia. So you can see how I was affected by all of these influences.

Some people knew my aunt as my mother. When I said, "No, she's my aunt," they'd say, "You mean your mother?"

"No, that's my aunt. My mother lives in the village."

"Oh, excuse me."

My mother didn't have much to say, except that she was my biological mother. My aunt felt she had two claims over her. So it was a tug of war over me.

If I said, "This weekend I'm going to the village," my aunt would say, "You were just there last week. What about your homework? What about singing in the choir at the African Methodist Church, where you're a soloist, where you go to prayer meeting every day?"

I managed to convince my aunt and my stepfather that going back to the village was an important thing for me to do. To convince them, I always had to be on my best behavior. I never resisted an opportunity to show them I was a good boy. I also reminded them that I needed to make my mother happy, you see. How did I, as a young person, manage to deal with all this? Well, under the guidance of my parents, strict as they were, I was able to handle it. Those experiences are still serving me today.

The Baptist Academy was one of the most famous schools in Lagos. It was ranked very high among the established schools, which included the Church Missionary Society Grammar School and the Methodist Boys' High School. All of these were missionary schools. The Baptist Academy was established by the Southern Baptist Convention. They also ran a teachers' college and a girls' high school. The academic standards were very high.

I lived in the district called Olowogbowo, not far from the mosque where the Muslim faithful were called to prayer every morning at five o'clock. I heard that, too. Religion did not divide people. One family could have members of different faiths. Many families had converts from Yoruba to Christianity, or to Islam, and they would still participate in traditional Yoruba practices even after converting.

Olowogbowo was not far from the marinas. It was a very popular area of the city. I lived at 27 Bishop Street. It was like living near Riverside Drive in New York City. You could see across the lagoon, just like from Riverside you can see across to Palisades Park in New Jersey. That's why many times, I take a sojourn, and just drive along the west side of Manhattan—it brings back pleasant memories of what the marina in Lagos used to be.

There were coconut trees planted all the way to the beach, where the lagoon and the ocean meet. That's how I developed into a long-distance runner. I'd walk about three blocks to the marina, and then run from there to the beach—about fifteen miles. Now all of that is gone. It's nothing but the concrete highway they built around Lagos. And they cut down all the palm trees. That showed no vision at all.

That was the city I arrived in. Those were the people who raised me, from when I was twelve or thirteen until I became a young man. So moving to the city was full of excitement and challenges, as well as opportunities to make something out of myself. Lagos was very exciting.

By the time I finished high school, many people probably expected me to become a minister. The upbringing my aunt and my stepfather gave me strengthened me at first, even though their strictness almost made me want to rebel against Christianity. But today I would thank them for standing firm and for showing me how to look at the other side of the coin. That helped me grow up and develop my own philosophy of life, based on my own experiences. That has helped me tremendously.

Our district was one of the historic areas in Lagos. It was where the city's most powerful people lived. The elders there looked out for the young. I was told that as a young man in that district, it was my duty to protect the women, especially the young girls. If you were a young man, you were expected to know who was coming to see the local girls, and to make sure they treated the girls well. If they didn't, you bounced them.

I was one of the leaders of a gang that was very protective of all the girls in the neighborhood. All the respect for womanhood that we had been taught from childhood, that's when it showed itself. We did not want to hear about any girl being mistreated by outsiders. There would be no battered young women in *our* area. Nobody was going to mistreat a young woman in our area, because if he did, our gang was going to get you.

I think I was respected among my peers because of my upbringing in the village. All the things that I'd heard about life—all the things I'd experienced, being with the old men, all the visitors coming to our house, bringing their problems to discuss with my grandfather, people coming to see my uncle, all times during the day and night—there was never a dull moment. All the women in the household were always cooking because you could never come into the house without being offered something to eat or drink. You were always told, "Sit down, relax, get something to eat, and then we'll talk. Have your breakfast. Mother of so-and-so, will you get the girls to prepare food for three or four people?" They'd finish and leave, and another group would come, looking for solutions to their problems.

The old man would do the same thing. He would gather himself to say, "Well, let me go and lie down. Maybe in an hour or two." Then another group would come by, and he would ask, "Have you stopped at such-and-such a chief's place to listen to him?" They would say, "Yes, but he can't help us." He'd say, "All right. If you can wait for another hour, I'll be with you." So all of that rubbed off on me, I think.

The church in Lagos where I was a member of the choir was near the fish market, and people who came to the market on Sundays would stop to listen to the songs. They would listen to how we turned the standard hymn "Onward Christian Soldiers"—which is usually sung so slowly—into a spiced-up tune with a four-four rhythm that people could dance to. People would stand outside and clap their hands while they were doing their marketing. That was also part of my growing up.

Lagos was where I started to develop my commitment to political involvement. This was around the time that Kwame Nkrumah returned to Ghana to fight for its independence, and that Nnamdi Azikiwe returned to Nigeria. Later he would be Nigeria's first president. He had been studying at Columbia University, and when he returned from there, he started a magnificent paper that took the country by storm, the *West African Pilot*. "Show the light and the people will follow the way." That was its slogan. It came out as a tabloid of four pages, and it showed a flare that he had learned in America, and it became popular very quickly in Nigeria. He would become one of the most popular citizens in the history of our country.

Demands for independence from Great Britain were becoming so intense that every young man with some education joined the fight in some way. Before I left for America in 1950, I became a member of the youth wing of Azekuwe's independence party.

Azikiwe had come back from Columbia with the idea that Africa must be united. He and Nkrumah both thought so. Both had studied at American universities, and both had been influenced by the American system of government. They used what they learned in the United States to enlighten the people about the fight for freedom. As a result of their efforts, all the political parties came together to free Nigeria from colonial rule. They had a unity of purpose, which they abandoned after independence. That abandonment is the main reason for the chaos and military rule that now exists in Nigeria.

But what really drew me into the movement was that a Jamaican man from England came to visit Nigeria and was denied a room at a Lagos hotel—the Bristol Hotel—because he was black. The National Council of Nigeria and the Cameroons called an emergency meeting at the Glover Memorial Hall on Marina Street, one of the most popular meeting places for political activities and speeches.

Azikiwe was loved and respected by everyone in all the ethnic groups because he spoke the three main Nigerian languages—Ibo, Yoruba, and Hausa. He had called this meeting to denounce the hotel's discrimination.

The hall held about five thousand people. Another ten thousand were gathered outside, so they installed loudspeakers to make sure people could hear him. When he was introduced to speak, he just said, "We cannot tolerate discrimination against any of our brothers or sisters from the diaspora in Lagos, Nigeria." That's all he had to say.

I was one of those people who left work at five o'clock and went to the hall. I couldn't get in. But I heard Azikiwe say, "We cannot tolerate discrimination against any of our brothers or sisters from the diaspora." There was an instantaneous response. All the people standing outside ran to the Bristol, just a short distance from the hall, and started throwing stones at the hotel. It took the mounted police to disperse us. I was one of those people who threw stones at Bristol Hotel.

These were the very beginnings of Pan-Africanism. The first step had to be freeing ourselves. Once you are free, you can embrace nationalism. Only after that can you really talk about Pan-Africanism. We had to form a nation before we could start thinking about a United States of Africa. Even so, it can be said that Pan-Africanism began with the return of Nkrumah and Azikiwe.

I was just out of school, and was among twelve people selected to be trained as labor officers. I was judged to have the demeanor, the style, to become a very good mediator. After working for a year or two, we would be sent to England to be trained as labor officers, as people who would negotiate between workers and employers. We would settle wage disputes.

I was now a young adult, and I needed to escape my aunt's overprotectiveness and become responsible for myself. It was time I learned to fight for myself, to defend myself. It was just getting too dangerous, the way my aunt would just cancel all the people she thought I shouldn't associate with. I thought she was going too far. She was interfering with my friends.

It was starting to get embarrassing, so a friend advised me, "Why don't you ask for a transfer, and go away?"

I didn't think I could do it, because she had so much power over me, as an elder, as a woman, and most important, as somebody who cared about me and loved me so much. She'd tell me not to do this and that, and this and that, and I'd just give in. Because she would never quit, trying to convince me to do what she wanted.

So I arranged for a transfer. I was transferred in 1948 to a city called Sapele. I told her a lie—I had to—that we were going for training for six months. It wasn't six months. Then she sat me down to tell me the rules. One of the rules was to be very careful about the women in that area. "Remember, you just can't have anything to do with just any ordinary woman. You have to be selective. You have to let us know who you are thinking about getting married to. Then we're going to have a meeting, and see whether this will be a suitable person for you."

It is often said that Africans select husbands and wives for their children. But I think this is a universal thing. Every good parent wants to know who their son or their daughter is associating with, who their daughter or son is going to marry. If I marry into your family, everybody in your family—your aunt's side, your mother's side, your father's side—they all become a member of my family and must be treated as such. It's a very strong rule. I could not escape it. I could not marry anybody without discussing it first with people in the family. It would have been sacrilegious. It was not done. They would have said, "You've missed one of the most important opportunities of your life." It's an opportunity where all your relatives on both sides of the coin come together to give you their blessings. Some of them are going to become your psychiatrist and psychologist, your advisor. Some of them are going to help you get on your feet. They have so much responsibility and so many parts to play in your life, so you can't take this kind of giant step in life by yourself. You need to remember that you are uniting not only two of you, but two whole families.

You hear this all your life. It starts when you show the capacity to understand what parents are saying to you. You start hearing it. So maybe some days you go out and you come in late, and they say, "You can't be doing that, because when you become a responsible person, trying to build a home base, to become a parent, is this the way you're going to be doing it? Just leaving home and coming back any time? How can people trust you?" You can't do things like that. You have to take members of the family into consideration.

I was in Sapele for two years. I was the vacancy officer, in charge of all job openings posted and filled. There was a plywood factory that had about five thousand workers. As a vacancy officer, I had to fill the vacancies as they arose, or as requested by the main employer or employers in Sapele and the district.

All people looking for work had to register with the government's Labor Department. At that particular time, before independence, there was a great exodus of people from rural areas coming into Lagos, looking for jobs. Some of them had stopped farming. So the government was trying to make sure these people got some kind of work so they would stay in their home areas instead of migrating to Lagos. Bricklayers, typists, people with different skills, all registered with the department. As the notifications came to us, I would go through the registration cards and pull out those who had been coming and renewing their cards every week. After I found someone a job, I would pull their card out and file it differently.

At the time I arrived in Sapele, there was a man from Lagos working for the Marine Department there. He noticed in the papers that an energetic young man was coming from Lagos by the name of Babatunde Olatunji, and that he was going to become the vacancy officer. This man had been working in Sapele for quite some time, and he knew everybody. He came to meet me, and invited me to his place for dinner, to welcome me. I didn't know that he was actually trying to warn me—so that what happened to the previous vacancy officer wouldn't happen to me.

My predecessor had been caught accepting a bribe. People want jobs. All of the vacancies go to the Labor Department, be they clerical or skilled. The Labor office supplied about five thousand skilled workers every month to the plywood plant in Sapele. Rumor had it that the chief of the town had arranged to send people in his town to this clerk. People looking for work would go to the local chief in town and gave him one guinea, which was equivalent to a little over five dollars. He'd say, "Well, I have connections." The chief would then send for these vacancy officers and say to them, "I want you to give so-and-so and so-and-so and so-and-so a job. And this is your share of what we get." This was how the corruption started. Quite a few clerks before me had been caught in the act, and not only dismissed but sent to jail.

So this man from Lagos working in Sapele came to warn me that he didn't want that to happen to me. He said, "Look, I don't know who you are, but since you are the new vacancy officer I just want to warn you that if anybody should come along looking for a job and offer you any money, please do not accept it because the government has arrested vacancy officers before you."

I thanked him very much, and said, "May God bless you. I don't think that I will get caught up in that anyway."

Sure enough, people started coming up to me and saying, "I have five guineas. Please call me when there is a request next time." That was very tempting. That was a very delicate situation. Here I was, a young man with a fear of creating lifetime enemies, and of course making sure, because of the way I was brought up, to protect my name. I had to think more than twice before I made any decision. I couldn't bring shame and humiliation to the family name. That was what I had to think about.

The government might want to test you. The money would be given to plainclothes men, who would come and register and then offer you money. If you accepted it, you would be arrested right there. So I told people, "Only people who have no money should come here looking for jobs." That was the first thing I announced to everybody.

They were shocked at first. Then they said, "Sooner or later, maybe you have your own money, but you're probably going to be tempted, too."

But I said, "I'm not going to get arrested. The government provides security for its workers. If you come here to bribe me, you will be the one arrested." So that went all right.

While I was there, serving as vacancy officer, I kept up my correspondence with my cousin Akiwowo, who was working at that time in the Treasury Department in Lagos. We decided to write to the Rotary Education Foundation of Atlanta, Georgia, to apply for scholarships. We put our curricula vitae together, and he drafted the letter and sent it.

I had a passion to see America. I had been involved in so many activities that pulled me in that direction. I had gone to the Baptist Academy, which was American sponsored. I had read about so many inspiring American events—the Boston Tea Party, Jackie Robinson. Americans can never understand what it's like to be outside America; you can't read and hear about America and not want to go there. They have no idea how enticing it is, how inviting it is, how tempting it is to do anything you can just to get here. America is painted so glowingly that you can't resist wanting to come.

As the years went by, I was sold on the idea of coming to America, instead of England, where I would have been offered a scholarship because one of my uncles was a member of the selection committee for British scholarships. He was the first Nigerian to own a pharmacy. But I didn't want to go to England. By the time I left the Baptist Academy, I was sold on the United States.

About three months later, we got a reply from the Rotary Foundation: we'd been granted four-year scholarships to attend Morehouse College. Because of the situation in the South, we wouldn't be able to attend Georgia Tech or the University of Georgia, but we could attend Morehouse, an all-black college, for four years, as long as we maintained a B average.

I immediately wrote back to my cousin: "If you're sure they mean it, we have to leave to be able to register for the second semester." At that time there were no planes flying from any part of Africa. The only way we could go was by ship.

I couldn't control myself after we got the letter. I started dreaming every day about coming to America and doing this and that. I became preoccupied with all the details, and with how we couldn't let my aunt know about it. My cousin promised he wouldn't tell any member of his family, because if any member of the family knew, my aunt would hear about it. So that's when I knew that my cousin and I would be doing things together for a long time.

I left Sapele to get back to Lagos. I told everybody that I was going on a month's leave. My department head, Miss Brucewait, from Great Britain, the managing director of the Labor Department, had just given me a promotion. She was very fond of me and my work, how I handled myself, and what I was doing. I lied to her so well that she expected me to be going to England soon to complete my studies to become a labor officer. Nobody knew about our plans. Akiwowo didn't even tell his father.

The last few days before we sailed to America were very interesting. I actually disappeared the last few days. I was fasting, and I went to the

Denge, used the *sakara* to sing the praises of kings and tell the history of his ancestors. I would take my *sakara* and sing lullabies to these boys. The little one would always fall asleep.

Every morning I would play my little hand drum, sometimes just to amuse myself. The ship was the *Del Oro* of the West African Berber Line, which brought all the cargo from West Africa to the United States through New Orleans. It wasn't a passenger boat. It had a few cabins that they would sell to passengers, but it was actually a cargo boat.

I remember the ship's engineer. He said, "A strange man in a strange land shouldn't sing a strange song."

But I was so excited. I was a Rotary Scholar. I was going to study to become a diplomat. I was hoping to be able one day to represent Nigeria in the UN, or as a diplomat or an ambassador to some country.

So for days, while we were at sea, we made good friends with these little boys, until we arrived in New Orleans, on 27 April 1950.

PART TWO

Adapting to a New Rhythm

4 | Jim Crow and College Life

A t Customs, that very first day in America, I experienced discrimination. Two gentlemen, the executive director and the assistant director of the YMCA in New Orleans, had been sent by our benefactor, the Rotary Club, to meet us. But when we arrived in New Orleans, they separated my cousin and me from our two little friends and their mother.

The two boys and their mother were on the other side of something that separated us. When I called the attention of my cousin to this, I was asked to leave it alone.

I called to one of the boys, "Mike, come over here."

He ran to me, and I picked him up. Just as I did that, a policeman walked up to me and said, "Put him down."

I turned to him and said, "What do you mean? You don't know him. Who are you to tell me to put him down?"

"I said put him down."

He was getting ready to put his hand on his gun. So I said, "Okay, what is the deal? What is the matter?"

He said to me, "You're not supposed to be playing with him." Then he said to the boy, "You go back over there."

I said, "What are you doing that for?"

The two gentlemen who had come to meet us interrupted the conversation and said, "Mr. Olatunji, please listen to us. Don't ask any questions. We'll explain to you what is happening."

I said, "But he doesn't know him. *I* know him. He was born in my country. I've been with them for thirty days aboard this ship. Why should I put him down? He doesn't know him."

They tried to calm me down and explain to me what was going on. I felt like turning right back and going back home. I didn't know about all this.

I said, "How can you stop somebody from playing with somebody? It doesn't make any sense to me. It doesn't make any sense at all."

These two men explained to me what was happening, that the policeman was just enforcing a rule.

I said, "Enforcing a rule?"

I was out of it, completely. I couldn't understand why two people who knew each other couldn't be together. I had never experienced anything like that in Africa. I thought, What kind of strange customs do they have here? It was a sleepless night for me.

That was the very first day. The next day at eight o'clock we were put on the Jim Crow train to Atlanta. It was a segregated train. Blacks could not go to certain areas of the train. They weren't served from the same car. The car that we went to was in the front or the back. It was just separate.

Then, when we arrived at the train station in Atlanta, we were told that we could not ride in just any taxi. We had to look for a black cab driver, who would drive us to the Morehouse campus. The journey from the Atlanta station to the Morehouse campus was fascinating. We got a guided tour from the cab driver, who took his bloody time to point out the different institutions to us along the road. "This is where Morris Brown College is. It's a co-ed college for young blacks, boys and girls . . . We're now getting to Atlanta University, which serves this whole area . . . And there's the Atlanta School of Social Work . . . You have Emory Theological Seminary, the place where Dr. Martin Luther King, Jr. got his ministerial training after finishing Morehouse . . . Then you have Morehouse College, an all men's college, and after that is Clark College, which is co-ed. And then, on the other side of the road, is Spelman College, which is an all girls' school, which happens to be the soulmate of Morehouse College."

Most of the Morehouse men found their girlfriends at Spelman. The administration arranged the social activities so that the Morehouse men would always be dating Spelman girls. That was like a tradition.

When we got to our new home, I told my benefactor, Kendall Weisiger, the story about what happened at Customs, and he said, "Oh, that's nothing. You have to adjust to the way things are in this country. A black man cannot play with a white child."

I said, "That's ridiculous. How does one make an adjustment to *that*? He doesn't know them. The child was born in my country."

Mr. Weisiger was the president of the organization that gave me the four-year scholarship to Morehouse. This man was the only white person, Southern white person, who served on the board of directors of Morehouse. He was right there to greet me and my cousin when we arrived on campus. He became my mentor.

He said, "Let me tell you. Do not let anything or anybody disturb your movement toward your goal. Here is the list of books that you need to read."

He guided me by placing in my hands the biographies and autobiographies of great men of all walks of life, black and white, American and foreign, for me to read. Lincoln, Sojourner Truth, Mark Twain . . . an orientation to the country.

And I'm glad he did. That's how I discovered what my friend, Mark Twain, had to say: "Millions of men and women are born, they struggle and fight for little advantages over each other. Age creeps up on them, infirmities follow, and shame and humiliation bring down their pride and vanities. And those that they love are taken away from them. Then comes at last, the ever unpoisoned gift earth ever had for man. And they perish from a world in which they were of no consequence. A world that will lament them a day, and forget them forever."

I said, "Oh, my God. I want to be of consequence. I don't want to be lamented a day and forgotten forever."

So Kendall Weisiger was right. He told me, "One of the main reasons you are here on the face of the earth is to help free mankind."

I said, "Me, free mankind? Doing what?" I couldn't understand in those days what he was talking about, but I always remembered what he said.

Quite a few things that people told me back then have turned out to be true. The truth in their pronouncements has become very clear to me. As my life developed, my activities would demonstrate this.

Once I arrived at Morehouse, it started really becoming clear to me that he was just telling me the law of the land. In one of his letters to us, he wrote: "I would have loved for you to go to University of Georgia or Georgia Tech. But because of the social situation in our state, I decided to put you at Morehouse College."

When we arrived on campus, we were introduced to all the staff. The news got around that the college had two more people from Africa. There was one African student who had come before us. His name was H. A. Oluwasomi. He graduated during my sophomore year. After Morehouse, he got his Ph.D. in rural economics from Harvard University. Later he would become vice chancellor of one of Nigeria's most important universities. At Morehouse, he would become my mentor. He was the first African student to be elected president of the student body, and I was the second.

As I looked around, I could see that eight out of ten of the students looked like my cousins, or my uncle, or somebody I'd known. I saw women who looked like women I liked very much, and men who looked like my relatives. I said, "You look exactly like friends of mine."

One of them, Maynard Jackson, Jr., became the first black mayor of Atlanta. He told me, "Don't you ever tell me I'm of African descent. I am a Negro. I was born in America."

I couldn't believe my ears. I said, "Your ancestors are from Africa."

He said, "I was born here. I don't want to be an African. I am a Negro."

They weren't even saying black in those days. So I said to my cousin, "What's wrong with these people? These are Africans. What is he telling me that he's not an African for? What is he trying to deny?"

I said to Maynard, "Just tell me then, where do you come from?"

He said, "From here."

"Nobody came out of a vacuum," I said. "Your ancestors came from somewhere."

"I'm from here. I'm not an African."

The questions began. Other students would ask me, "You're from Africa? What do you eat?"

"What do I *eat*? I eat the same things you do. We just prepare them differently."

"Are you sure?"

"Don't I look like a human being?"

The questions that I got about Africa embarrassed me at first. But I quickly changed my attitude. Within three days of my arrival, I started saying, "Come to my room when you have time, and we'll talk about Africa. Ask me all the questions you want to ask me."

So people started coming to my room. More and more students came to talk with me in my room, and this aggravated my roommate, who was blacker than charcoal. Later on he changed his room because there was too much discussion about Africa.

It went on and on and on, and I decided, "I have a job to tell these people about the rich cultural heritage of Africa. I better get on with this mission now." That's how I got involved in what I'm doing today.

I had to do something to maintain my sanity. Here I was, fresh from Africa, and I was looking at people who looked like those I left behind and they were telling me face to face that they weren't African. That was a big blow, psychologically. I wasn't too happy about it. I couldn't believe they really felt that way.

Hearing that on the college campus was mind blowing to me. I knew I couldn't take on the entire student body. So I slept on it, and decided the burden of proof was on me. I had to talk to them about it, to find a way to reconcile myself with them. I wanted to unite myself with them as one.

My approach was based completely on the education and training I got in my village and in Lagos. Those things had prepared me very well for this situation. I judged that these people really were not telling me these things to offend me. They were really telling me what they believed, what they'd been taught to believe. They had been brainwashed into believing these things. And that's a very dangerous thing.

I asked myself, "What will I do about it? What can I do to destroy the stereotypes about Africa and Africans?" I knew I had to do something about it. I couldn't start fighting everybody. And I wasn't going to go back to Africa just because of this. After a lot of careful thought and fervent prayer, I came up with the answer. I would have to take the cultural route, because I knew there was a cultural basis for our unity.

I asked my benefactor if he could arrange for me to speak in different places, and he arranged it. He sent me to speak at churches—white and black churches. When I went, I took my little drum. And I quoted from the bible, which is something I learned to do at the Baptist Academy, where we studied the bible from Genesis to Revelation.

All of that helped me deal with the kinds of situations that were trying to affect my sanity. I was able to develop an attitude that did not make me bitter. For every hurtful question, I learned to give a fantastic, unbelievable answer that would start everybody laughing.

I would be asked, "Is it true that lions run in the streets of Lagos?"

I would say, "Oh, yes. You see my little drum? When I play this rhythm, if any lion comes out of the grass and roars, I say some words that mean, 'I'm coming to get you.'"

And they would say, "Oh, get out of here!"

"Oh, but if I play this other rhythm, the female lions come around and they all start playing together."

"Get out of here! You can't call any lions by playing your drums."

"That's what you wanted me to tell you."

Then they'd ask me, "Is it true that Africans have tails?"

I'd say, "Now I know you have gone too far. You want to know if it is true that Africans have tails?"

Then I'd turn around and pull up my coat. "Can't you see?"

And everybody would break into laughter. They would say, "Now you really know how to fight back."

I'd say, "It's not a question of fighting." I had turned the situation around, so it would not end in bitterness. I knew now that "a soft answer turneth away wrath," as the Bible says.

I was able to rise above all the negativity. Soon after that I was selected to represent the freshmen class. That's how I started on the ladder. I represented my freshmen class, and then my sophomore class. By my junior year I was secretary of the student body. In my senior year I was elected president of the student body. I had become the most popular foreign student on the campus.

But we were late registering for class, so we wound up observing classes when we arrived on the campus on April 29.

They said, "You're too late to register now. How did you get here so late?"

I said, "No planes. We didn't fly here. We came by boat."

They said, "No wonder."

Then Mrs. Asher, the secretary to the director of personnel and a relative of one of the founders of Morehouse, a very proud, direct, and kind woman, said, "The president's office has just sent a memo that your name should be included with the students who are going to Simsbury, Connecticut, to work this summer. You know you're supposed to work, and save your money to buy books, and buy some clothes for yourself, so you'd better prepare yourself now, because you're going to work. I don't know what you did at home."

That's Mrs. Asher. So I said, "What kind of work is it?"

She said, "You're going to a tobacco farm."

I said, "Tobacco farm? I never picked tobacco before."

She said, "There's always a first time, and you're going to learn how to do it, and do it very well. Because you're going to learn fast how to do it, or you're not going to bring any money home. You're not paid that much."

"Tobacco is planted in rows," she told us. "And you're going to stand between two rows and pick those leaves, and lay them down. A bend is about one big street block long. You get ten cents for picking a bend. If you pick and pull, you get a quarter."

I said, "That's what I'm going to do. I'm not going to pick and let somebody else come and pull what I picked."

She said, "Great! How are you going to do that?"

I said, "I'll pull it myself."

She said, "How are you going to pull it?"

I said, "I'm going to pull it. I'm going to load them in the basket, tie two baskets together, manage with the third one on my head."

She said, "On your what? Is your head that strong?"

I said, "Ma'am, I'm going to have to do that to be able to save enough money to buy some clothes."

She said, "All right. You're going to pick tobacco."

I said, "It's nothing to write home about, but I'll do it. I've never done anything like that."

She said, "You've never done anything like that in Africa?"

I said, "No—not where I come from. I didn't have to do that. I can't even let them know that I'm doing that. My folks would be very, very disappointed that I came here to America to do that. They would say, 'You see? You see what he's doing over there? He's going to be a laborer. You were never to be a laborer there.'"

We left the first week of June, on a chartered bus. From Atlanta to Simsbury, Connecticut, it made only three stops.

I was amazed. I was so impressed with the road, I said to myself, "How long will it take us to have roads like this, that are so wide and clear and well taken care of?"

I nudged my cousin. I told him, "We have a lot of work to do in Africa." Now I was convinced that we really were almost five hundred years behind. But with the enthusiasm at home, once we become independent, we were going to go right ahead, building and rebuilding.

When we arrived in Simsbury, we were greeted by the farm manager. The farm was operated by Cullman Brothers, the makers of Lucky Strike cigarettes. We were taken to our residence, a big open dormitory with bunk beds.

I ran quickly to select the bottom bed, to make sure I didn't repeat what happened to me at Morehouse. My first night there, I slept on the top bunk and fell out. Coming from Africa, I had never seen a bunk bed.

The first orientation was conducted by the farm managers, who reminded us that to make any money, we would have to work very hard. I had decided by then to pick and pull my own. And that's exactly what I did.

Some of my fellow students asked me, "How will you do that?" I told them, "You just watch and see."

What I did was after picking my tobacco leaves, I put them in the baskets provided for us. I piled them up in two baskets. Then I tied the two baskets together. Then I filled the third basket, which I balanced on my head while pulling the first two baskets. This caused some kind of pandemonium among the students. They'd never seen anything like it. How could you balance this basket of tobacco on your head, and at the same time pull without it falling down? Well, you have to go back to traditional practices at home. When you are sent out into the woods to fetch wood to make a fire, and you have like a quarter of a mile to travel to get this thing home, you have to carry it on your head. I grew up doing that at home, so it came in very handy. That endeared me to many, many students, and to all the directors and managers.

So I became one of the top tobacco pickers that summer, and probably made more money than anybody else. With that kind of accomplishment, the manager invited me to come back the following year as one of the supervisors. But I had promised myself, without making any comment, that I would not be coming back to Simsbury, Connecticut, to pick tobacco. I had never worked that hard in my life, even though I'm from a fishing village.

I promised myself not to come back for many reasons. First of all, the summer heat in Simsbury, Connecticut, was far more severe than what I had known in Lagos. We were in open fields. There was no place to take refuge from the afternoon sun. No trees, no shade.

Second, I could not get myself to like the lunches we were fed. To this day, I never like bologna sandwiches and salami sandwiches. But that's what we got every day for lunch, with an apple or an orange, or milk.

Third, the pay for our hard work was a big reason. I was not going to come back as a supervisor if it meant helping the company exploit young people.

So when asked whether I would come back, I said, "I'll think about it and let you know."

But in retrospect, I learned a lot about hard work. I learned a lot about working with a group. I learned a lot about having fortitude, focusing on the goal, and knowing very well that work was not an end in itself, but a means to an end.

When the stay on the farm was over, I decided to spend a week out of the ten days remaining, before going back to school, visiting New York, the city that I had read so much about.

In Hartford, I waved goodbye to Akiwowo and my classmates and got on a different bus, a direct one that would arrive during daylight. Friends had written down for me the address of the 135th Street YMCA, where I intended to stay. I had selected the YMCA because of my background at home—I had gone to a missionary school and been a member of its choir. I knew about the Y. I was sure I would get help from everybody who worked there. They had to be Christian, God-loving people.

I was ready. I was prepared mentally, physically, and spiritually to go to New York and stay in Harlem, where, I was told, I would see many people who looked exactly like the ones I knew at home.

We arrived before noon in New York. For the first time, I was able to jump in the first cab at the taxi stand. It was quite a difference from my first experience in Atlanta. There, I had to be sure of who the driver of the taxi was. Was he black or white? Anybody could ride here. You could get into any cab and be driven anywhere.

What I didn't know was that taxi drivers are the same all over the world. I would learn that lesson as the years went by.

I gave the address to the driver. "I'm going to the 135th Street 'Y.'"

I had been told that the whole trip to 135th Street shouldn't cost more than three dollars. I wound up paying six dollars and fifty cents. The cabbie had taken me on a joyride.

I questioned the amount. I said, "Why does it cost so much? I was told that it should cost less than three dollars."

He said, "Didn't you notice there was traffic?"

I said, "I didn't see any traffic in front of us, but I saw you making left and right turns, almost in every direction. Isn't there a way that you could have gone from the bus station"—which used to be at 50th Street and 8th Avenue—"all the way to 135th Street?" Anyway, that was my first experience.

I registered at the Y, and asked the lady at the desk about the neighborhood. She gave me a map, which showed how the avenues went perpendicular to the streets.

I asked, "Where is Harlem?"

She said, "You are in Harlem. Right in the middle of it."

I said, "Great. I saw a lot of people who looked like people that I know at home."

She said, "Where is your home?"

I said, "Nigeria."

She said, "Where is Nigeria?"

I said, "West Africa. It looks like most of the people that I see here come from Nigeria or the West Coast of Africa."

She said, "Is that right? You think so?"

I said, "Yes. I know so. I'm going to take a walk out to lunch."

She said, "Good. When you get out of the Y, you can make a left turn and walk a block, and then make a right turn, and then you'll be walking uptown."

I said, "That's exactly what I'm going to do."

She said, "How long do you intend to walk?"

I said, "I'll walk as long as I can, until I get tired. Then I'll walk back."

As I walked, I saw so many people who looked like people that I knew, that I had seen all my life. I wanted to call and say, "So-and-so, and so-and-so, when did you get here?" I tried to contain myself.

I walked ten blocks from 135th Street, and came to the corner of 145th Street and 7th Avenue, and I saw "Lagos Bar."

I said, "Oh, my God! Lagos Bar! What a day! There's got to be somebody from Lagos there!"

My walk quickened. I stood in front of the place and looked again. "Lagos Bar." I had never been in a bar. There was liquor in there. I saw signs advertising Millers and Pabst Blue Ribbon. I laughed. I don't drink anyway.

I said, "Maybe I can ask them for juice or water." So I went in there with a broad smile on my face, so full of enthusiasm.

I said, "Good afternoon, gentlemen. Ladies and gentlemen. Good afternoon."

They looked at me.

I said, "I would like to see the manager."

The bartender said, "The manager is not here."

"I would like to see the owner."

"The owner is not here."

"Excuse me. This is Lagos Bar?"

"Yes."

"The owner must be from my city," I said, "because I'm from Lagos, Nigeria, the capital of Nigeria."

Everybody at the bar started laughing.

I said, "No, I'm serious, people. Lagos is the capital of Nigeria, and my name is Michael Babatunde Olatunji from Nigeria. The owner of this place must be from Nigeria." Then they busted into absolute guffaws.

I was so sad. "Ladies and gentlemen. Excuse me, please. This is a serious matter. I am not kidding you. I have just arrived less than three months ago. And I see that most of you look like people from my home—"

And they're saying, "Get out of here, nigger. Ain't nobody here from Africa. Get out. Nobody here from Lagos, Nigeria."

"But how did you get the name?"

"Will you get out of here, please?"

I said, "Thank you," and turned away, so disgusted, so embarrassed and sad.

I walked out of the bar. Across the street I saw another place. It was a miracle. It said "Zanzibar."

I said, "Zanzibar! That's an African name! Let me go over there. Maybe . . ."

So I walked across the street. The same thing happened. "There ain't nobody here from Africa."

I said, "Well, you look like somebody I know."

"Please. Nobody here is from Africa. I am an American Negro."

I walked back to my hotel—ten blocks to 135th and a left turn. I couldn't eat my supper that evening. Because of our traditional practices, I needed to consult an oracle to find out what had happened to me.

The next morning, I looked across 135th Street at the site where they have since built a residential complex called Lennox Terrace. It was just some old houses then. And right in front of one of the houses was a fortune-teller. I was tempted to go in there and say, "Tell me." Just like we consult the oracle Ifa, that tells the future.

I said, "I must find out what is it that has happened to me. Why is it that I should be experiencing such disappointment, when it had to be an African who came up with these names?" It must have been one of the sailors going to the Caribbean who stopped here, and jumped ship, and never went back home, because most of our people who came here did not come as slaves. I had all kinds of thoughts. I tried to put two and two together, because it was a very sad day in my life.

I walked in to the fortune teller. The lady said, "Come in." She asked me for a dollar.

I said, "It costs a dollar?" A dollar in 1950 was a lot of money to me, when I thought of what a dollar would buy in Nigeria. So I gave her a dollar.

She said, "You're a foreigner."

I said, "Of course I'm a foreigner. You can tell by my accent. That's no magic. Of course you can tell that."

She said, "You're a foreigner."

I said, "Yes, I'm a foreigner. I'm from Africa. What else are you going to tell me? Tell me about the future."

She said, "The future looks good. You are going to do well. That's all I can tell you."

I said, "I want my dollar."

"If you want me to tell you more, you can come back tomorrow and give me five dollars."

I gave her five dollars. I said, "When I come tomorrow, tell me exactly what happened to me yesterday."

When I went back the next day, the old lady was not there. It was her daughter or somebody else. And when she asked me to come back, I said, "No, I'm not going to do that." And then I told myself, "The best thing for me to do is to go back, kneel down, and pray." Then I remembered all of the things that I had experienced, going to prayer meeting, learning about the Psalms. The Psalm of prosperity: "The Lord is my shepherd, I shall not want." The Psalm of protection: "I who dwelleth in the sacred place of the Lord shall abide under the shadow of the Almighty." Another Psalm says: "I will lift up my eyes unto the hills from whence cometh my help."

I went back to my room, and I picked up the Bible, and I started reading. I was determined that I must not give up until I convinced these people, my people, that their ancestors came from Africa.

But I had mixed feelings coming to Harlem. I said, "I must return to Harlem one day." This was the place where I would need to start a program that would help people reclaim their identity with Africa, so that one day they would be able to embrace Africa, as the other ethnic groups that made up this country have embraced their homelands. Not until then would they become better citizens of America and of the world. I believe that now, just as I believed it then.

So that was my introduction to Harlem. I went back to 50th Street and 8th Avenue and took the Greyhound bus to Atlanta to begin my freshman year.

Morehouse College is a great institution. It was founded by a missionary society, and it has a Christian philosophy. Its faculty are carefully selected, and so are all its students. Its founders declared that those who came within its walls would graduate as men of strong character and tremendous courage. They would be nation builders. They would be honest people, and above all, they would be good Christians. By the time you leave Morehouse, you will have been prepared for success. You will be somebody who believes in himself, in the family, and in society. Above all, you will be a Christian.

During my orientation, both the president and the dean stressed all of the qualities that a graduate of Morehouse must possess. If you do not possess all of those qualities by the time you leave Morehouse, you must be promising. When I heard this for the first time, I told myself, "This is where I belong."

All the freshmen lived in Graves Hall, the most famous building on campus. Every morning when you went to chapel, you heard great speakers. The leadership of Morehouse was superb, starting with the president, Benjamin E. Mays, who was a great spirit, a great leader, and probably one of the most eloquent orators, teachers, leaders, and ministers I have ever heard. And he was black. He personified what we lack today in leadership. Leadership can always bring about change, but a leader must have vision, must be able to cope with change, must stay the course. Mays did. He helped produce men of strong character, like Dr. Martin Luther King, Jr., and so many other great Morehouse graduates. It has been estimated that there are more Morehouse graduates in leadership positions in America today than from any other black college, or even white college.

Mr. Mays laid the foundation. He was able to recruit a southern "liberal" Christian gentleman, Kendall Weisiger, to the Board of Trustees. Weisiger turned out to be my benefactor; later he became president of the Rotary Educational Foundation of Atlanta. He came up with the idea that to fight communism, there was no need for witch hunting, no need for

McCarthyism. What business people and intelligent people should do is bring people from all over the world to come and see democracy at work, to observe its growing pains. If you did that, you would defeat communism. He was right. That's the kind of man that Mr. Mays looked for, regardless of his color. He persuaded this man to become a member of the Morehouse board. That's how he was able to get a Japanese to be a student while we were there. He searched for the best. He expected nothing but the best from you.

He reminded you every time he saw you walking by: "Remember, the man of Morehouse is an achiever. You must keep your eye on the goal. You must be a Christian gentleman. You must be able to stand on your own." Every day in chapel, he reminded you of that. You were given all of this in little doses, every day. How could you fail? There was no way for you to fail, because you heard the message every day, relentlessly, from all the teachers, too. Teachers who didn't remind you didn't last long at Morehouse. The entire faculty was dedicated to the building of men of character. You were constantly reminded that one day soon you would be letting people know who you were, by the way you behaved, by the way you treated others. And you'd be told, as it says in the Bible, "How can a man light a candle and put it under a bush? It will go out." You heard this every day. You weren't going to succeed for too long if you were mediocre. People would find you out. Let people be able to say, "I can testify on behalf of this man. This is a Morehouse man." So it was quite an experience to be at Morehouse.

One of the things I cherish most in my life is that I was born in Ajido, a small fishing village, and that I grew up there. I remember my childhood as so rich, not materially but spiritually. I grew up knowing the importance of sharing. Morehouse was almost like the way I grew up.

I have been blessed in so many ways. My mentor, Mr. Weisiger, arranged four years of American college for me, in the early 1950s when it was not popular to sponsor people of color. He was a truly evolved man. His level of consciousness was so high. He is one of the main reasons why I say there are good people doing good work everywhere. No one ever wrote about Kendall Weisiger, and he never made the cover of *Time* or *Newsweek*. But when he became president of the Rotary Educational Foundation, he made a difference. In spite of the McCarthyism of the times, he encouraged people from all over the world to come to America.

One of the most important things my benefactor did was arrange for me to speak in many churches in Atlanta. And these were white churches, segregated ones. He made arrangements with pastors that, as a student from Africa, I would be talking about the work of the church missionary society in Nigeria and how I was involved. Most important, though, I always took my drum with me.

The first place I went one Sunday, the men said, "Tell us about your journey here, where you went to school, and tell us about Christianity in Nigeria." And then they asked, "What about the drum?"

I said, "In Psalm 151, it says 'Praise the Lord with all the instruments.' What I am going to present is how we worship in African churches. We sing the hymns with the piano, with the drums, and people can dance."

They said, "Really? You take the drums to the church?"

I said, "Yes."

They said, "Well let's see, let's try it this time. I don't know how the congregation will react, but we're going to do it."

I said, "Good!"

They called my name. I spelled my name and gave the meaning of my name. Then I told them the story of how the African Methodist-Episcopalian Church came into existence, and I went into the whole story of how Africans, after they accepted the faith, went to the Anglican Church, the Church of England, in Lagos, and they took drums. At first, the people said, "No you can't bring drums to sing the hymns." Hymns like "Onward Christian Soldiers" that were sung so slowly that people would even fall asleep. When they couldn't play their drums in the Anglican Church, they left and formed the African Methodist-Episcopalian Church. That was the church in which I grew up when I was in school in Lagos. What Africans did was jazz the hymns up, play them in four-four rhythm so that people could clap their hands.

I said, "If I sing 'Onward Christian Soldiers' in my language, you will be able to join me singing the same song in the English language." So I sang it, accompanying myself with the drums. Before I knew it the congregation were clapping their hands and people were smiling.

The minister said, "We are having a revival today in the church, not under the tent. Praise be to God." And a collection of four hundred dollars was given by the congregation. So I became like a king on the campus.

I did this maybe twice a month, and I always brought in money. People asked me, Where did you get the money from? Nobody was sending me money from home. It was taking about three months to get replies to my letters. My benefactor had arranged with the ministers that they would take up collections for me after my talks. This was how I was able to buy my books, some clothing, a new pair of shoes. That was how my benefactor contributed to a wonderful experience that has stayed with me.

Through the help of many, many people, especially our benefactor, we were able to see for ourselves that we could become beacons of light that would help bring about positive change in human relations. We became friends of African Americans, who welcomed us into their homes, poor families in the projects and middle-class families, too. Especially on Sundays, we could enjoy a home-cooked meal! Some of the students even dated their daughters. At every holiday, like Christmas and Thanksgiving, they always made sure we were part of the family. So it happened with the Harris family, where the head of the house held down two jobs, and the Henderson family, who were a middle-class African American family. Both Hendersons had a university education and taught at one of the colleges. We were able to relate to these two groups of people in this way. There were really three groups, the white group, the middle-class blacks, and those who were still struggling at the bottom of the ladder. We were surrounded by people who wanted to make us feel at home. All of these people were trying their best to make sure we did not feel neglected. We related to everybody there. It made our time at Morehouse very, very meaningful, and very educational as well.

From what we had heard about America, you would think there was a tree that dollar bills fell from and you could just pick them up. I found that in reality, there was an opportunity here for anyone who persisted. You read that it was the land of opportunity, but you were not told how difficult it could be for someone like me. Still, you could make it in time.

The greatest surprise to me was that the people I met from America who came to my country when I was in high school never discussed with us how deep and widespread the difference was between black and white. I was surprised they never told us about this. Also, it was a surprise that the majority of the people we met knew very little about Africa, except the negatives. In Africa we were able to read all about America.

My attitude was that I was here to get what I needed to get to be who I wanted to be. This was the place to do it. That was not going to come easy—I was convinced of that. If I kept my eye on the prize, I would achieve my goal. I knew I could rise to the pinnacles of achievement, but I knew it wasn't going to be easy. I had no illusions about that.

In giving so much of my time to being a cultural ambassador, I gave up some of my time for studies. My academic pursuits were already difficult because the British system of education is quite different from the American one. We were not used to the true-or-false method of answering questions. We were always asked to elaborate when we were asked a question. We wrote essays. So the first couple of semesters we were not doing very well. But I did everything possible to cope.

I will always remember my four years in Atlanta. They really helped me adjust, even though there were difficult moments, difficult times because of the laws of the state, which limited our involvement with other people. Despite that, we were able to relate to those who extended themselves beyond what the law permitted. That was very important for developing an understanding. There were people who would help us through difficult times. We were able to establish close friendships with both blacks and whites.

It was different in many ways, and very challenging. That's why I say that after I left Africa, the best four years of my life were in the South, at Morehouse. This is because of what I learned about life there. I don't mean just at college—I mean everything outside school, too, both the negative and the positive. First of all—and this was true of southern blacks *and* whites—people took time to greet one another. There was a kind of recognition of your importance as a human being. There was respect for age and for motherhood. I could see all of this in the behavior of African Americans, and I could really identify with it. They cared for every member of the family. There was a role assigned to every member of the household. This really seemed like the culture in which I grew up. I became very relaxed in the homes of African Americans because I would notice how the younger ones behaved with their elders. I was very impressed with the way the man of the house assumed his responsibilities. He was dedicated to making sure his family got the best he could offer. I said, "My goodness, these people are Africans but they don't realize it."

It was very important that I saw this. It was all a repetition of the lessons I learned growing up in my village. The lessons of love, affection, honesty, and determination. The lesson that I can be a success, that I have so much to give, and that if I give I will receive in return. Morehouse really helped strengthen the foundations I got growing up in the village, while going to school in Lagos, while being around all the people who did so much to nurture me.

So my first year at Morehouse was quite an exciting year. People showed me they saw promise in me, so much so that I told myself, "I must not let anybody down." That helped me maintain my sanity. It made me resolve not to overreact when people asked me painful questions about Africa. I realized that ignorance can be a dangerous bliss, and that my classmates sincerely wanted to know the truth.

I put myself in their shoes. When I read what had been written about Africa, like the Tarzan books and things like that, I told myself I wouldn't want to identify with Africa either if that was all I knew about it. I decided I would always emphasize all the things we have in common. All the traditions that I had been accustomed to and open to at home and that had always helped me tremendously.

After that first year, because of the way I responded to all the questions, and the way people responded to me, and because of the stories I told, I was on my way to becoming a respected voice on campus.

When it came to grievances on the campus, on the students' side *and* on the administrative side, the administration would always call me. "What do you think, Mr. Olatunji? What is going on? What do you think we should do?" The students would always ask me, too. I was representing the freshman class, and then the sophomore class.

I became the secretary of the student body. The president at that time always asked me to do all the talking, because he was a quiet, unassuming person. He said, "I know you will be able to convince them. You are the one who should tackle this." It made me a favorite to some day become president of the student body. That first year was the beginning of the whole thing.

I also became secretary of the campus YMCA. We arranged for all the Y's in the city of Atlanta, men and women, black and white, to get together. That was the first time that ever happened. The southern region of the YMCA and the YWCA convened in a hotel. That was illegal, and we got a telegram from Governor Talmadge, whose son later became a senator, saying we were violating the state law against blacks and whites meeting together.

Unanimously, all the delegates from the southern YMCA and YWCA meeting in that hotel in Atlanta sent a joint statement to the governor that we were meeting in the name of Christ—not in the name of Morehouse or the State of Georgia, but in the name of Christ. I helped draft that telegram to the governor. We didn't hear anything more about it.

In my freshman year, I went through a lot of changes on the human side of things, because my roommate was trying to brief me on how I should select a lady partner, not necessarily a girlfriend, but somebody I could always have to attend social events with. The first dance I went to was arranged by Morehouse with Spelman College, our sister college. That was the tradition.

My roommate said, "Tonight, this is what you do. You take a look at who you want to be taking to events. Whoever you have more dances with, she'll be the person you take to social events."

I said, "Why should that be based on how many times I dance with a lady?"

He said, "I don't know, but that's the practice."

"No. If I dance with a lady here, and I look over there and I see another good dancer, I'm going to ask her to dance. I'm just going to the dance to dance."

"Well, that's what we do."

We went to the dance and I spotted a lot of good dancers. I didn't dance more than twice with one person, but I danced with a lot of people that evening. They were surprised that I could dance, because the English style is ballroom dancing, and they were holding each other so close.

I'd say, "You're not dancing. What are you doing?"

They'd look at me and say, "Where in the world did you come from? Get out of here!"

"You're not dancing. Move around!"

"You don't know."

"You're just holding onto each other. That's not dancing."

So I became a subject of conversation the next day. They were saying, "Don't go near Olatunji when you're going to dance because he's going to come and bother you. He's going to tell you you don't know how to dance. He's all over the floor, turning the ladies around, and flipping here and there. I don't know where he came from."

They said, "You've got to learn how to dance, man, like we dance here." We'd laugh about it, and they'd say, "You'll learn how to do that one day."

I became friends with almost every student on the campus. Of course, by now I realized I was a little mature—I was twenty-one and most of them were seventeen, eighteen, nineteen. Just a few of them, the ones who had come back with the G.I. Bill, were a little older. So I was taking everything in stride.

I remember very well the first girl that I asked out. I asked, "What is your name?"

She said, "My name is Roseanne."

"Do you live on the campus?"

"No, I live in the city."

"Are you from Atlanta?"

"Yes."

"Can I have your telephone number?"

She gave it to me. I said, "Okay, I'll call you." She was also a freshman.

Back then it cost a nickel to make a phone call, and then you could talk as long as you wanted. So I got change for a dollar. That was what? Twenty nickels? That would last me how long? I wasn't going to be calling her every day. So it was going to last me more than a month. So I put the nickels aside.

The third day I went and dialed. I said, "Hello."

"Hello, who is this?"

"My name is Michael Babatunde Olatunji. I'm from Lagos, Nigeria, West Africa." Boom. She hung up. I looked at the number again. I said, "Did I make a mistake?" It was a lady, not the girl. And I said, "That's one nickel already, nineteen left. I can't afford to be making calls twice a day if my dollar is going to go a month."

But I used another nickel.

The woman asked, "Are you the same person?"

"Yes, I'm from Africa."

"Nobody wants to talk to you here. Nobody is here."

The next day I went and waited at the corner drugstore, where all the boys and girls came for coffee. That's when I saw for the first time that in a drugstore you can buy almost anything. Stamps. Exercise books. You can order food.

It was there that my roommate took me and said, "I'm going to treat you. Lunch this afternoon is horrible. Let's go to the corner drugstore and have something to eat."

So I sat down. He came back and said, "Here is a hot dog."

I said, "Hot dog? That's an insult. From where I come in Africa, we don't eat dogs."

So he laughed, and the next thing I did, I slapped him. I said, "Here you are, offering me dog. We don't eat dog in Africa."

He kept laughing. I hit him hard, and still he kept laughing. While I was trying to pick up a chair to hit his head with, to vent my feelings about all the other negative things I'd been hearing about Africa, I shouted, "To offer me dogs!"

Everybody came and said, "What's the matter? What's the matter?"

So he told them, and they all started laughing again. Then a gentleman who became my very good friend, the late Dr. Wendell Whalum, who was a sophomore at that time, a music major, who always asked me to sing folk songs to him, came and said, "It's not dog. They just call it that. The real name is frankfurter."

I said, "Frankfurter. What is that? What does frank have to do with dog? Is it from Frankfurt, Germany?"

Then he laughed again.

I said, "Come on. I'm so confused. Let me get out of this place."

He said, "Okay, let's go."

I later apologized to my roommate, and guess who became the biggest fan of hot dogs with mustard and sauerkraut? And always asked for a milkshake to go with it? I became famous for that.

It was quite an eventful year for me. After I fell off the top bunk my first night, Mrs. Asher felt sorry for me, and they gave me a bed to sleep in, so I wouldn't have to sleep in the top bunk. It was quite a wonderful year.

During the second semester, I tried to adjust to the system of taking exams. I found this new system very difficult. Instead of making A's, I made B's. I wasn't satisfied with that. I had to really buckle down, and I grew very frustrated. They didn't want you to think. It was another system for testing your intelligence. So I had to make an adjustment, and I didn't like the result. Some of the professors were not compassionate enough to understand that for those of us who came up in the British system, it was really difficult for us to understand true-and-false and multiple choice. We were used to essays. With essays, the professor could see how you arrived at your conclusions. Essays helped teach students how to think.

The second semester, I was determined to adjust somehow, but there was so much to adjust to, so much to understand, and there wasn't anything I could do about that. All I could do was work even harder. Then my extracurricular activities increased. The athletic department asked me, "Can you run?"

I said, "Yes. I used to run the mile at home. I'm a long-distance runner." So I joined the track team.

When I ran in those days, I ran barefooted. Win or lose, I always got mentioned in the papers because newspaper writers wanted to look at my feet. You know, "What kind of soles do you have, that you're running barefooted, without sneakers?"

I said, "At home, we learn how to run barefooted." And that's what I did. So I was always in the news, whenever we had a track meet, whether we won or lost.

I auditioned for the Glee Club. There was only one director of the Glee Club for both Morehouse and Spelman at that time. Most of the music lessons, for those who were majoring in music, were held on the Spelman campus. When I auditioned, the director, Kemper Harreld, who was also the chairman of the Music Department, said, "You have a good voice. You almost have a tenor voice. But you always change key." So they didn't choose me. That was one thing I couldn't join. Everything else, I was a member.

I was a member of the group that collected offerings at Sunday service. I became the leader of the ushers. That was early Sunday morning service, which was over at ten o'clock. Then we could attend other services in the city, where we were invited or where some of the students' parents were connected. Those started at eleven o'clock. Which meant that Sunday became a day that reminded me of home.

We had daily gatherings in the chapel. The administration arranged regularly to have different speakers on various subjects. People who were successful in business, in politics, in sports. Writers and actors came to speak to us—people from all walks of life, every day except Saturday. And then on Sunday, we had our services. I don't see any reason to be in bed on Sunday morning, so I was always there. And I didn't see any reason not to go to the chapel service every Monday through Friday, because I was always getting up to go to the prayer meeting. So all of those things I had learned at home were being reinforced at Morehouse.

The second year, I became more relaxed and more focused and tried to deal with different problems. But at the same time, I had not been able to date any girls. I had found no one particular person that I could take to events. When I went to an event, I went with three friends, three girls who were always friends. None of them could say, "He's my boyfriend." When I went to an event, or to the movies, I always went with two or three.

The ones I was really interested in didn't want to deal with me. So I told myself, "I'm not going to concern myself with this. I'd better focus on the reason why I came to Morehouse."

The second year, I joined the football team. I was always fascinated by that game. I didn't understand why they should be knocking each other down. But I really enjoyed the calling of the plays, how each play was diagrammed to be different from the others. That, to me, was quite a skill. I wanted to know how they figured out when the quarterback was going to fake. It looked like he had given the ball to somebody else, but he was still holding the ball, fooling the opposition, and then he'd throw the ball and somebody would catch it and make a touchdown. I think when a play is well executed, or when a running back cuts through all those big guys and makes a touchdown, it's one of the most beautiful things you can watch. It's almost like magic. I've always loved that.

But I only played one game, and then I gave it up. The coach said, "You're a runner. We're going to make you a running back." In practice, before the first game of the year, I got the ball at midfield and ran it to the thirty-five-yard line. They caught up with me. I went down and everybody piled on me. When I looked up, I saw four or five of my teammates on top, too.

I said, "What in the world are you doing? What is this? You're not supposed to be on top here."

They said, "This is the only place we could fall. This is where the whole play ended."

I said, "I'm not going to be in this. This is too much weight on me."

So I gave up football and became a cheerleader. The coach said, "We need your spirit, so come and talk to the football team."

The Morehouse football team never won anything anyway because there was so much focus on scholarship. We never recruited many students with athletic skills. Even when they did have athletic skills, they never had a chance to display them because they were expected to be scholars instead.

But baseball was my favorite. I'd brought my overseas radio—the one I used to listen to in Lagos for the overseas news—and I used it to listen to baseball games. I used to listen to the Voice of America on that radio. What is broadcast on VOA to other parts of the world is never played in the United States. That's very strange. I didn't play baseball. I liked it, but I didn't have time to play—I was in everything. We developed one exciting pitcher, but he never got drafted. In those days, no black players had been drafted into the majors. And the athletic department had no money. We didn't have a building, or enough equipment to really develop good, competent athletes.

There's a wonderful story about how Morehouse built its gymnasium, which now has everything you need to build a strong athletic program. It happened in my junior year. I was secretary of the student body. Morehouse had always selected its homecoming queen from Spelman. I noticed in my freshman year that all the girls who were selected were either fair-looking girls or girls who had never done anything for Morehouse. I said, "This time we want somebody who has served Morehouse. We don't want to select somebody who most of the students believe is beautiful because of her long hair, because of her complexion, or because she can always pass for white. That's not beauty."

That started a controversy in my junior year. That year's search committee for the queen recommended two names. Neither was a girl that most students would say, "Oh, very beautiful." One of them was Laura Williams, a young lady who had a beautiful voice, who sang with the Spelman and Morehouse Glee Club. That was the first year we stopped them from selecting people based on who was fair, who had long hair, and all of that.

Also, it was the first time that we refused to spend the student fund allocated for the dance. The administration was refusing to let us hold the dance off the Morehouse campus. All we had was a barn, but the barn wasn't going to be big enough, because all the alumni were coming, too. We usually held the dance outside, at Magnolia Hall, which holds about 2,500 people. Because of an incident the previous year, when one of the Spelman girls had one or two drinks, and the dean found her wandering into the men's dormitory, he wasn't going to allow us to hold it there this year.

I said, "I'm going to be responsible. I'm going to make sure that doesn't happen during my administration." But Dean Brazil still refused. So we took a delegation to see him.

We said, "What the last student administration did is past. We are promising you that we will be able to handle it. We will make sure that none of these kinds of incidents happens during our term. The men want to hold the dance outside the campus. You have no place. You've been raising money to build an athletic complex that we can use to hold things. It has not been done."

So I called an emergency student council meeting. I said, "You have two choices. You either go along with the administrator's plan to use the barn, or you have to force this administration to take action. A Morehouse College student has never been on strike. You might have to do it this time to drive the point home."

Everybody looked at me and said, "What are you trying to do? Go on strike? It's never happened in the history of Morehouse!"

I said, "Well, do you want to go to Spelman for the dance? I move we vote on it. If you don't want to, it means we have to go on strike. It means we are not going to have the dance this year. We're going to take the money—we have about three or four thousand dollars—and we're going to donate all of it toward the building of a new complex. The administration will get the message that we are serious. We must have the facilities. If not, there's no justification for them to stop us from going."

The executive committee voted that we weren't going to Spelman. So we took it to the student body. The executive committee's decision was that if the student body went along with it, we'd go on strike. No homecoming dance. Can you imagine that? The word got around, and the dean called me and I told him—I said, "Well, it's a democracy. We have a constitution. The students have to act. The administration has refused to listen to our promise that the student leadership this year will make sure that the incident of last year doesn't happen again. So we'll leave it to the vote."

The executive council prepared the presentation. Then the different fraternities met and the administration was trying to lobby important student body seniors and juniors, and they were trying to tell people that they shouldn't let one or two people mislead them, that Morehouse had never experienced any kind of student strike, that it would be a sad situation for the alumni coming home not to be able to have a dance.

I called them back again and I said, "The best thing is we are giving you the money allocated for this dance so that you can go out and raise money and build a place for us. We really need for that to happen."

So a special meeting for the student body of over thirteen hundred was called, and 99 percent said, "Yes." If they didn't allow us to go to Magnolia, we were not going to Spelman to have our homecoming dance. We were going on strike, and we should give them back our money. And that's exactly what happened.

The administration couldn't believe it. And the alumni said, "How do you let this radical from Africa come and dictate to us, and stop the tradition? That has never happened in the history of this institution. Leading the student body on strike!"

But the executive council was right behind me. They said, "We all decided we are not going to do that, and we're giving the money back."

You know, within a year, the administration raised enough money and built a complex with a gymnasium that holds four thousand people, and an Olympic-size swimming pool. With those athletic facilities, two years later, a Morehouse man made the Olympic team.

Mrs. Asher, my constant critic, called me and said, "Now that you've won your heart's desire, are we going to have peace on this campus?"

I said, "It's not finished. We're going to do something about the food service in the dining room, too. We might go on strike about that."

She said, "You're not going to do that here. We're not going to allow that to happen."

I said, "It's not me. The students are going to call for improvement in what is being given to them to eat."

"You're not going to come here and change things around here."

"I'm not trying to change things here. I'm trying to help make things better. For this institution to remain a great institution, we must right the wrongs. Just like you see that I make sure that our student body doesn't walk on the grass, so the campus will remain as beautiful as it is. I'm not telling them what to do. The students are making this decision, not me. It is my job to steer the board in the right direction."

So went the third year. When I became president of the student body, I was sent around to black colleges in the area, to Talladega College, Savannah State College, and many other places. People were proud that Morehouse students had selected a foreigner as their leader.

It was also the year when, on my travels, I got to a place called Lookout, Kentucky, and met a gentleman who looked exactly—*exactly*—like one of my uncles at home. I was so pleased. I said, "Do you know, you look just like my uncle."

He said, "Maybe I am. Maybe I'm from your family."

"You talk just like my uncle, too," I said. "I have a few questions to ask. Why is it that they call some black people Uncle Toms?"

He laughed, and said, "Well, my boy, I must tell you. These days, you might find it very necessary to B.S. your way to survival."

I said, "To B.S. your way to survival? You mean that in order to survive, you have to get a Bachelor of Science?"

He guffawed. "Oh my God. Now I believe you're from somewhere else. You just don't know. You have to talk trash if you want to survive. You don't want to get killed. Men are human, you know. Wink your eye at him when he laughs, but if you want to survive, you better find something to say that will make this man leave you alone."

So I thanked him. I never forgot that. His name was Mr. James.

There was another James in my life—Willie James, the authority on blues, who actually discovered me. Willis Lawrence James was his full name, and he was an assistant to Dr. Herrald, who later became chair of music at Spelman. Professor James saw me many times in the corner drugstore at Morehouse. He noticed that my hands are always flipping, and playing something. He came to me and said, "You're musical, aren't you? What instrument do you play?"

I said, "I play drums."

He said, "Do you sing?"

I said, "Yes."

I hadn't told him yet that I had tried to join the Glee Club at Morehouse. So he said, "Sing something to me."

I said, "I heard some songs when I first came here, on the radio. Songs like 'When I Lost My Baby, I Almost Lost My Mind.' That sounds like an African song, and I can put the beat to it."

He said, "Really? What else?"

"I've heard songs like 'Babalu.' That's a Yoruba song from my language. It is a prayer by young women who get married and want a child. They're saying a prayer: 'Father, Lord of the world. Please give me a child. Let me have a child to play with. Let me leave the world a copy of myself. When the fire dies, it leaves its ashes. And when the banana tree dies, it leaves its offspring.' Desi Arnaz sang it on the *I Love Lucy Show.* They say he's from Cuba. There must be Yoruba-speaking people there."

He said, "Tell me some more."

That's how Willie James took me under his tutelage. He was the one, in my sophomore year, who took me to the Tanglewood Music Festival in Massachusetts and presented me to wonderful composers and musicians. It was there that I met the members of the Modern Jazz Quartet, who had just started their group in 1951.

It was also there that I met and performed with Candido, one of the great bongo players from Puerto Rico. I met Fred Ferber there, too, the man who established the first ballpoint pen company in Englewood, New Jersey. He later gave me a job and the opportunity to work any of the three shifts available at his factory, to support my education at NYU. I also met people there who took an interest in my career later on, and who suggested to me that if I made any move at all, I should consider coming to New York, because that's where I would meet a lot of people who would be willing to help me. I followed their advice.

It was Willie James who gave me my start and who encouraged me to continue on my way, on my musical career. He also told Wendell Whalom, who later took over the Morehouse Glee Club, to give me an opportunity to compose some of the songs that have since made the Morehouse Glee Club very popular. Every Christmas the Morehouse and Spelman Glee Clubs would join together to sing carols at Sisters' Chapel. One of the songs sung every year is one I composed, "Bethelehemu."

I had little time for a social life at Morehouse, but when I met Rosa May Johnson, a student teacher from Clark College, who was teaching dance and getting a degree in sociology there, she became a lady friend, and the one that I decided would one day become my partner.

I told her, "Please be patient. I cannot pay you too much attention. I'm here for a purpose. But after graduation, I will offer you an engagement ring."

In my final year, I attended all the campus events with Rosa May. When I graduated, I fulfilled my promise to her. I went to Rich's and bought her an engagement ring for three hundred dollars—which probably is worth about a thousand or two thousand today—and gave it to her before we left Atlanta.

I said, "I'm going to New York to attend NYU. I want to start a group."

She helped me. In 1953 I recruited a group of African Americans from Atlanta University. I had to go there—none of the students at Morehouse would perform with us. None of the girls from Spelman joined, either— only the graduate students at Atlanta University, who were a little more mature. Most of them came from New Orleans, so they were really culturally oriented.

They helped me put together the group that in 1953 gave the first African show in Atlanta. That brought white people from downtown Atlanta to Davage Auditorium on the campus of Clark College, now known as Clark University. It brought white people to a black campus, and Ralph McGill, the editor of *Atlanta Constitution*, mentioned it in his column.

That started a great chain of events, as far as blacks and whites being together and experiencing a tremendous awareness created by the richness of African cultural heritage.

Rosa May went to Cleveland, planning to join me before I began my first term at NYU. But then I heard from her in August. She returned my engagement ring, telling me that her parents were now past sixty-five. They had told her they were too old to travel such a long distance to come and see her in Africa, so she should consider very, very strongly whether she should get into this kind of relationship that would take her away from them. Well, here I am, still in America.

I returned the engagement ring to her. That was tradition. Her name had been called on that ring, and she could do whatever she wanted with it. I could not give this ring to another person, and I would have been wrong to hold on to it, according to family tradition. She still wears the ring today, and she never got married. It's kind of interesting. Once in a while I'm still in touch with her. I think she's very disappointed that she didn't make up her own mind. People would ask her, "Why don't you get married?" She would say, "I don't think I will ever find somebody like this man again."

One of the things about Morehouse that makes me proudest is that even though I didn't graduate at the top of my class, there isn't a single student from my freshman year, or from the seniors and juniors ahead of me, who will ever forget Babatunde Olatunji.

When I was running for president of the student body, I defeated a man who became a very prominent doctor and in 1988 the U.S. Secretary of Health and Human Services under President George Bush. That was Louis W. Sullivan. Then I turned around and made him the president of our class. So we are good friends.

We had many other distinguished Morehouse men from that time, like Peter Chatard, who is now a plastic surgeon, one of the best in the country, and who lives in Seattle. And Major Owens, a congressman from Brooklyn.

I am proud that I have lived up to the expectations of Morehouse men. I won the coveted Most Christian Gentleman Award for four years at Morehouse, class of 1954. I am very, very proud of that. When I think of that, I hesitate to do anything that will tarnish that particular honor.

I will forever remember some of the families in Atlanta who helped African students. Besides the first family of the college, Dr. Mays and his wife, a couple who were absolutely dedicated to the welfare of all the students, especially the foreign students, always making sure that we were on the right track, that we were physically, mentally, and spiritually stable, there was also the Harris family. They were not a middle-class family. They lived in the downtown projects, but they helped all the African students who ever came to Atlanta.

Mr. Harris worked in a factory and took on extra jobs to take care of his family. He had two beautiful daughters, Ola Lee and Genevieve. Ola Lee is the oldest. Her first name is a syllable of my name. We'd say, "Where did you get this name?"

They'd say, "We are Africans. We know we are Africans."

So you can see the difference between them and the college students. In the Sea Islands of South Carolina and the Gullah districts, you find the remnants of African culture. It's all there, the way they greet people, the way they care about one another. The Harris family reminded us of an African family. At the time, this family lived in a three-room apartment in the projects. That is where we'd go. They would invite us every Sunday to come and eat a home-cooked meal. We didn't ever eat supper at Morehouse unless it was absolutely necessary. We'd go to the Harris family, four, five, six of us, turkey dinner with greens, home-baked bread and pie, cookies to bring back to the campus. They demanded nothing from us, and they made us feel at home. They remain our most celebrated, most remembered, most loved family today.

Why one of us who met them didn't marry one of their daughters, I don't know. I know they didn't try to force any one of us to marry them. They just made sure we were well taken care of. I was so preoccupied with doing well in school that I wasn't thinking about that; I had promised myself that I wasn't going to get involved in a serious relationship. I was very lucky that the first attempt I made failed when the woman hung up on me and wouldn't let me talk to her daughter. I said, "That's it." Not until my junior year, when I met Rosa Mae, did I even think about it.

I believe the Harris family has been blessed through the good deeds they have done for other people. Today, Mrs. Harris has a big church in Atlanta, and a big home. She has a room that is Babatunde Olatunji's room. She welcomed my daughter to stay there when she attended Spelman College a few years ago. Today Mrs. Harris drives a Cadillac. God works in mysterious ways. She calls me "my son."

One of the most important people in my life, and especially in what I do, was Mrs. Marjorie Johnson, who was a teacher at the Atlanta University School of Social Work. Mrs. Johnson also hailed from Cleveland, and worked in the area of communication and dance there. She developed dance programs at Karamu House, which produced several stars of theater, dance, and music. She also introduced Roger Mae Johnson to me. They are no relation but have the same last name. Marjorie Johnson knew Roger Mae Johnson and her family and her sisters from their participation in dance programs at the Karamu House. When Marjorie came to teach at the School of Social Work in Atlanta, she got Roger Mae to come to Clark College to teach dance and then work toward a degree. Marjorie helped us select participants in my first dance program. She was another one who helped make our dreams come true.

Then there was the Henderson family, who were middle-class. Mrs. Henderson was a teacher at Spelman College. Freddie and Jed Henderson opened their home to us on weekends. They were always inviting us to social functions in their house. When they gave parties, we were always invited. It was through our relationship with them that they developed the African Travel Agency. That made them pioneers—the first blacks in America to develop an African travel agency. It has been in operation since the 1960s. We always felt welcome in their home. It was a place to dance when we got feeling homesick.

That's also where I met one of my oldest friends—Bill Lee, who is Spike Lee's father. I have known Spike since before he was born, before he became a good friend of my son. I've known his mother, who is a Spelman graduate, since when Bill was dating her. We all used to go and have home-cooked dinners at Spike's grandmother's home.

Dr. Martin Luther King, Jr. was at Morehouse two years before me. He graduated in 1948. While we were at Morehouse, the African students, myself and a few others, started this whole black awareness program through our activities without even knowing it. By our second year, we were able to convince some of the students to put on traditional African dress. We would lend them some of our colorful robes, and then we would get on the bus that came from downtown to Fair Street, which passed through the university district. We just walked on the bus and sat anywhere, and no one said anything.

The next day we made sure the same driver was on duty. Then we put on our regular clothes. He said, "No, fellows. You can't sit there. You've got to go to the back." And we said, "We are the same students as yesterday who sat on your bus, and you didn't say anything. We sat right here. Now you're telling us to go to the back?"

He said, "If you don't move, I'm going to stop and call the police."

We did that a couple of times, and refused to sit in the back. Then they called the police and tried to lock up one of us. The Morehouse president called to have him released.

We started the protest quietly. That was three years before Rosa Parks and the Montgomery bus boycott. We were part and parcel of the struggle for freedom before the 1960s, more so than anybody can imagine. We took chances. Dr. King at first didn't want to take any action. Nonviolence was his approach. But somebody had to do that. That's why people rallied behind him, because leadership can bring about change. If leaders are determined, strong, and committed, and believe in what is right and wrong, and remain steadfast, things will happen.

Baba, a civil servant in Labor Dept. at Port Harcourt, dressed regally for a party, 1949. *Photos on this page from the personal collection of Dr. Akinsola Akiwowo.* **B**aba, circa 1950.

Mr. and Mrs. Olowu's
send-off for Akiwowo and
Baba, Lagos, Nigeria, 1950.
*Lagoku Studio; all photos on
this spread from the personal
collection of Dr. Akinsola
Akiwowo.*

Baba and Akiwowo are
welcomed by representatives
of the New Orleans YMCA
(Negro), on arrival in the
USA, 1950.

Baba, lead drummer for the Osisiganyan Culture Night performance, Atlanta University, 1951.

Baba in his sophomore year at Morehouse College, 1952.

Morehouse men: Fidelis Obi, A. Akiwowo, Harrison Tucker, Nathanial Olaku, and Baba, 1952. *Photos this page from the personal collection of Dr. Akinsola Akiwowo.*

Baba as Best Man at Akiwowo's wedding reception, Cambridge, MA, 1959.

Drums of Passion Recording Session, Columbia Studio, New York, 1959.
From left to right: Deloris Parker, Barbara Gordon, Baba, Helena Walker,
Aida (Bee Bee) Kapps, Helen Hayes. *Photos this page by Bob Henriques,
courtesy of Sony Music.*

Drums of Passion Recording Session, Columbia Studio, New York, 1959.
From left to right: Baba, Akwasiba Derby, Afuavi Derby, Taiwo Duvall,
Deloris Parker, Helena Walker, Barbara Gordon, Chief Bey, Aida (Bee Bee)
Kapps, Helen Hayes.

LEFT:
Mrs. Amy Olatunji, holding daughter Modupe with son Kwame and daughter Sade (on tricycle), 1962. *From the personal collection of Dr. Akinsola Akiwowo.*

BOTTOM LEFT:
Poster of the John Coltrane Performance at the Olatunji Center of African Culture, 1967.

FACING PAGE, TOP:
Baba and Michael Manley, Prime Minister of Jamaica, 1979. *From the personal collection of Baba Olatunji, photographer unknown.*

FACING PAGE, BOTTOM:
Baba and Drums of Passion opening for the Grateful Dead, Oakland Coliseum, New Year's Eve, 1985. *Credit: Ken Friedman.*

Baba, promotional shot, 1985. *John Werner © 2004.*

Baba leading chant at Harmonic Convergence, Telluride, Colorado, 1987. *Credit: Ken Friedman.*

Baba, Carlos Santana, and Mickey Hart, World Music in the Schools Program, Petaluma, CA, 1987. *From the personal collection of Baba Olatunji, photographer unknown.*

World Music in the Schools Program, 1987. © *Jay Blakesberg 2004.*

Baba and Drums of Passion with Carlos Santana, Jerry Garcia, and the Grateful Dead, 1987. © *Jay Blakesberg 2004.*

Della Flack, Baba, and Drums of Passion Band, Ashkenaz, Berkeley, CA, 1992. *John Werner © 2004.*

Armando Peraza, Baba, Giovanni Hidalgo, Mickey Hart, and Zakir Hussain at Mickey Hart's studio, 1993. © *Jay Blakesberg 2004.*

Alala Day, Baba, and Joan Baez, Baba's 75th Birthday, Palo Alto, CA, 2002. *John Werner © 2004.*

Akiwowo at Baba's Award Ceremony, New York City, 2002. *From the personal collection of Dr. Akinsola Akiwowo.*

Baba at Esalen, Big Sur, CA, 2002. *John Werner © 2004.*

5 | Harlem on My Mind

After graduation, instead of going to California, where I had been accepted by the University of California, or to Boston, where my cousin Akiwowo had been admitted to Boston University, I decided to go to New York. This decision was not an easy one. First of all, it would mean separation from my cousin. We had left Africa together, and had spent our four years at Morehouse College together, giving each other moral support when it was necessary.

It was also difficult because I was treading on new ground. I didn't have admission to any schools in New York. I was on my own. But I went. I gained admission to the New York University Graduate School of Public Administration and International Relations, but there was no scholarship offer, and no promise of any departmental grants. This meant that I would have to work.

On the other hand, when I visited New York City the first time, before starting my freshman year at Morehouse, I was so impressed that I said to a friend of mine, "I love New York. The whole world is in New York. I believe this is the place where I will be going when I finish Morehouse. It is the place where whatever you do can be seen, heard of, talked about by the entire world in no time. It is quite an exciting place."

I had found many people in Harlem who looked like people I knew in Nigeria. I believed that one day I would be able to establish a school there. New York is where my whole musical career started. The world was there, waiting for me. The world was there waiting to listen to what I had to say musically.

There was one thing I could be very thankful for—a promise from a dear friend. I say dear friend because he promised he would help me if and when I needed it. I had met Fred Ferber, an immigrant himself, who came to America and became a successful businessman, while I was still a student at Morehouse. He started probably the first ballpoint pen factory on the East Coast, in Englewood, New Jersey. When I wrote to him and expressed my desire to come to New York University, he promised he would help me by allowing me to work as long as I wanted to, as many shifts as I could, and as many days as I wanted to. He said he would also introduce me to other people who could help me with a better summer job when school was out of session.

With this kind of assurance, I decided I must be on my way. Harlem had been on my mind since my first visit. I had read stories about how Harlem was a place where people, both black and white, used to come to discover great talents. Most importantly, the vivid picture of the people I saw during my first visit in 1950 remained on my mind. They reminded me so much of almost everybody I had known in my life before I left Nigeria. I knew I had to go there.

I had heard people say that if you make it in New York, if you achieve anything in New York, it will be known all over the world. I agree with them. Because the whole world is in New York. Almost every ethnic group you can think of in this world is in New York City. It reminded me a little bit of what Lagos was when I left the village to go there. I noticed the pattern, the repetition, of events that have followed one another in succession and have played such an important part in my life, in my development. So I summoned up the courage and determination to go. After all, I was a Morehouse man. I felt that I would make it in New York and be known all over the globe.

With just a few possessions, I left the driving to Greyhound, and arrived in New York. By then, Fred had made arrangements for me to stay in Englewood, where he lived. That, he said, would make it easy for me to work the first shift, from seven to three, take the bus from Englewood to the Medical Center on 160th Street in Manhattan, get on the subway, and take the A train. Twenty minutes later I would get off at West 4th Street, walk two blocks, and be at NYU.

Having to work in order to take care of my education was the most difficult part. I didn't want to live in New Jersey, I wanted to live in Harlem, but I couldn't do that because I had to work at the factory in Englewood. So I reluctantly moved there, and rented a room for eight dollars a week. If I felt anything at that time, it was loneliness. And it was difficult for me to put my schedule together so that I could study and make good grades. But I got used to the fact that this is what I had to do—go to work from seven to three, go to school Monday through Friday, and work all three shifts both Saturday and Sunday. I would take a Sunday off every month to visit International House and to relate to other African students in the city. It was quite a schedule for me to maintain, but that's what I had to do to pay my tuition, which in those days was only twelve dollars per credit.

Where I was living, there were two senior citizens of African descent who were not too open when they discovered that I was from Africa. Once again, I was faced with the ugly Hollywood image of Africa that has persisted so long in the minds of millions of people, both black and white, in America. I was told I could not enter their house through the main door— I would have to come through the side door. And I could not use their main kitchen—I would have to do all my cooking downstairs. Old cooking pots and pans that had not been used for years were brought out for me to use. And I could not use the living room to entertain any of my friends who came to visit me. It was very difficult for me to work around this, so that it wouldn't affect my performance as a student. I was raised to respect my elders. To avoid any confrontation with them, I didn't tell anyone about these things until I met a wonderful young African American couple, Calvin and Mary Vismeel. They were delightful. They helped me to relax a little bit, to take my mind off the treatment I was getting with the other couple.

But most of the time I still could only come home through the back door. I would go to the attic, sleep, and then start the next day at seven o'clock, picked up by Mr. Epps, one of the African American managers at the plant. He was a slow-talking, humorous man, very kind, astute, and compassionate. Fred had asked him to pick me up every morning at seven so that I could get to work on time. Afterwards he would drive me home to get ready to leave Englewood for classes at NYU.

Eventually, I told my story to a few friends, and I was introduced to the Johnson family at 268 Harliman Road. What a contrast—they were a wonderful couple. And the grandmother of Mr. Johnson, who was a contractor and a builder, reminded me so much of my great-grandmother. She laid down the rules in the household. Mrs. Johnson was a very strong, dynamic, beautiful woman, who asked me to share meals with them whenever I was there.

The grandmother made sure I was well taken care of. Anybody who called and asked for me had to tell her what their relationship with me was. She made it very clear that she would be asking them what they wanted from me when they called. It would have to have something to do with my education. If it didn't, she would not deliver their message. She was amazing—quite a contrast.

So I said to myself, "The Creator is really smiling on me. If I'm patient enough, the Creator will send those who will help and aid me on my way to success. Truly, the Lord is my shepherd. I shall not want." So I didn't have to worry.

This was right after *Brown vs. Board of Education*, the Supreme Court decision that outlawed segregation in the United States. People were beginning to mobilize from the grassroots, and the NAACP was becoming a vanguard for social justice. One of my main reasons for moving to New York was to promote cultural awareness. So immediately I established the Olatunji Center of African Culture, without a home or space to meet in, just a name, and began recruiting people to become part of a performing group. All of these things were going on at the same time, including my involvement in the NAACP Youth Program. In the meantime, Mary and Calvin Vismeel took over the organization, almost supervising my rehearsal schedule for me. So I was on my way.

That was how I was introduced to the minister of the Baptist church in town, Reverend Taylor. He became a fan, and later on, with the Vismeels, I organized a fundraising event using the new dance company to raise money for their new church building. I became a good friend of Reverend Taylor, who later on became a political force in Englewood, when he was elected the chairman of the Englewood Chapter of the NAACP. This propelled him to the forefront of the new group of young, energetic African American leaders, who were determined to bring about change in America. With his help, my new dance group become one of the performing arts groups that was most requested to appear at meetings and rallies. This went on for years. We became known as the Kings of Benefits.

All this was happening while I was still a student at NYU, trying to complete my dissertation. After three years in Englewood, I met the lady who would become my wife.

I met Amy one day in the library. The first thing that attracted me to her was her hair. Here was a young and beautiful, light-skinned African American woman, similar to the ones who at Morehouse would have been most likely to be selected Homecoming Queen, because of their complexion and their hair.

Well, here was this light-skinned woman, but with a crew cut like an African woman. Now, who in the world was this? She had to be a rebel. Where did she come from? She couldn't be from the South, because no woman in the South with her complexion would have this kind of haircut. I knew I had to find out who this woman was. Little did I know what I was getting myself into.

She was a librarian. I said, "Good afternoon, my name is Olatunji."

She said, "My name is Amy."

I asked, "Where are you from?"

"I'm from Alabama."

"You're from where? Alabama? You can't be from there."

"Yes, I'm from Alabama."

"Where in Alabama?"

"All over Alabama."

"Are you kidding?"

She said, "I used to live in Tuscaloosa with my uncle who is a dentist, and with my aunt. I have folks in Birmingham. I have a brother-in-law in Mobile. I went to Talladega College."

"Talladega? I was there. I went to speak to the student body there. What's your last name?"

"Bush."

"I met a young lady there named Bush."

"My sister is there."

So that was my wife's sister. "What a small world. May I have your telephone number?"

She gave me her number, and I told her I lived in Englewood.

I lost her number. Because of my schedule, I didn't call her for months. She didn't call me either, because I didn't have a telephone, and I rarely gave people the number of my hosts. I felt embarrassed sometimes when Granny gave all these people a grilling.

But I went on, and things began to get a little clearer. I had decided that I would do my doctoral thesis on the impact of colonial administration on the communal ownership of land in Nigeria, and how it affected capital development and capital formation between 1900 and 1950. I wanted to make it clear that the policy caused the flight of capital from Nigeria and encouraged the exodus of millions of people from rural areas. This created overpopulation in Lagos. Rural people were looking to make good in the city, but in doing that, they were leaving behind a great opportunity to develop the land so that it would feed the people and support the economy of Nigeria as a whole.

By the time I finished my course requirements and my program was nearing an end, requests for my group to appear at social gatherings were increasing tremendously. The dance company was growing. I had been able to recruit a few drummers. Around that time, I attended a party given by a Morehouse graduate, who was two years my senior but who had been a great admirer of mine when he was at Morehouse. When he was a senior, I was a sophomore. So I attended the party, and there I saw Amy again.

I told her, "I'm sorry I didn't call you. I lost your telephone number. I wished you had called me."

She told me she had called me once, but the lady who answered the phone asked her so many questions that she hung up, telling her that she would call me back. But she was determined not to do that. Granny had grilled her till she couldn't stand it. But she didn't want to insult an elder.

I said, "I understand."

"But I must tell you, she was looking out for you. Really, you need to have somebody like that in your corner."

So we started to get together, and we became very serious. In 1957, we got married in Tuscaloosa, Alabama, with Akiwowo as best man. Then we moved into a five-room apartment in Brooklyn. Amy was working at that time in the children's section of the Brooklyn Public Library.

I have great respect for the institution of marriage. I think it is one of the most important institutions in the world. I was brought up to recognize the importance of family life. I was raised to respect and recognize the significance of womanhood. As I mentioned earlier, my biological mother and my aunt—my second mother—made it clear to me that every woman, no matter her age, is a potential mother. That was why I had to remember to show respect in all my dealings with women. I still do believe that, and I will always do whatever I can to show my respect for any woman that I deal with.

At the same time, I am the kind of person who deliberates on the extent of my involvement in anything I do, and I have always believed that I must pursue vigorously and without hesitation anything or everything that I believe will make me happy while I am doing it as long as it does not harm other people. So I am calculating, very calculating, in making choices. That was why it took me so long when I was in college to even have a date with a woman to attend social functions, especially in the South, where the women I was interested in weren't attracted to me. At least, until I met my wife.

My wife came from a very respected family of doctors, dentists, educators, school principals, and so on. She was raised with a silver spoon in her mouth. She knew what she wanted and she was a very determined soul. She was a rebel, as I suspected. I found out that she had challenged the whole state of Alabama. She grew up in Tuscaloosa, where the University of Alabama is located. But she was denied admission for graduate studies there after finishing at Talladega College, a black college. Instead, she was offered a scholarship to any university in the United States outside Alabama. In those days, the State of Alabama refused to admit African Americans to their university. But they also said they would pay for any student to do graduate studies anywhere else in the United States. As a black woman, she decided to test them on that. Her family told her, "You don't have to—we can send you anywhere you want to. You don't have to do this." But she told them, "No, the state said they would do it, so let them pay. And I am going to go to Syracuse, New York."

In the end, the State of Alabama paid her transportation, her room and board, and all her fees. They spent thousands and thousands of dollars on her education for her master's in library science and a minor in languages at Syracuse University. So now you know how very strong and determined she was.

She said, "That was good for me."

I said, "Wow!"

Those were the circumstances when I married Amy in 1957. And like almost all Africans, I started a family right away, even without a steady job, or a high-paying one. I was attending NYU, we had moved to Brooklyn, and I was working at the Institute of International Education as a clerk, doing mailings to all the scholarship students from Europe under the sponsorship of IIE.

Our first child was a boy, whom we named Kwame Ayodele. We named him after the president of Ghana, Kwame Nkrumah. Kwame means, "born on a Saturday." Ayodele means, "Joy comes home." I wrote Nkrumah, asking him to be the godfather of my son, because he was such an inspiration to so many of our generation. Nkrumah had attended Lincoln University in Pennsylvania, then had gone back to Ghana, organized the people, fought for independence, and been jailed. Later he was given the opportunity to organize the first state government headed by an African. Ghana became independent in 1957.

In the meantime, at my new job, which was near the UN, twenty or thirty calls would come in to my division, and out of those calls, more than one-third would be for me. People would ask when I could come to speak, when I could come to perform, when I could come to talk about the role of the drum in our culture.

With all of this going on, I said to myself, "I must make a decision, and fast."

Between 1954 and 1957, so much was happening in all aspects of society. There was tremendous opposition building up in the country over segregation, and over separate but equal education. The NAACP was leading the fight. Roy Wilkins came in as leader just around that time, and one of the first things he did was see to it that there was a very strong youth division in the NAACP, and to make sure there was a nationwide effort to galvanize young people and recruit them to the fight for equality.

In the mid-1950s, organizations like the NAACP started recruiting young people. While I was president of the Morehouse student body, I spoke to about five thousand young people about the NAACP meeting at the Statler Hilton in New York.

By the time I moved to New York, I was already known, and word got around that our group was being asked to perform at various rallies. The Southern Christian Leadership Conference, which brought Dr. King to the forefront of this whole movement; the Student Nonviolent Coordinating Committee (SNCC), headed by Stokely Carmichael and later by H. "Rap" Brown; and the Congress on Racial Equality (CORE), headed by James Farmer, all of these organizations were working to achieve the same thing. And at the same time, the Nation of Islam selected Malcolm X to be its spokesman. You can just imagine the tremendous impact that all of this had on the whole country. And all of these organizations called on us to perform at their functions.

There were no institutions offering grants at that time that would support my research for my dissertation, so in money terms I was stranded. When we were asked to perform, the only thing I was being offered was transportation for the thirty members of the group. Nobody was offering to pay us to perform. We were always being called on by different organizations for fundraising events, but they never offered us compensation.

I was still trying to finish my dissertation, but my life now revolved around bringing Africa to America, planting seeds in the minds of people, reawakening people's interest, trying to make true Victor Hugo's prediction that Africa would one day be seen in its true reality by all eyes. I was trying to restore some kind of pride in our people, to show that we were kings and queens, that we were beautiful people with a rich cultural heritage. People of African heritage had to destroy the stereotypes that had permeated American society, they had to regain and reclaim their share of what this society had to offer, their contributions to the economic, political, and social development of America. Through, as Churchill put it, the blood, toil, tears, and sweat of their ancestors, this country had become what it became. I included all of this in our presentations. Our performances served not just as entertainment that brought cheers and applause. They always reminded African Americans of their glorious past, and forced them to think, to reject their present condition, and to move forward, knowing that they had a part to play.

While all of this was happening, we participated in the first album made by UNICEF. It was a recording of children's lullabies from all parts of the world. Akiwowo came from Boston to join me in recording a song that had been sung to us as children:

Oh, do not cry, my little children.
Remember, I am your mother.
I am your father.
Oh, do not cry, my children.
Surround me. Come around me. Gather around me.
Like stars gather around the moon.
Do not cry, my children.
I am your father.
I am your mother.

We were not paid anything, but our contribution represented Africa. That recording brought me into contact with members of the UN Choir, which was conducted at that time by a gentleman named Ralph Hunter.

I had been invited to a Christmas party in 1957, at Miss Odell's house on West 4th Street, not too far from NYU. She was a member of the choir and had a roommate who was a girlfriend of one of the African students from Algeria. I had just married in March, and my wife was expecting our first child. I went to this party, taking my little drum, not knowing what would happen, but it was destined to happen. Ralph Hunter was there. At one point during the party, he stopped everything and said, "We want to hear a folk song from every part of the world."

We all told him, "This is going to take all night. We might as well start now."

He said, "I'm not going to start alphabetically. There are some people I'm going to save for last."

I said, "Oh, my God. When are we going to get home tonight?" I was hoping he would start with A, for Africa. But I was the last one.

In introducing me, he said, "Let's ask the gentleman who contributed the folk song to the UNICEF album."

I did the English translation first. Then I sang it in Yoruba.

Then he asked me, "Can you do any of the chants?"

I did the chant to Shango, the God of Thunder and Lightning. The applause went on for about five minutes.

When that was over, he said to me, "I'd like to introduce you to a friend of mine at Radio City Music Hall, by the name of Ray Wright. He's the musical arranger for the Radio City Symphony Orchestra. I'm going to tell him about you, and then I'll arrange for you to meet him."

He did just that. He gave me Ray Wright's name and telephone number, and I gave him mine. Soon after that, Mr. Wright called me and arranged for me to go see him at Radio City Music Hall on Rockefeller Plaza.

Suddenly I knew what I had to do. I resigned from my job. After that, one Monday morning, my wife said, "Are you going to work?"

I said, "No. I quit Friday."

"What are you going to do for a living?"

"I'm going to find out. Maybe in six months we'll know. People call me every day to come and perform for them. I'm going to start asking them to pay me something for what I do. Maybe I'll be able to put some money together to go home and do this research, and write my dissertation.

Remember, NYU said they would publish my dissertation. The subject matter is so interesting. We'll manage."

I was able to calm her fears. She was still working at the Brooklyn Public Library.

So I met with Ray Wright. I gave him some folk songs, lullabies, and chants. He said, "We can put something together for the orchestra, so that in the fall, when we have our new show, maybe you can be part of it."

I said, "Really? Good."

The whole thing started in February. In March, Mr. Wright told me we had enough to put together an overture that would last twelve minutes. The orchestra would play this piece before going to the other parts of the show.

Since I cannot read music, I told him I could put the songs together by using the English "do, re, me, fa, so, la, ti, do." And I could give him an idea of what I wanted the trumpet to sound like, and what I wanted the other instruments to sound like. We practiced for three months. He painstakingly put together this overture, and scheduled the show to open with the premiere of *Cat on a Hot Tin Roof*, a wonderful movie starring Elizabeth Taylor.

From September 18 to November 21, 1958, for seven weeks, I was featured with the Radio City Symphony Orchestra, four shows a day, seven days a week. I made five hundred dollars a week. That was my biggest break in the business, because it gave me an opportunity to be heard by millions of people. And I had just quit my other job! So dreams do come true.

This led to excellent reviews in all five New York newspapers. In the *New York Times* I had a quarter of a page, with my picture. They called me the Doctor of Drums. In the *Daily Mirror* there was a column by Walter Winchell. The *Daily News*, the *New York Post*, the *Herald Tribune*, and the *Amsterdam News* all had reviews.

The Radio City appearance also got me on *The Ed Sullivan Show*, *The Today Show*, and practically all the major television shows of that era, including the game show *To Tell The Truth*. That show's producers went to the embassies. Ghana was the only country that was independent, so they selected a brother from the Ghanaian Consulate and an African American. They bought suits, new shoes, ties, everything, for all three of us. I was the guy to be identified.

All of this got me an agent—Monte Kay, Diane Carroll's husband, who handled five great talents at that time: the Modern Jazz Quartet;

Chris Conner, a vocalist; Herbie Mann; the Afro Jazz Sextet; and Drums of Passion.

And I was on many different radio shows. On one show in 1958, the young producer, who had just been hired by Columbia Records, his name was Al Ham, tapped me on the back and asked, "Are you putting an album together?"

I said, "Yes."

That was the beginning. He became my producer. I was on my way now. But you have to remember, I'd been in New York since 1954, and I'd started the group as soon as I got there.

In retrospect, I would say that the first five years of my marriage were the most enjoyable ones. They were the five years when I received the most attention and help in the pursuit of my mission, which was to promote African culture—or the African personality, as Nkrumah called it—by disseminating the rich cultural heritage of Africa. At a conference in 1958, I had promised Nkrumah and the other delegates that I would do just that.

Had I known, I would have parted ways with my wife right after those five years, because they were the most glorious five years of support that any man could enjoy with his partner. The fifteen years after that were a struggle for both of us because she felt that the mission, the job, was too much for me. She was probably right, because according to her, I had not been given the right tools, or enough support, to continue the job after Nkrumah's death.

As someone put it, Amy was married to my drums, to my vision, to doing what I enjoyed doing the most. So it was a stormy marriage. The way I understand it now, we had a "clash of cultures," in the sense that people develop certain characteristics in their formative years that remain with them forever.

It is said: "Teach a child in the way he should go, so when he is old, he will not depart from it." The seeds of virtue sown in youth eventually reap habits. Little things that the African considers important mean a lot.

The clash of cultures started after we were married. She would serve me leftovers.

I would say, "This is part of what I ate yesterday."

"Yes, but it's all dressed up now. You'd better eat it."

"What I am trying to say is, I grew up in an environment where there was no refrigerator. When you cook something, you have to eat it all. And when it is time to eat again, you start fresh again to cook."

"But there's no time to do that. I have to go to work. So you have to learn to eat leftovers."

But it took time for us to reach that level of dialogue.

"For you to say, 'Just eat it,' you didn't find out why I don't like it. I like pea soup, but I don't like to look at the green peas on the plate."

"Whenever I serve you peas, you always separate them, they are good for you. Why is that? The other day I saw you ordering pea soup."

"Why don't you ask me why, instead of saying, 'You should eat it'? You ask people why they don't do this or that."

"Then, why?"

"Let me tell you. My second year here when I was in college, I worked for Bird's Eye Frozen Foods Company. They put me in the fields to load trucks with bags of carrots and peas eight hours a day in Geneseo, New York. A little town, nothing to do. I went to the manager and said, 'I need to work twelve hours. I have nothing to do in this town. I have to make enough money to buy books and clothing to go back to school.'

"He said, 'Oh, you want to work twelve hours? Well, we will put you in the factory.'

"And where did he put me? In the section where I had to test the peas for twelve hours."

She laughed.

So I said, "So, you see why I don't like to see the peas? For a whole summer that's what I did. But if you take the peas and break them up and cook them I will eat them. It's psychological. When I see them, I want to set them aside. They remind me of that job."

A clash of cultures. "You don't ask me why, you just make comments, and I react to it."

We were beginning to argue over little things. Little things mean a lot.

With all this, the contract to record *Drums of Passion* came along.

6 | Drums of Passion

The mid to late 1950s were a vibrant, vital time for me. So much was happening all at once. I knew I was really alive then, in so many ways. I was adjusting to marriage and deciding on a career. I was at the same time very disappointed that there was no interest in Africa, and no money available for me to travel to Africa and England to do the research I needed to do for my Ph.D. dissertation. I was depressed for a few months about not being able to complete my dissertation, which probably would have earned the respect of my colleagues in the academic world.

But I snapped out of my depression when I got an invitation from the President of Ghana, Kwame Nkrumah, to attend the first All-African Peoples Conference to be held on African soil, in December 1958. This first meeting of African leaders to discuss the future of Africa and the idea of Pan-Africanism was very important. Among the famous people attending were W.E.B. Dubois and Vice President Richard Nixon.

As president of the All-African Students Union of the Americas, I was invited to bring my wife. Our son, Kwame, stayed with my sister-in-law in Cleveland while we were away. It was the first time I had returned to Africa since I left in 1950.

I was able to afford the trip because I had just finished a seven-week engagement at Radio City Music Hall with the sixty-six-member symphony orchestra performing my "African Drum Fantasy." I made five hundred dollars a week. I had never earned any money like that. I had also just appeared on *The Ed Sullivan Show* and other local TV shows.

The conference was held at a time when the independence movement was underway in Africa, beginning with the independence of Ghana the year before. At the conference, I read my paper proposing the creation of an African cultural center in every major city in America; these would help destroy the stereotypes and ugly images of Africa that persisted in the minds of millions of Americans through Hollywood movies and incredible stories, of the kind that would not encourage anybody to embrace anything African. The cultural centers would disseminate information about the heritage, culture, and traditions of Africa through performances, presentations, classes, and other events. President Nkrumah invited me to come to his official residence to discuss this vision with him. He knew that I was currently pursuing my education to become a diplomat. It was just my wife and I with him and one of his aides.

He said, point blank, "Why don't you consider being a cultural ambassador? You're already in New York. Why don't you begin there? What can we do to support you?"

It took me by surprise. I didn't know what to say, but I told him, "I need the instruments. I have no money."

So he made all the arrangements for the drums to be shipped from Ghana. And you know, these are the instruments that we used in recording *Drums of Passion*, the same ones that were used during the performance given in honor of the guests and representatives from all over the world at the conference in Ghana.

It was also at this meeting that Nkrumah agreed to be the godfather of my son, his namesake, Kwame Ayodele Olatunji, and that he made known his hope and prayer that my son would one day work toward the liberation of all of Africa—not just his father's country, Nigeria, but the whole continent. That had a tremendous effect on my life at the time. It really raised my spirits.

The next few months after I got back to New York from attending that conference were unbelievable. Everything happened so fast, and so smoothly, just as if it was meant to happen. I was definitely in the right place at the right time to pursue my vision. New York was where it was all happening.

This was a period of divine intervention in my life. By answering the call that was meant for me, which was to show people that there was a cultural basis for our unity, I was given the opportunity to illustrate how wonderful and important our heritage is, how energizing and meaningful it is, and how the tradition serves us so well.

I knew that the success of this idea, to present the culture of Africa through music and dance, would depend on the caliber of the people I selected, and that they had to be willing to sacrifice a lot, because there would not be instant remuneration. They had to understand that, right from the beginning. It was not my intention just to entertain people. I wanted people to get beyond the stories of wild animals, safaris, and the Nile, which are so dear to many, including Africans. I wanted them to see Africans as real people, part of the human race, and to understand their values, beliefs, traditions, and standards.

This vision to educate Americans about the real Africa was a heavy load for me. But I picked it up consciously, willingly and very deliberately. This vision was the driving force that motivated me. I wanted people to see in me a real African, what my greatest teacher, Kwame Nkrumah, called the "African personality," which is who I am in my essence. Because I have my own essence, I am just like every other person on the face of this earth.

When I arrived in New York in 1954 as a graduate student, I was determined that I would continue what I had started in Atlanta. So I immediately put together a dance group. This was a fascinating period in my life, a most invigorating and challenging time. What made it so was the selection of members of the group.

I went about it the way I read in the Bible how Jesus Christ selected his disciples. I made sure that those I talked to about it were people I could put my trust in. So I approached developing the group—which became the foundation for what we later established as the Olatunji Center of African Culture—with a sense of hard work, determination, and purpose.

The members came from very different backgrounds, though they were all African Americans. They came from the South, the Caribbean, and Latin America. But they all had one thing in common: they had a huge thirst for learning about their ancestors. That was the important thing. It is what made them so dedicated, so energetic, and so willing.

Only two members of the group were directly from Africa. The rest were African Americans. They were so diverse, so different in their orientation, yet so dedicated to learning about African music. They grasped everything with passion and dedication. It is the kind of commitment you don't see from those who are eyeing the culture today.

Mary and Calvin Vismeel, the wonderful young African American couple that took a liking to me, helped me organize my group as soon as I told them what I had done in Atlanta. They were so proud that I would be able to start a thing like that.

So right after the semester began, they told me about two wonderful sisters, Alfreda and Joan Derby, whose parents were from Surinam in South America. They were raised there before their parents came to the United States. Their background was actually West African, because the blacks in Surinam had come from Ghana. They went home to visit every year, and they were thoroughly informed about the traditions of the drum—about what the dances meant in their society. They still make drums in Surinam like they have made in Ghana for generations.

I introduced myself to these two wonderful sisters, and quickly won their affection and their interest in helping me develop a dance company. They were very, very wonderful dancers, because of their talent and their background in African dance, which is part of the heritage that has taken root in places like Surinam, Brazil, the West Indies, and Latin America. Those countries have helped preserve African culture in this part of the world.

Mama Derby, whom we all knew as YaYa, was so strict with those two girls that they'd go nowhere alone. When you saw one you always saw the other. For rehearsals, she would put them on the bus in Fort Washington, New York, to come over to Englewood, having given me strict instructions to meet them. After each rehearsal I had to call and tell her they were on their way back home.

These two young women immediately became the original members of my dance company. They formed the pillars of that group. It was not hard to teach them—they knew the power of the drum. They helped me greatly to select other members of the group. They even changed their names. That was another process we went through, having naming ceremonies. It was like an initiation. Alfreda became Afuavi, which means "born on Friday," and Joan became Akwasiba, "born on Saturday." Those two taught many others who now do African dance.

One of the drummers, who was also a vocalist, had been offered a part in a Broadway play. He had a beautiful voice, but because he lacked a college degree, he was not given the lead role.

When I heard him sing, I said, "You've got to come with me."

"What are you going to teach me?"

"I am going to teach you African chants."

He had a deep voice. I asked his name.

"James Hawthorne Bey."

I said, "You are Chief Bey."

That is what he has been called since 1956.

He had such a strong, commanding voice. When he spoke, you just had to listen to him. I got him to do the chants to the different deities, and to do what has long been such an important part of African American heritage, the call and response. That was featured in many songs on *Drums of Passion*, with him coming in to blend with my tenor voice. His deep voice really demonstrated how our people have utilized their African heritage in this country, as in the call and response of gospel music.

The other drummers were Montego Joe, whose parents were from Trinidad, and brother Taiwo DuVall, who was an excellent painter, and who painted all our backdrops showing beautiful African dancers and drummers. He changed his first name, too. Taiwo means "first-born of the twins." And he became very much more involved. He helped me tell more significant stories, not only about drumming and dance but also about African history and culture.

Every one of the members of the group came ready. They were eager to do something, to learn something. They became believers. Every one of them was highly dedicated and anxious to know about their heritage. Their dedication, and the intensity with which they pursued the knowledge they had been denied for so long, was unbelievable, just phenomenal.

All of the singers were very special, too. Sister Ida Capps, Helen Haynes, Barbara Gordon, and Helena Walker were all very dedicated African Americans whose introduction to Africa was through the Drums of Passion Dancers and Drummers. They learned to practice the traditions, and they even started wearing African dress. They started wearing the head tie and letting their hair grow naturally; they contributed to the new fashion that way. And there was Dolores Parker, a tall, beautiful woman who just by coming on stage could arouse the instincts of any faithful man in the audience.

Helena Walker, who is still active today as a teacher, performer, and facilitator, was one of the most important members of the group. She was so energetic, and she could improvise in any situation. She had a unique and powerful stage presence. When it was time for her to do her solo, she would walk on stage and say, just by her expression and her presence, "This is my time, I want you to pay me the utmost respect, and know that I am one with you." She knew how to bond with her audience, how to take command of the stage, and how to tell a story with her movements. She could bring out the uniqueness of African dance and music almost without any effort. She knew how to illustrate that every movement is synchronized with the beat of the drum.

All the women in the group, about twelve of them, were just so tremendous and unique in their own right. The same thing was true of the drummers. And that was the message, the story of what this whole effort was about—that everyone who embraced it would become proud of it and proud of themselves. I credit myself for succeeding in what I set out to do, but they were the ones who actually made my vision become a reality.

One of the most important characteristics of the original members was their dedication. When rehearsal time came, everybody was ready—they all knew what they were supposed to do, what they were supposed to say, where they were supposed to be. It was not a question of "What do we do next?" They knew what to do because they were doing it every day. They were from different backgrounds, but they all had the same things in common: faith and determination. They talked about what they were doing when they ate and when they traveled. That was all they talked about. That is what made the group so successful. Even though I am very proud of all of my groups, there is no comparing the ones I formed later with that original one. The difference might be that we were doing something new then, or that those first people had been denied for so long the opportunity to really express themselves. Not that the present group cannot be seen like that, but today the interest has shifted slowly to the commercial side of it. There would never be another group like that first one.

Later on, when we became a full group, we rehearsed at Michael Studios, one of the most popular studios that African American dance companies used to rehearse. It was at 57th Street and 8th Avenue, not too far from the old Madison Square Garden.

Seven days a week we would rehearse, even on Sundays after group members attended their local churches. Those who were strongly religious, who were good Baptists, good Catholics, would bend a little and say, "If I have to rehearse on Sunday, I will come after church." We would rehearse from two until six in the afternoon, from two until eight when we had shows.

I insisted that in order to learn the culture, they would have to learn the language. They were going to be singing a new language, so I had to teach them how to pronounce the words right, what their meaning was, what was involved in African dance, what dance means to our society, how the music covers all the passages of life, how it is central to all life. They had to know all of that. They had to live it, and talk about it, until it became part of them.

I would give lectures about the traditional ways of doing things, the role of the child in the traditional African home, the relations between brothers and sisters, between young and old, between all community members. I would explain to them about all the different African deities and the chants the practitioners sing at their gatherings. Then we would discuss it all. I started with the lectures, and only then did I teach the dances I knew.

In my presentations, I would have them think about Africa before the First World War and after. There are really two very different maps of Africa. The original map of Africa had no borders. If you take the whole of West Africa, people used to travel from one end of it to the other, from what is today Senegal all the way to what is now Nigeria. People were going back and forth, exchanging ideas and cultures. They really have so many things in common. Not until after the First World War, when the European powers divided up Africa, did the problem of Africans not knowing who they are begin to arise. They lost the knowledge that they are all one. I have always known that all of the drums that can be found, even though they may come in different sizes and styles, are common to all of the countries of West Africa, if not the whole continent.

I have been called a taskmaster, and many other names, too, because I am such a strict disciplinarian. I make sure that if you are in my group, you do not get on stage to perform until you know what you are doing. Everybody who performs with me is ready to perform with any group in the world. First of all, you have to go through the process of learning what the dance and the music are all about. I make sure you understood that. If you don't, there is no way you can stand next to me on stage to perform.

I still require attendance at rehearsal, even today. If you don't rehearse, you don't perform. No matter how good you are, if you stop coming to rehearsals I am not going to put you on the stage. People know I strive for perfection. No matter how good I am, I still strive for perfection. That way of thinking, maintaining that principle, has helped my groups a great deal. People know that it has nothing to do with my relationship with you, but if you don't rehearse you don't perform in the next show. That is one of the most important things that the members of my groups learn. They know that rehearsals are whenever we can get together. If we can rehearse every day, we will. With my first group, all I was trying to do was let them glimpse what their culture was all about and solidify their belief in it. If I could give them that, they would appreciate it more.

This group, which I put together between September 1954 and January 1955 while I was a student at NYU and living in Englewood, later became known as the Drums of Passion Dancers, Singers, and Drummers. Its members were so dedicated, so talented, and so eager to learn that it took no time for us to become known all over New York.

Our company introduced a lot of people to African dance. It also influenced a lot of people and helped start what is now known as modern jazz. We were also able to catch the attention of quite a few important people and promoters in town.

That was when I met Alvin Ailey. He was just forming his own company at the same time we were starting to rehearse at Michael Studios. We rehearsed at the same studio, and he came to watch us many times. He became a very good friend who had a tremendous respect for me as a person and for what I was doing.

Alvin drew one of his most celebrated dance works from African sources. In many of his works he used movements he had seen during our performances. In one of his dances, *Revelation*, which was a gospel-style dance, he borrowed some of our movements. That became one of his masterpieces and is still very popular today. In fact, the Derby sisters, who were the first two members of my company, also danced for Ailey's original company. They were dancing with both groups simultaneously.

Alvin was a lovable, friendly person who most of the time didn't have much to say. You really had to push him to get him to talk about things. He was also a wonderful teacher who made sure you did the right thing. He insisted that whatever story the dance was telling, you interpreted that story in such a way the audience would understand it. He was a very talented young man who really believed that what the black experience has been in America could be told in a dance format. He could really tell the story and bring out the point people needed to see—that the struggle of African Americans in this country had evolved into a fight for freedom.

He was very good in selecting the right person for the right parts. He could, without any prejudice, select the dancer he believed would actually portray what he wanted to put out to the audience. In other words, he was not a biased leader. He really believed that the parts should be played by the right person. He would make sure that that happened. He had the knack of knowing what a particular dancer could do and could become with enough hard work. He produced so many great dancers, like Miss Judith Jamison, who is now the director of the Alvin Ailey Dance Company. He could tell she had abilities that needed to be brought out by just pushing her a little bit, by encouraging her to work on her technique.

Other young choreographers in the mid-1950s used to come and watch us, too. Like Elio Palmeri, who was trying to start a company, and the legendary Jean Leon Destine, a vibrant, talented male dancer who was the leading exponent of Haitian dance, which had to do with the history of vodun. They would marvel at the performances we were putting together.

Around this time I volunteered to perform for one of the pioneers of African dance, Asadata Dafora from Sierra Leone, who was the first to perform African dances in the New York area before my arrival in the fall of 1954.

Choreographers like Agnes DeMille were winning Tony Awards for their work, after they auditioned so many African dancers around New York, New Jersey, and Connecticut for so long. They observed their movements and put together what they saw for Broadway shows. But Africa was never given credit for that.

It's the same kind of thing with clothes designers: they go to Africa, take pictures of the cloth designed by traditional African cloth makers and weavers, then take the designs to be copied in European mills. But they never go back to compensate or replenish their sources. This has always been the experience of Africans, and can really been seen as the rape of Africa. This has worked against the development of Africa, against the reduction of illiteracy in Africa. Africans themselves need to make their voices heard in the capitals of the world. This rape has been going on for centuries, and it needs to stop.

If Alvin Ailey had lived longer, he probably would have done more things with me. *Drums of Passion* influenced a lot of black choreographers at that time, and maybe it still does. All the dance teachers, black or white, used *Drums of Passion* to teach their classes.

So for three straight years, my dancers rehearsed, remained dedicated, and maintained tremendous interest in African folklore and traditions. They studied the songs, learned the rhythms, and read about traditional

African ways. Then they were asked to apply those ways to their own lives.

All of this was happening while I was trying to adjust to family life. And I was still a student at NYU, looking for money to research my dissertation in England and Nigeria. But at least I had been offered the chance to be heard. Finally, all of a sudden, I was able to put it all together and produce a recording.

The recording contract with Columbia Records followed my seven weeks at Radio City Music Hall, where I was featured with the orchestra in "African Drum Fantasy," a twelve-minute overture. Al Ham, who became my engineer at Columbia, attended one of the performances, and made it clear what he expected of me. He gave me the go-ahead to do whatever it took to make the album the best I do. I succeeded. *Drums of Passion* is just that—the best I could produce, and probably the best I will ever produce.

I signed that first recording contract as Michael Babatunde Olatunji. That is my Christian name. When I left the village for Lagos and joined the African Methodist Church, I was baptized as Michael Gabriel. That is how that name came about.

Al Ham likes calling me Michael. He was a very sensitive, intelligent young man, with a wonderful gift for knowing how to treat his artists. He asked so many questions. He asked, "What would you do at home?"

I told him that when we wanted to do something of this magnitude, we prayed first, and we performed our rituals.

He said, "Go ahead, do it."

He didn't question anything. He was right there, ready for us to do anything.

When the time came to go into the studio, according to tradition, we came together to perform the appropriate rituals. I made sure the group understood what I meant by rituals. That they were done to unify us, to bring us together as one, so that we would have a singleness of purpose. This venture would show how unified we were in our purpose, which was to record an album that would probably make us or break us. If you knew and understood that, you would put your whole self into it. There would be no competition between singers and dancers, no competition between drummers. Everybody would have to stick to the parts they had been given. Egos, including my own, would be forbidden.

The traditional ritual called for pouring libations and calling on the spirits of the ancestors through the Creator to guide us through the production and thereafter. It called for a feast to be served to the people of our community, so we held one. We slaughtered a goat, and cooked it and served it with rice and beans and drinks. This was a celebration of the project we were about to undertake.

We decided we would dress for the recording as if we were performing for a big audience, as if we were representing a whole village. It was almost like psyching everybody up to say, "Look, when you go to the studio you are not there by yourself. All the spirits of the ancestors are present, helping you. Just imagine that you have hundreds and hundreds of people in the village watching you doing something that you will never regret, doing something that represents all of them. All the people in the village are right there, they are clapping for you, they are urging you on."

When we arrived at the studio, dressed as if we were performing on the stage of Carnegie Hall or Radio City Music Hall, wearing traditional dress, with our best earrings and jewelry, the production staff at Columbia Records were totally surprised. They asked, "What is happening?"

I told them, "We are recording an album. But we are actually performing. We are going to imagine that we have hundreds of people here. So we are really on stage. We don't know anything about how you set up your studio, but right here, in our imagination, we know that the spirits of the ancestors are here."

Al Ham, who was brave enough to have offered me a contract, really was a man of vision. He said to me, "I have never seen anything like this. You have it. Go for it. Do whatever you have to do to record this album."

A year or so later, Columbia fired this young man, who had so much vision, so much taste. I don't know how record companies can do that.

Many people have asked me how I came up with the title for *Drums of Passion*. I have always maintained that no idea is new. If you wake up one day and have an idea, somewhere, somebody has had the same idea. Maybe they did not express it the same way you did, but somebody had the same idea somewhere along the line. No idea is new in the universal order. Ideas are ongoing, and we build on them.

Drums have been used for many purposes through the ages in societies all over the world, in all cultures. It is nothing new when we talk about rhythm. Everything we do, we do in rhythm. Everybody walking down the street walks in rhythm, in their own rhythm, in their own way. You see some with the left arm next to their thigh while the right one is swinging up and down. You see others swinging both arms simultaneously. You see others swinging both arms simultaneously and then kind of moving at their waistline as they walk. You see some taking smaller steps than others. But they are all doing it in their own rhythm.

Your own rhythm affects the way you think and the way you approach things. When you are out of rhythm, it affects your passion, the way you feel. Do you feel sad when you get out of rhythm? Do you feel happy when you make certain gestures? Do you become exhilarated when you approach things in certain ways? When you really study the human anatomy, you see that everything affects other things.

In the Yoruba tradition, there is a saying: "What affects the eye affects the nose." You cannot escape rhythm; it is a natural fact. So when people stop doing things in rhythm, that is when they get into trouble. Drumming is like that. The spirit of the drum itself, when it is played well, creates not only captivating rhythm, but also the kind of passion that will heal you. The rhythm gives you that passion. It is the kind of passion that will help you forget your suffering, that will give you confidence to continue and to rely on your inner strength.

Interestingly enough, this recording got its name through the contributions of two other people, my agent and a friend.

They asked me, "How do you play the drums so well that everybody wants to listen to them?"

I said, "When I play, I play with passion, I am completely involved in it."

He said, "Well, okay then, that's what the album will be called—'Drums of Passion.'"

At first, the executives at Columbia really did not like the name. "This is 1959. You can't be using the word 'passion' so freely. What do you want young people to think about when you say 'Drums of Passion'? Do you know what passion means?"

They disliked the title so much that when the PR department recommended spending money for us to go to schools, they would not approve it. They told me that if I wanted to go to schools, I shouldn't call my record *Drums of Passion*, I shouldn't talk about passion. That was very interesting. But as time went on, people began to grasp the true meaning of passion. They were able to distinguish what we meant by passion with regard to the drums as compared to other meanings that could be attached to it. But passion was so natural to me.

It is very interesting that the recording was made on the East Side of Manhattan in an old church with beautiful acoustics. Columbia had turned it into a recording studio. The pews and the sanctuary weren't there any more, but even so, it was quite appropriate. It was like being in a House of God, in the temple of one of the deities, because of some of the songs we recorded. "Shango" was a chant to the God of Thunder. "Odun de! Odun de!" was a song and dance to celebrate the harvest. And there was "Baba Jinde," a courting dance that celebrated the ritual of selecting a future wife. Another was "Akiwowo," a chant to the Trainman. An important piece was "Jin-Go-Lo-Ba," a composition of mine based on the way Nigerian women danced. In my home country, there was no expectation that you had to be slim to be a dancer. Some of these women were quite large, yet they would join the circle and dance with dignity. That piece has a rhythmic pattern that is sensuous, energetic, inviting, and very stimulating. All the body movements are synchronized with the beat. It is actually a duet between the mother drum and the *omele* drum, each one speaking a part.

The songs on the album were the ones I had heard as a child. All I did was set them to music. The selection was perfect. They all had significant stories to tell about the culture. That is why *Drums of Passion* is such a unique album and why it is such a classic today.

So everybody arrived for the recording session in African attire, to the great surprise of all those who had been invited to watch the recording. We would warm up, we would do the chants, we would pour libations, and we would all say "Ashe," the Yoruban term for blessing.

The recording of *Drums of Passion* was a unique experience for everyone involved, especially for the members of the group, who were committed to making it the best recording ever. They had been preparing every day for more than three years. The group's preparedness must have impressed all concerned, from the record company executives to the marketing department.

The recording was done in three sessions in one week. It was very easy to record, for two reasons. First, every member of the group knew exactly what needed to be done, knew every number backwards and forwards, so it was very easy for them to record the album almost to perfection. Most of the numbers were "one takes." Second, we were totally prepared both ritually and spiritually.

After the recording came the arduous task of mixing, and preparing the liner notes. My cousin Akiwowo—now Professor Akinsola Akiwowo—and I collaborated on the liner notes, and I participated in the editing and arranging of the songs.

We performed the same kinds of rituals when the album was released. Friends gathered together, poured libations, and prayed that this album would be accepted and would help break the misconceptions people held not only about drums but about African culture. One other very important fact is that in the entire group, there was only one other African directly from Africa. That was Akiwowo. The rest of the people on the album were African Americans or people from the diaspora.

The company launched its promotion of the album. My cousin and I visited almost every small record store in Brooklyn, Manhattan, and Queens to persuade the owners to order CL1412, as the album became known to the famous record store, Sam Goody's.

The contract with Columbia came at a time when I was depressed about not getting a grant to go to Nigeria or London to do doctoral research. The excitement of becoming a Columbia recording artist, of being talked about in all the New York dailies, of being on *The Ed Sullivan Show*, *The Today Show*, and all of the other regular television and radio shows at that time, led me to overlook some important contract details, especially relating to copyright. But those things also helped me get over my disappointment at being unable to complete my dissertation.

When I signed the contract for *Drums of Passion*, I was so thrilled that I didn't bother to get any advice from anyone. There was no one to whisper in my ear about what went on when you signed contracts. The pieces on the album were all based on traditional folk songs. Even so, I did most of the arrangements and created most of the rhythms for them, so I should have made sure I at least got mechanical rights.

If you don't fill out the forms saying they are your songs, you are not going to get paid for them. I did that somehow for one song, "Jin-Go-Lo-Ba." I claimed full ownership for that. I also clarified that I had written it and had arranged the music for it. I said that the others were traditional folk chants, chants to the God of Thunder, and that the words were not written by me, but were chants that people passed on from generation to generation. All I did was set them to music. But I should have gotten credit for that. I should have made sure I collected something for mechanical rights. But I didn't clarify my contribution. "Jin-Go-Lo-Ba" was the only one I got 100 percent royalties for. I didn't even get 50 percent for the rest of the songs.

That would have brought in a tremendous amount of money, when you consider the number of albums sold. By the time I knew what to do, the company was not promoting the rest of our albums as strongly as "Drums of Passion."

Columbia gave me a 3 percent personal royalty, but included in the contract that the 3 percent was going to go toward the cost of the next album, which would have to be recovered before I got anything. Three percent wasn't enough. I didn't know how much it cost to record *Drums of Passion*. Neither did I know how much it cost for the second album, the third album, the fourth album, or the fifth album.

I really didn't know the business side of it, though I should have. Artists need to know. They need to ask, "How much is it costing you to record my album?" It should be negotiated that if your album does do so and so and so, you get to renegotiate your royalty percentage. Instead, throughout my contract with Columbia, my royalty was 3 percent. I never finished paying for one recording before the next one came out. I was forever owing *them*.

Nevertheless, I rejoice that I was able to bring about some recognition of African heritage, which for so long had been so greatly ignored by Americans. *Drums of Passion* became the talk of New York, and from there the talk of the nation. Then it gained international recognition as a significant contribution to understanding Africa's rich past. All of this really helped soften my disappointment over not being able to research my dissertation.

If I have any regrets, it is simply that I had to wait twenty-eight years according to the copyright laws to acquire control over this album. Twenty-eight years without royalties prevented me from fulfilling my other goals, the ones relating to establishing cultural centers in every major American city. That is what I had envisioned in 1958 when I attended the first All-African People's Conference in Ghana.

Drums of Passion became so popular in the 1960s that Murray the K on WNEW would open his daily radio show with the song "Akiwowo." He would play it and say, "The chief is here today. Change is coming. Look out, you guys." Students on college campuses, both black and white, were listening to *Drums of Passion*. I was given credit for the cultural awareness that increasing, among African Americans and among all young people, both black and white.

On WADO, Symphony Sid—one of the greatest supporters and promoters of jazz—would play two or three cuts from *Drums of Passion* on his show every night. Murray the K and Symphony Sid, and other famous radio programs in New York City, helped popularize *Drums of Passion* among high school and college students in the tristate area—New York, New Jersey, and Connecticut. It was Murray the K who introduced my album to the Beatles. I heard later that at one point they considered recording one of the tunes on it. But they broke up just after that, which was very unfortunate.

Every dance company, and almost every dance studio in the country—New York, the South, the West Coast—used *Drums of Passion* for rehearsals or to teach classes. This, the album's general popularity, and the tours the group made around college campuses all over the country, enabled us to open the Olatunji Center of African Culture.

Many of the songs on the album were sung in the Yoruba language, and African Americans who heard the album couldn't believe that all of us on that album didn't come from Nigeria. They thought I brought everybody over from Nigeria or West Africa. But I told them some came from the diaspora, and some were born right here in the United States. Remember, it took three years to prepare this album because of my insistence that people who wanted to join the group would have to learn the culture first—they were not going to be just playing drums. They would have to go through the whole cycle, going back again to Africa, really learning what the family means, what coming together to do a project means, what it means to have a unity of purpose. Everyone's whole life changed, in that first group.

Africans couldn't tell, because the group members pronounced the words so well. People would say, "There is no way that all these people didn't come from Nigeria or Ghana."

I would tell them, "Yes they did. Their ancestors came from there, but they themselves were born in America or the West Indies, and had to go through the process again."

Somehow I got the idea that they would have to learn the language. When we established the school, one of the things we did was offer courses in twelve African languages. You know, when your language is taken away from you, you have lost practically 90 percent of who you are, because in the process of learning a new language, you forget your own way of doing things. You have to learn how to talk in the language of whoever the master is. You have to learn how to think like your master, how to approach things like your master. You have to forget your whole self.

My performers had to regain what Nkrumah called "the African personality." That was the real secret to the success of *Drums of Passion*. That album proved that African Americans really can go back and relearn Africa and be reconnected to it and become sanctified by it, that they can become rejuvenated by reacquiring their rich cultural traditions.

We proved it with that album. It was not easy, but we did it. A lot of people applied to join the group, a lot of performers who became big names later on, but I didn't let them in. I won't name any names—it might be too embarrassing. I would explain to some of them who have since become very good friends of mine, "But I have the best, and there is no room for anybody else anymore." I had eight wonderful men, real men, strong dancers, and twelve beautiful women.

Miles Davis was one of the best-known artists on the Columbia label, with very successful albums, especially *Sketches of Spain*, a beautiful album and a favorite of mine. It was released at the same time as *Drums of Passion* and shared the same recognition. For weeks, those two albums ran neck and neck on the Billboard Top Ten.

Miles was a giant in the history of music, especially jazz, and not just in this country—in the entire world. He was one of the most celebrated artists of his time, and one of Columbia's most respected and perhaps even feared artists. Everybody knew that any time he wanted, Miles could just walk into Gary Lieberson's office—that was the president of Columbia, and a very liberal, compassionate man. When Miles wanted a sports car, he would just go in and say, "I want to buy me a sports car." And the next day he would come in for the check and buy his car. Whatever Miles wanted from CBS Records, he got.

Miles was very talented and imaginative. To me he seemed haunted by some things, but you would have to know more about his background, his childhood, which I don't. He played with finesse, intensity, and authority, and you knew he had something to say. He wanted to say what he had to say the way he wanted to say it. He didn't want anybody else to tell him how to say what he had to say. He knew what he wanted to say, and believed he was the only one who knew how to express himself. It showed in his playing.

Miles was complex, but simple, too. After a rendition of a beautiful solo, he'd get a standing ovation. What would he do then? He'd turn his back to the audience. He wouldn't take a bow. You'd think the audience would say,

"Get out of here!" But no, they'd applaud. When he was finished, he'd walk off the stage.

When somebody asked me, "What does that mean?" I'd say, "Well, he is saying, 'There is nothing to what I am doing, I am just expressing myself. What is all this noise about? I am just expressing myself. You want me to take a bow now? I'm going to turn my back. Leave me alone. Don't bother me. Let me do what I have to do.'"

Once you knew him, you realized that Miles wasn't really like that. When he walked off the stage like that, he wasn't mad at anybody. But he was always guarding himself from you. It took all this energy and time before you could reach him. When you were working together, that's when you got to know him. But he was very particular about his associates.

What was going on around him was too much for him to cope with. It takes willpower to say no to so many influences. He just couldn't deal with them. So many evils came running toward him, drugs, alcohol, and he couldn't handle them. He knew they were wrong, but many times he let them affect him. You really have to be a strong person to deal with all of them.

He was a musical master. He revolutionized the whole field of jazz. He was responsible for so many advances in it, so many new approaches to it. And he knew what he had to do to bring out his own genius. His A&R man, Teo Macero, the one who put all his recordings together, was the only one who could actually understand Miles. Many others couldn't deal with him. Teo knew that when Miles said, "I am finished today," he was finished—you might as well pack your bags and go. Say the session had just started an hour-and-a-half ago and you were supposed to be in the studio for six hours. He'd say he was going home, didn't feel like playing. Teo would say, "Okay. Will you come back tomorrow to play? What do you think?" He'd say, "Yeah, we'll come back tomorrow. I don't feel like playing. I don't like what is happening. I don't like the vibrations around."

Miles' sessions were very expensive for Columbia. It's a good thing he sold so many albums. Sometimes he'd do twenty takes for one tune. Sometimes he'd spend a whole three hour-session on one song. If he didn't play it to his satisfaction, that would be the end of the session, after twenty or twenty-five takes. But that's the kind of determination he had. I think it shows that he believed in what he was doing and that he was striving for perfection.

I believe that Miles would not have left CBS for RCA if Teo Macero had still been there. His next producer, George Butler, couldn't deal with Miles, and Miles couldn't deal with Butler. George wanted to establish himself as an A&R man who could control his artists. Miles had been there a long time, and he asked for things that George couldn't get him, so Miles left. I believe that was one of the most painful things for Miles, having to leave CBS. That was a sad ending to such a long relationship with a recording company.

Miles made an enormous contribution to that label. He really kept the CBS jazz line intact for many years, more than any other artist. During the 1960s and 1970s, CBS was busy trying to promote the masterpieces of great classical composers like Bach and Beethoven. Their PR division was trying to get Bach's picture on the cover of *Time*. Many artists were left uncared for or not promoted. That is why Aretha Franklin left CBS, and why Tony Bennett was about to leave, too—they weren't doing anything for him either. It had nothing to do with black or white, it's just that those executives in those days didn't have any idea who to promote or not.

They were spending a lot of money promoting people like Andy Williams, who came out with the single, "Go Away, Little Girl." The jazz lines were not really taken good care of. The pop lines weren't being promoted much, either. So Aretha left, and she became a bigger star in pop after she left Columbia. They didn't know how to take care of talented people.

Drums of Passion could have sold even more than it did, and in more places. But they hesitated. I had no place to go—I had to stay there. They got rid of Al Ham. Then I fell into the hands of a great man, John Hammond, who had a tremendous record for discovering talent. He's the one who discovered Billie Holiday and so many other great artists. John was a big name at Columbia. He knew talent. He became my producer there, and I was really glad to have him.

It was John who brought Bob Dylan to Columbia. I was right there in John's office when Bob Dylan came in with his big boots on like he just stepped off the railroad and a big cowboy hat and a bag over his shoulder. The bag was filled with more than two hundred songs he had written. John had to go from his office on the fourth floor to the CEO's office on the seventh floor. At the time, Columbia didn't have their thirty-two-story building on 6th Avenue. They only had the one on 7th Avenue, seven floors.

John went to the seventh floor to talk to the CEO, and he was gone for two hours. He was trying to convince them to sign this talent. I was right there. That is how I became a good friend of Bob Dylan.

He didn't say much. He said, "Where is the goddamn man? What the hell is he doing?"

I said, "He's upstairs talking to the high falutin' CEOs."

"He better come down here quick, 'cause I'm gone."

"No, wait. John *is* coming back."

"No he's not."

"He has been very good to me since they got rid of my A&R man," I told him. "He will take care of you. Let's go for lunch downstairs at the coffee shop."

The coffee shop was next to a Chinese restaurant called HoHo, where most of the Columbia executives usually ate lunch. So I took him there.

We had lunch and came back up. John was looking for us.

I said, "You were gone so long. I had to take this young man somewhere."

"Thank you very much! I thought he was gone!"

They signed Bob that same day. He would have taken off, he was ready to go. Bob Dylan became a major artist for Columbia.

With his first album, I became one of his favorite people in the world. People still ask me, "How do you know Bob Dylan? He said you were one of his favorite six people in the world." That was on his first album.

John Coltrane became my number one fan, and didn't hide it. He let me know that he really appreciated my contributions and would really like to do projects with me. He always came to see me whenever we performed.

'Trane was a quiet storm. He was so deep and vast, like the River Nile. He was a deep thinker but a man of few words. When you looked at him, you could see the pain seeping out of him. You could tell something terrible was bothering him. He looked ready to burst from it. You need to be able to talk things through and let them out.

I don't know if he had any close friends he could reveal himself to. But he did some to me. He told me in no uncertain terms, "I really admire what you've been doing. Every chance I get, I come to see and hear you. And when I do, I listen close to every move you make, everything you play. So one day I want to come a little nearer and learn something from you."

"From me?"

"Yes, brother! I'm serious."

At that time in his life, he was beginning to learn more about African language and chants. In 1962, in my honor, he recorded "Tunji" for his *Coltrane* album. With that piece he began bringing African forms into jazz. He wanted to express his interest in African traditions. That piece started simple and then built up and became complicated. He opened it with a four–four rhythm and turned it into a polyrhythm.

When the Olatunji Center was being established, 'Trane was the only musician to offer financial help. Every month while we were making repairs and renovating it to be a school, he sent us a check for 250 dollars.

'Trane was a determined man in every way. It was a period when we were going through so many changes. He did not appreciate what young jazz concert promoters were trying to do. Jazz promoters were able to borrow money from their cousins, rent Carnegie Hall, or whatever other venue, and pay an artist like him $3,000 or $4,000, and then they would deposit $75,000 into their own account from the concert proceeds. He didn't appreciate that. He felt that musicians should be compensated more than they were.

That was one of the reasons he stopped playing. Another was he felt there was nothing more he could learn about jazz from his Western orientation and training. He wanted to go back to his roots. He wanted to come to the center to learn the language. He wanted to learn about the music. He wanted to learn about the culture and how all of it tied together with the family and the music of the people. He thought he might be able to do a lot of creative things with the music, with his experience in the Western tradition. So he didn't perform for two years. Instead, he came to me to listen.

He was hoping to do an album with me where half the compositions would come from me and half from him. Whatever I composed would fit into what he was doing, and vice versa. He would write jazz pieces, and I would create rhythmic patterns for them.

He came up with a plan. He called Yusef Lateef. He said, "Let's join Brother Olatunji. The three of us could get together and give a concert at Lincoln Center. We could hire somebody to promote the show. We could get more money for ourselves and our groups if all three of us did a concert together. And we could tour the entire country. Then we'd be able to establish a center like Baba's in every major city, like he's proposed."

Can you imagine what would have happened if 'Trane had lived? I know that if he was alive today, I would have cultural centers in every major American city.

Yusef agreed, and they made me secretary–treasurer. But what to do next?

They said, "Okay, let's go ahead and book the first show." 'Trane gave his part of the money, and we paid a thousand dollars to Lincoln Center to have a show in January 1968.

'Trane passed away during the summer of 1967. Before he passed, he performed at the Olatunji Center. That was his last performance. More than three thousand people came and jammed the place, so we had to do two shows. How much did we charge? Three dollars a ticket.

'Trane was a man of conviction, a man of action, a very determined person. He knew what he wanted and knew how to go about it. He was really a giant of a man. Very intense, very serious. Only God knows why it didn't happen. Since then, nobody has come to me to do anything similar. I realize now more than ever before that John Coltrane's death was a big reason why the center had to close in 1984.

Drums of Passion played a significant role in all the social change taking place around that time. It was the first percussion album to be recognized as an African contribution to the music of African Americans. It also came right at the beginning of the Civil Rights Movement. This meant we were recognized as pioneers in the "Black is Beautiful" movement. The whole idea of "black power" came along at this time, too. And so did the wearing of the *dashiki* and natural hair.

We found ourselves right in the middle of this, going from one rally to another, sponsored by different organizations fighting for freedom. From the NAACP to CORE to SNCC to the Black Muslims. This era was so full of excitement and challenges to everybody who was alive and part of it, black or white.

So *Drums of Passion* became part of history. It became a number one album, right there on "Billboard's Top Ten" for weeks and weeks. It was very well received, just like I expected. The reviews it got—the best reviews any album could enjoy—and our appearances on local radio stations, on national television, and in magazines, all made us a very hot property. All of that, and our appearances across the country, and the friendships we made great musicians, gave me many wonderful opportunities.

The way I saw it, the album had been well planned and produced, so it had to be successful. I knew it was for real. I had put together a group of people who really believed in it and shared its purpose. It was the fruit of a very positive and disciplined program of training and preparation. The group was learning something very new to them, something that was a great challenge, and they were all totally committed to it.

That first group of young men and women recognized this music and dance as something new to them. They were determined to learn about it—not just a little bit, but all they could. They learned the songs, the rhythms, the traditions and practices, everything.

Whenever we got together, we would hold hands and say these words: "As we get together today may we unify ourselves with Mother Earth, may we unify ourselves with the universe, may we unify ourselves with everybody who is in the reach of my voice. It is through this togetherness, through divine order, that we will eradicate all negatives from our words, from our minds, and from our actions."

Before we did anything else, we would say that prayer. And after a rehearsal or a performance, we would join hands again and say that we would be back again, even stronger in our conviction that we would succeed in whatever we said we were going to do. That was the traditional African way when people got together. I had learned it in my childhood when I saw people come together. At no moment did the group ever forget the learning they had undergone at the very beginning.

I haven't the words to describe the joy and satisfaction that I felt when the album became the talk of the town. Privately, I pledged to myself and prayed that it wouldn't turn me into someone else, that I would be able to handle the success. Not that it made me any money. That created quite a few problems for me. Everybody, inside and outside the family, believed I was rich. They concluded that there was no way I could not now be a millionaire. But I knew at that time that I was selling a new commodity that had to be promoted. I knew I would not be given what I deserved, but that it would be what I was able to negotiate. Even those in a position to negotiate, those who represented me at that time, didn't have any idea how to market my talents. Even they were not so sure about the validity, importance, or marketability of what I was doing.

But I was very satisfied that I had made my point in letting people know that Africa had contributed to the development of world culture. I knew at that time that I was on my way to fulfill all the promises I had made to those who helped me, and that I would continue to preserve the rich cultural heritage of Africa, come what may. It was a time I truly felt renewed, reinvigorated, and rededicated to the vision that I had seen of myself years before, and that the preacher on the beach saw for me before I left Africa.

PART THREE

Passing the Rhythm On

7 | Social Change and Civil Rights

have always been very mindful of how I treat and relate to people. My years in the village taught me to have respect for the elders, beginning with those in the immediate family and extending to everyone in the village. I was brought up to always be ready to lend a hand, try to make the other person happy, try to share with the other person whatever I had if I could afford it. I was taught that if I followed the golden rule, doing unto others as I would like others to do unto me, my life would be better and happier than I could ever imagine.

Many stories were told to impress upon me how important it is to have reverence for life, to always take a look at the other side of the coin, and most important, to always ask, Why? When? Where? How? and What?—of everything.

With this in mind, I became very inquisitive about almost everything. I wanted to know the answer to everything that puzzled my mind. I remember during my childhood always standing on a little soapbox to repeat something or to address my friends who gathered around to play. At some point I would get their attention by asking everyone present some kind of question.

I grew up noticing that many of them always wanted to know what I thought on all subject matters. They probably thought I had the right answers to everything, and that I was going to ask everyone the important questions.

I had not been prepared for everything I experienced in America, however. I was not surprised that I found a different America than I had read and heard about. But on the first day of my arrival, I was confronted with a social situation that I had not known before: segregation of the races.

The cultural revolution that started in the early 1950s contributed a great deal to the social change happening in America. It created an awareness among African Americans, for the first time. It was like an awakening from a deep lethargy. It's like suddenly realizing who you are, why you are, and what you can become.

The 1950s, as powerful and challenging as they were, had to be the most difficult years of my stay in this country. They were the years when the winds of change were blowing so hard, not only in Africa but also in the United States. Those winds could carry you away if you lacked commitment, dedication, faith, and, most of all, belief that adversity is what makes a man.

Those were the years when social change in the United States coincided with the freedom movement in Africa. This was the time when colonialism was about to become a thing of the past, only to be replaced by what Nkrumah called "new colonialism." This was the time when most African countries became independent. But the colonizers had done almost nothing to prepare them for it, and had not given them the help they needed to cope with the enormous changes that were coming so suddenly to so many countries in Africa.

The fight for independence in Africa had a tremendous impact on the way I looked at and participated in the Civil Rights Movement. Before I left Lagos, I'd been involved in a civil rights protest. I'd been a member of the Zikist youth movement. One of our leaders, Nnamdi Azikiwe (later the first president of independent Nigeria), had gone to Lincoln University in this country and then to Columbia University and had come back to Nigeria to establish a newspaper, the *West African Pilot*. He also became general secretary of the National Council of Nigeria and the Cameroons, which welcomed other organizations to help in the fight for Nigerian independence. As general secretary he spoke openly and directly about what was going on. At one rally, after hearing him talk about how we as an African nation could not allow discrimination against any of our brothers and sisters from the diaspora, we left the hall without hearing the rest of his speech and marched off to stone the Bristol Hotel, where a young man from Jamaica had been discriminated against. I was one of the ones who broke this hotel's windows, before the crowd was dispersed by mounted police. I remembered that day vividly.

In the 1950s I participated not by throwing stones at any hotel or by disrupting anything, but by taking the cultural route—by supporting those who were on the front lines. This was similar to the sit-ins conducted by the Student Nonviolent Coordinating Committee (SNCC), headed by Stokely Carmichael and H. Rap Brown, who were testing the laws against segregation.

So it was within this global context that a new generation of African Americans acknowledged their heritage, spoke out loudly against the injustices that they had suffered for over four hundred years, took action, struggled, and sacrificed to show others that they truly were citizens of this country and had contributed to the development of America. They were beginning to fight against the psychological impact that segregation and prejudice had had on them over the years. This was the time when different organizations were trying to convince their members that they were the ones that could lead them to the promised land. The leaders of the African American community were pitted against one another—Dr. Martin Luther King, Jr. against Malcolm X, or all the other leaders against Muslims. All of them were really trying to tell the world there were many ways of skinning a cat, and that to rid themselves of the dangers of what the changes had brought and would bring in the future, they needed to think collectively.

Social change started right on the Morehouse campus, with my impromptu African awareness sessions in my dorm room. This had quite remarkable results. I was able to win the friendship of many of the students and faculty. Every year I was there, I was an elected representative of the student body.

With the first public program of African music and dance that we gave in 1953 using the student body from Atlanta University, we attracted white people from downtown Atlanta to the campus of a black college theater.

With the Supreme Court's 1954 decision *Brown v. Board of Education*, and with my election as president of the student body, I was placed in a position of leadership—one that was noticed by many people beyond Atlanta.

I became aware only gradually of what my mission really was. It didn't come with one event, but gradually after a number of events, including the assassination in 1961 of Patrice Lumumba, the first president of the Congo, and the assassination of JFK in 1963. The constant obstruction by those who were against social progress built up an awareness in me that much more had to be done, that my dedication to change must be unwavering, and that it would take time to achieve not only my own goals but also the ones set by those others who had been working day and night to ensure a better life for all people.

I decided that I would always do the Creator's work, whatever it took to bridge the gap that had existed between people for so long, whatever it took to accomplish the difficult task of building and rebuilding. I have always had the faith that this effort will succeed, that all of us will one day be able to sit down, laugh, and clap our hands in jubilation, that things are going to be better than they are now.

My work with the NAACP started while I was at Morehouse. Roy Wilkins became that group's new executive director. He was determined to develop a youth program for the NAACP. He named a young African American, Herb Wright, who had just graduated from Howard Law School in Washington, to direct the youth program.

I was invited to speak to five thousand young people in New York at the Statler Hilton Hotel. I took the bus to New York and addressed this tremendous gathering on the importance of joining the NAACP and becoming future leaders of that organization. I spoke about that time as one of growth and development. I told them they needed to be concerned about the future, because they *were* the future.

I was involved in social change even before Dr. King was propelled into the leadership role, which he accepted with great reluctance.

By conducting protests at Morehouse, like sitting at the front of the bus, we African students were testing the boundaries and expressing our solidarity with our American-born brothers and sisters. We were also telling the authorities that whatever affected them affected us as well, and that just because we were wearing our African garments, we were not to be given preferential treatment.

We were testing the segregation laws at Morehouse even before Stokely Carmichael and H. Rap Brown, representing SNCC, were doing the same thing elsewhere. At the time, many young people felt that the NAACP had not done enough to test the law.

After Rosa Parks, the young people said: "To test the law, let's sit down in the restaurants and see if they'll serve us or not. Until we do that, we won't know whether we're obeying the law or not." The law had to be tested. GAT, an umbrella students' organization that had been in existence for a long time, did a lot of things, like organize rallies and hold benefits to raise money for different organizations. We entertained people. We did that to energize them, to unify them and let them know we supported their work.

The *Drums of Passion* years were a very interesting time in my life because I had the opportunity to introduce many people to African music, including some who later became advisors to heads of state in Africa. It was a time when many other groups, of many colors and religions, joined the struggle for freedom. It was when all of the minority groups in this country began to work together to demonstrate a unity of purpose, to come up with positive programs of action.

One of these efforts resulted in a march to the UN in April 1960 to protest the Sharpeville massacre in South Africa, when more than half of the three hundred demonstrators were killed or injured. You could look around and see almost all the major organizations representing different ethnic groups coming together, Jews and Gentiles, blacks and whites, to demand that South Africa be ousted from the UN. I was the one who carried the sign that read, "We insist that South Africa be ousted from the UN." Nobody wanted to carry that sign.

A photograph of me carrying that sign was printed in papers all over the world. All the people who believed I was just a student radical—who even accused me of being a communist—those people are now leaders, advisors to African presidents. They are now shaking hands with Bishop Desmond Tutu and Nelson Mandela. When I was carrying that sign, in April 1960, Mandela was not even in jail yet.

If the UN had taken that strong action against South Africa, the fight for freedom would not have been so prolonged and costly, in terms of both dollars and human suffering.

This was also a time when new young political leaders were beginning to emerge. People were looking beyond America, they were seeing the world in its entirety. That meant they were becoming aware the role that Africa was playing in the lives of people all over the world.

Around this time, our dance company performed for the United Jewish Appeal at the old Madison Square Garden. This show was put together by

Harry Belafonte and his wife Julie. We were involved not just in African American civil rights, but in social change for all minority groups.

It was in 1960 that young people began taking over the leadership of this country. John F. Kennedy emerged as the challenger to Vice President Richard Nixon, who was the heavy favorite to become the next president. Kennedy was young, well liked, and from a well-respected family. His main challenger for the Democratic nomination, and the "establishment" candidate, was Lyndon Johnson, the very powerful Senate Majority Leader, who years later, as president himself, would push through many important civil rights laws.

Kennedy chose New York City as the place to announce that he would be running for the Democratic nomination. The venue was a $500-a-plate dinner at the Waldorf-Astoria. My group was asked to participate.

I knew the emcee of the show quite well. He had watched me perform over many years. He said, "I'll give you fifteen minutes. This is not a cultural dance or anything. This is a very important political meeting. You have fifteen minutes to do whatever you want to do. I'll close the curtain on you if you do more than that."

I said, "Yes, sir. I'll do just fifteen minutes."

Well, after I finished the first number, Kennedy and his wife, who later became First Lady, stood up and called, "Bravo! More, more, more!"

That's all I needed to hear. I went ahead and performed for another twenty minutes.

The next day, a newspaper headline read, "Culture and Politics Mix."

That's how the John and Jacqueline Kennedy became big fans of mine. Later on, I wrote a song telling the story of the First Lady's family, how connected with culture she was, how she spoke French and Spanish, how beautiful she was, and how great she was as First Lady. That song, "Lady Kennedy," came out on the *High Life!* album and was turned into a single.

There is a story about the Kennedys and the Peace Corps that I can tell now. Who knows what would have happened if JFK had lived longer? He probably would have changed the world because he was so progressive and had so much foresight. He wasn't satisfied with just sending ambassadors to represent the country. Many ambassadors couldn't even speak the language of the country they were being sent to—the ambassador to France couldn't speak French, ambassadors to Spanish countries couldn't speak Spanish. He set up the Peace Corps to help developing countries all over the world.

But where did the idea of the Peace Corps come from? I can tell you, because I was involved.

The idea of the Peace Corps came from what is called "Crossroads Africa," which was established by a minister of the Church of the Masters in Harlem. Many Africans from Nigeria attended that church because their girlfriends went there. These Nigerians told their minister that they needed to send books to their villages in Africa for people who really wanted to read. So people who had books that they didn't want to read, or had already read, should bring them to the church. The minister announced that. And that brought books in from everybody. The minister said, "If you bring two books, you need to give me at least five dollars for more than one book for me to mail these books to Nigeria." That is how the concept of Crossroads Africa started—with the books being collected at the Church of the Masters.

Almost all African American leaders—ministers especially—were Democrats in those days. They were so happy that someone like Kennedy—a young, vibrant leader—was asking his countrymen to think of what they could do for their country and not what the country could do for them. They liked that slogan. Kennedy met all of these people and turned the idea of Crossroads Africa into the Peace Corps. My dance company performed at the first fundraiser for Crossroads Africa at Columbia University. I was given a check for thirty dollars to buy subway tokens for the group. It was the early 1960s—a challenging, rewarding time, when many people felt they were helping the president, the leader of the free world, maintain that leadership.

Because the Kennedys were fans, I saw the First Lady many times. She made sure I participated in fundraising events in Manhattan that she was involved with. I have had my picture taken with many celebrities over the years, but one I cherish is is one that was taken by chance. I am told that for one of the fundraising events she was supporting, she asked the sponsors to have me come with a few drummers and singers and to pay me for my effort. I was paid handsomely for a three-hour job—what I would have gotten in a week. I was happy about that.

The people told me, "You've got to stop playing as soon as she gets to the door. We oversold. We're trying to arrange for people to be in another room where they can hear what she has to say. But she has to go straight upstairs where three hundred people are sitting down for lunch, and another two hundred are on the second floor. She is coming right on time for her to go upstairs, we don't want her to stay downstairs. Please stop playing the drums as soon as she gets here."

I had rehearsed with the group to sing "Lady Kennedy," which goes: "First Lady of USA, Lady Kennedy. From the Family Bouvier, Lady Kennedy. Par lé bucai Français, Italian, and Español, Lady Kennedy? Gracious mother of Caroline, Lady Kennedy." That was the song we were singing, and people seemed to like it because it was in English and in my native language together. They could hear all the words and what I was saying about her and her children and the family, and how she was a real First Lady who really lived up to her role.

They said, "When she comes, you have to stop."

I said, "Okay," and I did.

As she entered, we were on the left side of the room. She looked over and saw me and came over.

She said, "What's the matter? You're not playing."

I said, "Sure I will."

And she stood there for another ten minutes, and when I finished she gave me a big kiss on my left cheek. I was very happy about that.

Later on, I also met John, Jr. He was brought to see me perform at the 1964 World's Fair at the African Pavilion. The Kennedys have shown that kind of interest. It has been a wonderful relationship.

I had been taught in the village to care for people and to help out when it was needed. So it wasn't anything new to me. Even so, many people—including my immediate family and especially my wife—thought I was trying to carry the whole world on my shoulders.

I was asking myself, "Why am I here? Why was I created?" I had to discover that. My answer was, "To be of service," because "service" is the greatest word of all. It can make or break a man or woman, not to realize who you are and what you are about.

During the 1960s, this period of so much social change, the dream of establishing an African heritage center was uppermost in my mind. And it was breaking my heart that I couldn't find backing for the idea. We had the opportunity to teach, and many people were interested, yet the financial support for a place just wasn't there.

Even though *Drums of Passion* was enjoying a great popularity in the early 1960s, it wasn't making any money for us. So we couldn't develop a positive program of action to satisfy the people's needs. We were finding it very difficult to rehearse in rented studios every day.

Also, we were suffering from what I call a "black backlash." At one time, universities had sponsored our shows and paid us from general funds. Not any more—now we were referred to the campus black students' organizations. But those organizations were not given enough money to sponsor more than one or two groups over the whole year.

For example, every year we used to play twice at Kent State University. The $10,000 that cost used to be paid from the student body's general fund. Now, Kent's black students' organizations were supposed to pay us, but their total budget for the year was only $15,000. Obviously, they found it impossible to allocate $10,000 of that to us. So we could not go back there.

Social change was also doing us harm, especially between 1962 and 1964. In 1962 there was not a single week that Drums of Passion did not perform. But in 1963, we had only eight weeks of performing over the whole year. That was because the booking agencies were shelving our group to promote another African group. Either they were using one group to sell the other or they were shelving one group to promote the other with an identical act. So 1963, compared to 1962, was awful. It was tantamount to a no-income year. Yet we had been the first to promote African culture in America.

Then, for the New York World's Fair in 1964 and 1965, we were selected to perform at the African Pavilion. We became the number one attraction at the African Village. Two groups shared that venue with us: a group from Ivory Coast, and the Royal Drummers from the palace in Burundi, the Watusi.

It was the African American ambassador to Liberia, Dr. Samuel Westerfield, who had been my economics professor at Morehouse, who told the organizers, "Whatever you do, be sure you include Babatunde Olatunji and the Drums of Passion at the World's Fair. He is very well known and will be the greatest attraction." I will always be grateful to Dr. Westerfield for convincing the organizers that I would be a great asset at the African Pavilion.

But at the fair, something changed. People were growing tired of wearing the *dashiki* and cutting their hair natural. The whole emphasis had now shifted from, "I am black and beautiful," to something we couldn't get a handle on.

With some money I'd saved from the performances at the fair, I was finally able to establish my old dream, the Olatunji Center of African

Culture in Harlem. It was designed to be a place where people could learn about the music, dance, language, folklore, and history of Africa. The center would offer all kinds of classes and would eventually establish its own recording company and booking agency.

We rented a building formerly occupied by an optical company. It had left behind the optical equipment and everything.

The landlord told us, "You have to take this as it is. You know what that means—you have to clean it up yourself. We are not going to do that for you."

That was a lot of expense. John Coltrane was the only performer to help out. We wouldn't have been able to do it without his monthly checks. We had to put parquet floors in for dance. We had to have mirrors. We had three dance studios, and rooms in the back for language classes. It was a big endeavor.

We wanted to make it affordable, so we taught dancing classes for two dollars. We offered twelve different language classes for two dollars each. Drumming class was two dollars for an hour and a half. We weren't setting this up to make money. Even so, we had an impressive roster of teachers, many of them from West Africa. We had a teacher's training program to teach teachers how to go into the schools to instruct children in African dances, songs, history, customs, and folklore.

I had two lawyers, fresh from the Harvard University Law School, African Americans. I asked them, "How best can we put this together as a nonprofit organization?"

At first, they didn't think it should be that way.

I said, "It will have to be nonprofit."

Then we changed things around. We had to get a grant to establish our nonprofit status with the IRS. We wrote to different foundations. There was only one foundation, the Rockefeller Foundation, that responded.

I wrote to the foundation, reminding it that early in the 1950s my group had participated in its fundraising efforts. The foundation supported schools in West Africa, especially Liberia. We had been invited to the Rockefeller estate in Tarrytown. I reminded the officers of all that, and got a reply signed by Debbie Rockefeller. David Rockefeller was a fan, and he said, more or less, "I remember with pleasure all the occasions of our meeting. With regard to your letter, please call the Rockefeller Foundation at 30 Rockefeller Plaza, telephone number so and so and speak to so and so and send your application."

The Rockefeller Foundation was the only one that ever gave us a grant—for $25,000. That was how we got our tax exemption. After that, all the other foundations, including the Ford Foundation, always wrote back saying they did not support our kind of program.

We also set up a publishing program for all the people who taught the different languages. We said, "Write a book about yourself, about your language, so we don't have to use a book by Europeans."

One gentleman was able to do that about Swahili. We went to the printer and got a contract, and we published our own book on Swahili. Every year we sold at least five thousand copies of the book, for five dollars each. The writer got 50 percent, and the center took part of it to print more copies. We were not making any money.

We were revitalizing interest in African culture, and helping destroy the ugly image of Africa that had been planted in the minds of millions of Americans through Hollywood movies and so many books and articles about Africa and Africans.

But the struggle to keep the center open continued. We wrote to foundations. The reply always came back: "We do not support your type of program." We were never told what kind of program they were looking for. That went on for about ten years before we started going around asking people for support. We tried to start programs that would put us on stronger financial footing.

The independence of Nigeria, the largest and the most populous country in Africa, in 1960, followed soon after by the independence of the Congo and many other countries in Africa, rekindled the demand for social change in America. JFK's victory in the presidential race was a beacon of hope and inspiration for many civil rights leaders and for those who wanted change in America. Until his election, the United States had never developed a clear, positive policy toward Africa.

JFK came in with the idea of creating a New Frontier for the United States to conquer, of improving America's relationship with the Third World. African leaders welcomed American policies and agreed to support programs like the Peace Corps and to maintain close relations with the West. This impeded the Soviet Union's campaign to win the new African nations to their side.

The confrontation between the American government and the government of the Soviet Union reached a boiling point with the Cuban Missile Crisis. But by then, things were not going so smoothly in Africa either. Leaders must show their citizens that they can deliver the goods, that they can bring about social as well as economic change, and Africa's leaders found themselves unheeded when they approached their Western allies, their former colonial masters, for development aid.

For example, Ghana is a one-crop economy. The price of its cocao is controlled by the world market. Ghana needed to diversify its economy in order to grow and to feed its people. So it drew up an agricultural program that would enable it to do both. Nkrumah came to the United States to appeal for funds to carry out its program. When the Americans denied his country aid, he had nowhere to turn but China. As a result, in 1966 he was overthrown while visiting China to ask for development money.

The overthrow of Kwame Nkrumah, the first president of Ghana, was one of the most painful moments in my life. That event virtually dashed all hopes for a United States of Africa.

The last straw was when Patrice Lumumba, a protégé of Nkrumah, was assassinated in the Congo's Katanga province. He appealed to the American government for help, telling it that the Belgian colonizers had left nothing in the Congo's treasury when they pulled out. The Congo desperately needed foreign help—there were fewer than two dozen people in the country with administrative skills.

Lumumba spent a whole week at the Biltmore Hotel in New York, lobbying without success for financial help. Yet right after he was assassinated by his opponents Tsh'ombe and Kasavubu, the Moral Rearmament Organization sponsored a visit by Mobutu to the United States. The winds of change blowing through Africa brought political independence but no economic emancipation.

I remember so well the words of my son Kwame, may his soul rest in peace, who saw me cry for the first time when the news of Lumumba's death was announced: "Daddy, Africa is gone."

I wrote a song for Lumumba and recorded it as a single. It was banned from play on radio stations in New York, but was finally given to a group of newspaper writers from Zaire to be distributed to the people there. Thankfully, that song has been included in the CD box set of all my recordings, put out by the Bear Family Record Company in Germany.

Just before that, in November 1963, JFK had been assassinated. That was a terrible blow to efforts to bring about a more balanced economy both for Americans and for people in developing countries. At the time of his death, his idea of a New Frontier for America was just beginning to show signs of success. His death slowed down considerably all the progress toward peaceful coexistence between developing countries and the West. This progress was impeded even further when President Lyndon Johnson intensified the Vietnam War.

The 1960s were a very critical time. So many events had a tremendous impact on the political situation in the United States, the Soviet Union, and the newly independent African nations. Also, the American public was deeply divided over Vietnam. America itself was going through tremendous changes. And we cannot forget President Richard Nixon's visit to China. It was almost a political miracle. I believe that Nixon's visit will forever be remembered by historians as a watershed in the struggle to dismantle communism.

During the 1960s, social change inspired many Americans to visit or at least think about Africa. Everybody was talking about Africa. But at the same time, polarization increased, even among blacks who had been so proud of wearing the *dashiki* and growing their hair naturally. Most black men went back to curling their hair, most black women started going back to hairdressers instead of cutting their hair short.

It seemed as if Black people were not so proud of Africa anymore, or so interested. Faculty on campuses began debating the usefulness of Black Studies programs. Educated African Americans could not agree on a curriculum for Black Studies.

Around this time, support for the Olatunji Center of African Culture almost vanished. From the start, it never enjoyed national support from middle-class African Americans. By hook or by crook, a few of us kept the center going, finding ways to maintain the quest and disseminate information about Africa's rich cultural heritage.

By now, I had committed myself to helping other organizations. I was traveling to Boston every Monday by bus to teach fourteen classes in two days. Then I would come back on Wednesday morning and fly to Cleveland, where a station wagon would pick me up and drive me to Kent State University, where I was teaching Wednesdays and Thursdays at the Institute of African American Affairs, which Professor Edward Crosby had established in 1969 with my help. Later, in 1976, this became the Department of Pan-African Studies. Then I would return to New York on Friday either to perform on the weekend or to teach at my own school.

I kept this up for fifteen years. The Boston program was at the Alma Lewis School of Fine Arts, in Roxbury. Fifth-graders would leave school at three p.m. and come straight to my classes, where they learned African drumming, history, and language.

I dedicated myself to offering programs in various cities, including Boston, Philadelphia, and Washington, and to performing with our dance company at around five hundred schools, colleges, and universities. Those efforts helped build a strong interest in African drumming and dance.

Many wonderful things happened around this time, but so did many discouraging things, which slowed the momentum of the Civil Rights Movement. The 1960s were the most memorable years of my time in America. So many things were happening that I really can't rank their importance now. The Drums of Passion group participated fully in all of the social change of those times. Our first and second albums were released just as the whole Civil Rights Movement was launched, so we were often asked to perform at civil rights rallies.

We did close to a hundred performances for the NAACP. We performed for the United Jewish Appeal at the old Madison Square Garden. We performed at the Town Hall to help raise money for clinics on the West Side and the East Side. We played more than fifty rallies for the Congress of Racial Equality, chaired by James Farmer. We performed for Dr. Martin Luther King's organization, the Southern Christian Leadership Conference. We performed for SNCC, led by H. Rap Brown and Stokely Carmichael. We were just everywhere. We were not getting paid for what we did, but we were making our presence felt.

We were the only group to accept an invitation from the Muslims to appear at their bazaar, which was modeled after an African market. It was a place where people could come together and do all their shopping in one spot. Malcolm X used this approach to demonstrate the economic power of African Americans.

In those days, you were making a controversial statement just by going to hear Malcolm X speak. People were afraid they would be labeled, and many people were in fact labeled. *We* were labeled. Once people knew you were associating with the Muslims or even just going to their lectures, they wouldn't even want to talk to you. We were the only group to accept their invitation, and Malcolm gave us a hundred dollars to transport all our drums. We had thirty people in the group. We did that performance in Harlem in a big place on 158th Street that could hold three thousand people.

All of these organizations existed to make sure the law of the land was adhered to. They were holding rallies in almost every major city in America.

The Drums of Passion dancers and drummers became heavily involved in these organizations by presenting cultural shows before or after their rallies.

Around this time, many minority groups that had been discriminated against at one time or another were coming together to support one another. After all, they had a common bond, a common enemy, a common goal to fight for.

We did a lot to raise awareness that "Black is Beautiful" and to bring African traditions to African Americans. It was really something to watch black Americans slowly change their self-perceptions. When I first came to America in 1950, the blacks here saw themselves as "Negroes." After that, they began seeing themselves as black Americans. Then finally they settled on the image, "I am an African American." That was very important.

We campaigned for the first black mayor in Newark, New Jersey, touring the whole city with drummers and dancers on trucks, urging African Americans to get out and vote for him. When another black was running for mayor in Boston, we were there to campaign for him.

Over those years, I got to know the leaders of the Civil Rights Movement. Men like the Reverend Martin Luther King, Jr., whom I admire very much; Malcolm X, with whom I developed a very close relationship, until I knew him even better than I knew Dr. King; and Stokely Carmichael and H. Rap Brown, the leaders of SNCC. Those two young activists were seen as uncompromising and aggressive. Dr. King advocated nonviolence; and Malcolm X believed in achieving equality by any means necessary.

And here I was, surrounded by all of these people, and admired and loved by all of them. Whatever their differences, they were linked by a common culture, and because my basic belief was that there is a cultural basis for our unity, I got along with all of them. I understand where they were coming from, because I believed, and still do, that there is always another side of the coin. I was brought up to think that way.

I have always believed that there are three sides to the story: your side, my side, and the side of the truth. And that everybody is always trying to pull the side of the truth to their side.

So how do I deal with these people? Stokely Carmichael, H. Rap Brown said, "Test this law. It is the law of the land that there should be no segregation. In America, you should be able to eat wherever you want to eat and not be segregated. The NAACP is pussyfooting around—they refuse to test it. So let's test this law and make sure that every American understands that they just cannot do this to their fellow citizens."

Well, there I was, in 1958, attending the All African People's Conference in Ghana. Tom Mboya, a wonderful friend, had been elected in absentia to be the conference chairman. Mboya was president of the All African Students Union. The strong leadership of Kwame Nkrumah, the president of Ghana, made this happen. He wanted to shift the spotlight from Ghana to East Africa because Ghana had already been in the news every day since independence in 1957.

Ghana was the only newly independent country with an ambassador at the UN. That meant it represented all of the Third World—not just Africa, but the Caribbean, too. So Nkrumah said, "Let's elect Tom Mboya." Mboya was in London negotiating the release of Jomo Kenyatta, who had been imprisoned by the British for fomenting the Mau Mau uprising.

Mboya wanted to come to America. The Reverend George Houser, president of the American Committee on Africa, was also present at this conference, and asked me, "Olatunji, please sign this visa application for Mboya to come visit." That is how I became a friend of Mboya. He came to America and spoke to Dr. King, telling him that I wanted to see East African students coming to America. It was very important to have students from there as well, not just West Africa. Dr. King told him we needed to go around the country and ask for scholarships for East African students.

Dr. King came to New York and met with Mboya. I followed them as far as I could, to Atlanta. On the stage at Morehouse College and also at Spelman, while I was sitting there, both of them appealed for scholarships for East Africans. After that they went around the country making the same appeal. I did not go everywhere with them, but that is how the tour started. Together, they arranged four hundred scholarships for East African students.

The American Committee on Africa arranged their visas. Once those students arrived, I was chosen to show them the Statue of Liberty. Most of those students are now legislators, lawyers, doctors, and community leaders in Kenya.

This was during the 1960 presidential campaign between Nixon and Kennedy. Nixon was considered the odds-on favorite to win. The East African students were scheduled to arrive that year. It was customary for the State Department to arrange for transportation for anything that had to do with the State Department. The White House could easily have ordered it. The whole scenario had changed, and the government of the United States was willing to involve itself in the independence movement. But a few Democrats thought that if the White House arranged a plane for them it would give the Republicans—and especially the Nixon campaign—a tremendous boost. So they didn't want the American government to foot the bill—that is, to send a plane for these four hundred students.

Some African American leaders and celebrities, including Jackie Robinson, Sidney Poitier, Nat King Cole, and Harry Belafonte, came up with an idea of raising money to charter a plane. They did not want the government to bring the students over because it would give Nixon too much good publicity.

They didn't want the Republicans to get credit for anything. They drafted a letter that would go to seven people to come up with the money. I was right there while this was happening. But for some reason, they weren't able come up with enough money.

So who did pay for it? The Kennedy Foundation paid for that flight to bring four hundred students from Kenya. Those guys couldn't raise the money, but they didn't want the Republicans to get credit for it. African Americans have always been loyal to the Democrats, but I don't believe that the party has ever done enough to earn that loyalty. If they really wanted to earn it, they would put Jesse Jackson on the Democratic ticket. That's what I think.

I attended the March on Washington in August 1963. No one realized how big it was going to be, but I knew I wanted to be there. I was on tour with my group. I drove my station wagon back from Los Angeles with my drummers, dancers, and singers, hoping we would have the chance to perform there. Too late—by the time we arrived, all arrangements had been made.

We had to stop in New York before going on to Washington. On the day of the march, we were delayed along the New Jersey Turnpike by the Highway Patrol. For some reason, they were stopping maybe six out of ten cars traveling on that road toward Washington. They weren't stopping cars coming the other way, but they were stopping all these cars going to Washington, so the drive took longer than it should have.

So our car was stopped. They were just checking people's IDs. I wonder if there is still any record of how many cars were given tickets that day. They were giving tickets for speeding, but there was no way anybody could have been speeding because there were too many cars for anyone to be going anything above 65 mph. We still got a ticket.

Finally we reached Washington. The room I had reserved had already been taken because we had arrived so late. But after the march was over, I tried to go to where the leaders were staying. I didn't have the documents that would have allowed me to meet Dr. King, because I had been away for a month performing on the West Coast. With those documents, I would have been able to see him that day.

Soon after that, Dr. King came to New York. Friends had arranged for him to meet Malcolm X, believing it was important for those two to settle their differences. I was there, and I will always remember it. As long as two people are working toward the same goal, there can be a meeting of the minds, no matter what their differences are. I continue to regard both of them as great, great men of history, great souls indeed. I have tremendous respect for both of them.

Those years, every time the Southern Christian Leadership Conference asked me to appear at a rally, I went. And I also said yes when Malcolm X called me and said, "We want you to appear uptown New York at the first African bazaar."

I loved that. You have to remember that at the time, anybody who associated with Muslims, or with Malcolm X, was automatically ostracized— musicians especially. It was a very unpleasant situation, even for Max Roach, with whom I recorded a protest album, *We Insist* (as in, "We insist on freedom"). For a couple of years after that album, no jazz club in the New York area would book him.

The second time we performed for the Muslims, I was given a stereo/tuner as compensation. At the time, stereo/tuners were just coming onto the market. From that time on, I was always welcome wherever he was speaking. Our families became very close. Our wives became very close friends, and his children became very close friends of my children.

On New Year's Eve of 1963, the press was looking for Malcolm to ask him what he meant when he said, "The chickens have come home to roost," after Kennedy was assassinated. They had been looking for him for almost a month. "Clarify yourself," they were telling him. "People are attacking you. Say something about this."

All Malcolm meant by those words was that violence had become a way of life in America. What more proof did anyone need? People might not want to face it, but violence could happen even to the president of the United States, and something needed be done about it.

That particular day, I was with Malcolm. He was attending a small get-together just to take his mind off all the publicity his statement had generated. The reporters still hadn't found him.

That party was where I got a better understanding of what Malcolm had meant when he said about drugs, "Stop it downtown, and it won't come uptown."

He said, "Look, you're wasting your time arresting all these little guys, the little guys in Harlem who are selling five and ten cent marijuana. The people you should really go after are the bankers, the big names, who are helping to bring drugs into America. Now we all know who they are, we know the source, so it's not really profitable or wise or really necessary to just go after the peddlers on the street. You have to go to the people who are making billions, who are laundering drug money on an international level."

That's the way Malcolm put it. You had to really be around him to see how he simplified things when he talked. "Stop it downtown, it won't come uptown." That's street talk. You really had to listen to him to grasp the meaning, the power of his words. That's why I listened to him talk whenever I could. He would put things in such beautiful, simple ways for the average person to understand.

Malcolm was labeled all kinds of things by the press. He was accused of being a racist, of not liking white folks, just as he was trying to show people who he really was. He was saying that the color of your skin didn't matter— that if you are not good, you are simply not good.

When Malcolm visited Africa, it changed his thinking. He felt the love and affection of the people, and the genuineness in how they treated him. He really felt their admiration for him and for what he had achieved by bringing African Americans closer to their African heritage. I think the African leaders recognized that he had done that. In Nigeria, they gave him the name "Omowa'le," which means a child who was born away from home and who has returned home. He was recognized for what he had done to bring African Americans together. This was very important to him.

Later, Malcolm would demonstrate to African Americans how powerful they were economically as well as politically and socially. He borrowed the African concept of markets, where people with different goods come together to buy and sell. He started a market in Harlem, which the people operated by circulating existing currency from one person to the next. This was very important. I wish this had been included in the movie of his life.

Malcolm was trying to do in America what many were trying to do in Africa—bring all those of African heritage together. If he could do that, there would be less confrontation; people would get to know one another and be in a position to solve their own problems. They would stop blaming their brothers, and stop pointing the finger at other people. They would remember that whenever they did that, there were always four fingers pointing back at themselves. That would be a very great day, because no longer would they point a finger, saying, "It was a white man. It was a yellow man. It was a foreigner." That would be a glorious day, because Africans would then start to help themselves. They would realize that they could no longer ignore all of the things they had in common with the rest of the world. They would be able to—be compelled to—negotiate as equals at the bargaining table.

Malcolm was right, because most people and most countries depend on the outside world or on a particular group of people to carve out their destiny for them. Where do we, as Africans, fit in the global concept of things? Malcolm said the same thing that Nkrumah said: Africa must learn how to redistribute its wealth to benefit all its people. Once it has learned that, it will have enough left over to share with the rest of the world. This is what Pan-Africanism is all about.

Malcolm was always perceived as someone who hated all white people, who called all white people devils. Actually, he was only coming up with a new way of thinking about people, one that dumbfounded many, including Elijah Mohammed, the leader of Islam. Malcolm's new approach was interpreted—wrongly, I believe—as a break with Elijah Mohammed. People thought he was abandoning his leadership role for the sake of antagonizing against anyone who disagreed with him.

But this was not so. In *The Last Temptation of Christ*, Nikos Kazantzakis declared that Jesus was just anyone else until he assumed Christ's spirit. At that point he was no longer Jesus—he became Jesus Christ. The way I see it, Malcolm went through that same kind of rebirth: he saw that not just black people go to Mecca. I thought that was a wonderful thing to point out to others. When you find out the truth—when the truth really becomes naked—it isn't a half-truth anymore, it is the whole truth. Malcolm really should have been rewarded for proclaiming that truth.

That man came to see the light. He discovered a new reality, a new truth. And then he said, "I'm going to use this truth to bring about change." But he was never allowed to demonstrate his discovery to benefit other people. We lost a great deal because we misunderstood him.

After he had traveled to other parts of the world, and had made his pilgrimage to Mecca, and found people in Islam of many, many wonderful ethnic backgrounds and colors, he tried to let it be known that he discovered this truth of unity. He was a changed man—he was ready to let people know that it is possible for an individual to discover the truth and change course as a result of that.

But he was not given the chance to do that. And Kennedy was not given a chance to put through his New Frontier for America. It looked like America was moving back toward an era of isolationism. But isolationism cannot hold in this world of global economics, global communication. Everything is global now.

In hindsight, the activism of Stokely Carmichael and H. Rap Brown was misunderstood. Young people were saying, "We, too, have a role to play. We, too, belong here. We, too, must have a share, a slice of the pie. We must enjoy the results of the blood, toil, tears, and sweat of our ancestors. We also are here now, and we should be reckoned with and we should be part and parcel of what happens to this great country. We should contribute, and we can contribute even more if we are given a chance to make this country a better, greater, more powerful and prosperous country."

Today we are experiencing the deterioration of values. We are experiencing a lack of respect for womanhood and a lack of reverence for life. Too many of us no longer fear the Creator. In this regard, the 1960s were a dangerous time in American history. This country was founded on the firm declaration "In God We Trust," and it seemed like nobody was embracing those words anymore. To believe is to act. When you believe, you feel compelled to act. And our actions are always reflected in our relations with one another.

The home is always where children receive their spiritual education, and an understanding of values, but too many children today are going without that learning, because too many homes now have only one parent. There must be two parents. There is no way that one parent can raise a child. The mother and father have their own contributions to make to the child's development. The home is the place for that, not the classroom. That job cannot be delegated to teachers. It must be done in the home. Until that happens again, what we hear and see happening between families will continue to happen, and social catastrophe will be unavoidable in the coming century. You cannot help but see the impact of single-parent families on America and around the world.

Going back to the early days of independence in Africa, the leaders forgot why they had fought for independence, or they pushed those reasons to the background. They lost their unity, and they forgot their purpose, which was to improve the lives of their citizens, to fight illiteracy and disease. Somehow, they forgot their own people and began satisfying their own selfish ends. Like their counterparts in the West, they are now neglecting their citizens.

Once these leaders came to power, too often greed got the best of them. They formed alliances with forces outside Africa, with forces in Europe, America, and other parts of the world, and helped them go on stealing Africa's natural wealth, with no compensation for their people. And they tried to copy Western institutions too closely. These were some of the worst things they could have done.

For example, in Nigeria, at the very beginning of independence, when television was introduced, stations began airing programs from abroad that did not reflect African ways. Stations were buying foreign programs like *Have Gun, Will Travel*, and programs that showed people how to hijack cars. These programs had a tremendous impact on people's behavior. Car hijacking became something new in Nigeria. Today, they are going about it just the same way it is done in the United States.

We could have used television for education, to combat illiteracy. Even now, 85 percent of Nigerians—and there are 122 million of us today— cannot read or write. We have been left ignorant to the point that Western countries are exporting their products to us that have been condemned to warehouses in the West. Those goods should have been destroyed; instead, they are being sold in Third World countries. The government has placed bans on almost all the products you can imagine, yet somewhere in Nigeria, you can always still buy them. How can these goods still be coming in?

Outside forces were playing havoc with the lives of ordinary Nigerians, and pushing back the gains that people enjoyed in the first years of independence. This is leading to anarchy and to the kind of ethnic cleansing that happened in Rwanda.

Africa's entire wealth is controlled by just a handful of people. As a result, in places like Nigeria, Liberia, Sierra Leone, and the Congo, people are now worse off than they were under colonial rule.

But getting back to what was happening in the United States, the Drums of Passion dancers, drummers, and singers enjoyed tremendous popularity right after JFK was elected. G. Mennen Williams was named Secretary of State for African Affairs—the first person in any American administration to hold that position. This enabled us to present an African program at the State Department, which was attended by the secretary himself.

After we performed at the State Department, one of the employees there, Warren Robbins, got the idea that the arts could help bridge the gap between Africans at home and abroad. It was he who brought forward the idea of establishing a Museum of African Art in Washington, which later became part of the Smithsonian Institution.

Around this time, our group was traveling all over the country, performing on college and university campuses. We traveled in two station wagons, presenting shows in the South and all the way to California. This experience gave the members an opportunity to appreciate what a great country the United States is.

In many states, we encountered what seemed like insurmountable obstacles. Many times, the state troopers stopped us when they saw our New York license plates. Sometimes they delayed us for an hour before telling us to move on. Despite these confrontations, we kept on, and we succeeded in presenting exciting programs. College students across the South welcomed and admired us. These national tours we made in the 1960s and 1970s helped start what has since developed into a widespread interest in and respect for African music.

This was also a critical time in American history. The assassinations of the 1960s almost stopped all progress in civil rights. The Vietnam War did not help either. It was a time of polarization.

This social climate affected all institutions of change, including the Olatunji Center. We stopped getting as many invitations to perform on college and university campuses—performances that were necessary if we were to continue the Center's work. The Center was a nonprofit organization and charged only two dollars for almost all of its classes, so keeping it open was a struggle. We were faced with the very real possibility that we might have to close a place that had served so many ordinary Americans over the years.

The Center was operating out of a big loft at 43 East 125th Street, near Madison. The building was owned by Maloot Ellis, who lived in Englewood Cliffs across the river. His company owned more than three hundred buildings in Harlem and was known by the local people as a slum landlord.

The Center got through that period by arranging a tour of the Caribbean. We performed all over that region, including St. Thomas, St. Kitts, Jamaica, Trinidad, Guyana, Surinam, and Curaçao. In Curaçao we saw an American-owned refinery that was processing half the oil the Americans bought from Nigeria. Its production was then shipped to many South American countries and even to South Africa. That was an interesting discovery.

In Guyana, a group of Yoruba people who had been in Guyana for more than one hundred years traveled fifty miles to see our show, bringing with them traditional foods to welcome us. From there we went to Trinidad and Tobago. We were given a royal welcome in Tobago, which I remember as Little Africa. Trinidad is a very interesting place, too. At its northern end, we heard people still singing songs to Nigerian deities.

In Surinam, seventy-five miles from the airport, we were amazed to discover Ghanaians who had settled there years and years ago. They still carved instruments the Ghanaian way. They still practiced the traditional ways of their ancestors. That was quite a discovery.

The only setback during that tour was that our agent disappeared toward the end with four thousand dollars of our money. We never saw him again.

But that didn't rob us of the joy we felt at meeting so many people who wanted to hear us so much. In Barbados the entire public school system was closed so that we could perform for all the schoolchildren at a football stadium. That was an experience I will never forget. I invited the students onto the stage to join me in singing one of my songs. They all wanted a piece of my robe. I had to be rescued by the police.

When we returned to the United States, we tried to get funding from many different sources, but they all refused us. We appealed to those of our African American friends who were in a position to help financially. But nobody seemed interested in saving a cultural institution. Maybe it was because of the political situation, maybe because of the social polarization that was developing at the time, with so many leaders being assassinated who had been speaking out for constructive change in America.

But I continued to struggle to keep the Center open. We were offering twelve languages there: the three main Nigerian languages—Yoruba, Hausa, Igbo; the three main Ghanaian languages—Twi, Ga, and Ewe; an important South African language, Xhosa; and the main East African language, Swahili. Swahili was the language in greatest demand at the Center. We wrote a Swahili textbook that was later adopted by quite a few African studies programs. It was written by Felicia Njuwa, a Kenyan who came to work with me at the Center. By then, the Center was consulting on quite a few programs at different colleges, including Manhattan College, where I taught, and Kent State, where I served as an outside examiner for the Department of Critical Languages.

Many things that happened to us while we traveled through the South, many of our experiences there with segregation, are beyond imagination.

I remember we were driving down Highway 1 when the speed limit was 65. We had driven hundreds of miles and all of a sudden, as we got to the top of the hill, within two hundred yards the 65 mph changed to 35 mph. Coming down the hill, while we were coming into Texas, there was a state trooper. He pulled us over and asked us to show our licenses.

I asked, "What's the matter?"

"Didn't you know this was 35 miles an hour?"

I said, "I just came down the hill. There was no time for me to slow down."

"You we still speeding—look at the sign."

He told both cars to follow him. He took us off the highway and turned right onto a side road that led to a holding jail.

He said, "This is where you spend the night if you don't have enough money to pay."

I asked, "What are you talking about?"

It just so happened, luckily enough, that when we got to the desk, the man facing me who was going to take our information asked, "What is your name?"

"My name is Michael Babatunde Olatunji."

"What?"

"Olatunji."

"What do you do?"

"I am a musician."

"What do you play?"

"Drums."

"Did you make that album, *Drums of Passion*?"

"Yes!"

"Well, what are you doing over here? Okay, you're supposed to pay a hundred dollars for each car for speeding, but pay $50."

I couldn't believe it.

He said, "Yeah, I heard of your album when I was in high school. What are you doing here? Where are you going?"

"I'm going to Houston to perform. I'm just coming from Atlanta."

"Be careful, now. Watch the signs very close. Slow down on your way. If you don't, you're going to be pulled off the highway again."

I said, "Oh my God, thank you very much!"

You can imagine how it felt to me that the album had become an identity, I don't know what else to call it. Something people will always remember. Like people say, your fame precedes you.

That sure came at the right time, because we didn't have two hundred in cash.

And other experiences, like going to a store, when one of the musicians wanted to buy milk. They told him they couldn't sell him milk, but that he could buy chocolate milk.

He stood there arguing, "I see the milk here, I don't want chocolate."

"Well, that is what we're going to sell you, chocolate milk."

Incomprehensible, little things like that, enough to discourage people from pursuing whatever goals they had set for themselves. But we moved on.

As time went on, it became more and more difficult to run the Center with just the money we made from performances, without any other funding or income. We tried to raise money by launching a Sunday afternoon program that presented highly regarded jazz musicians, to bring back old memories of the time when people came to Harlem to see great acts.

We started with John Coltrane, charging three dollars a ticket, calling it 'Olatunji Center Presents.' 'Trane, Yusef Lateef, and Pete Seeger all helped out. All of this was before the book *Roots* was written by a great friend, Alex Haley.

That wasn't money enough to support the ongoing programs at the Center and to pay the secretaries and, especially, the rent, which the landlord raised at will. Every two or three months we would receive an eviction notice and would have to go to court to block them. We were able to do that with the help of a supporter and family friend, the lawyer Morton Sarnoff. Usually he would ask one of the younger lawyers in his office,

Michael Wolfson, to go to court on our behalf and make sure the landlord didn't take any action until we were able to raise the rent money.

Finally we got some support from the National Endowment for the Arts. But those funds were for teacher training programs, not for administration. So we had no money to hire administrators. And we could not use the federal money for any other purpose except that for which it was given.

In that situation, we could not help ourselves, and I saw that sooner or later I would have to close the Center. This deeply saddened me, and drained my energy. People could tell that I was getting ready to give up.

By now, my marriage was also in trouble. Amy reminded me that she had warned me long ago that I could not save Africa by myself, that I needed to look out for myself first, that I couldn't always be carrying Africa on my back—it was too much of a load. She was telling me I'd been spending almost all my time trying to save Africa, and needed to spend more time thinking about myself and my family.

So I was really getting it from both sides. All day I had to deal with the public, with the landlord, with the group, with uncertainties about the Center's future. And when I got home from all that, there was very little support or consolation waiting for me.

Finally, the Center was forced to close when the landlord refused to offer us the first option to buy the building after we had been there for over fifteen years. We couldn't come up with a $25,000 down payment. We couldn't get any grants to do it.

What would I do next? This was during the Shagari regime in Nigeria. Shagari was a northerner, and I knew his vice president well.

Shagari's vice president made a state visit to the United States, and I attended the reception held for him in Washington. I was standing with a group of other Nigerians when he saw me from across the room.

"There's Babatunde! My goodness! Well, make sure you follow the entourage to my hotel."

"Where is the hotel?"

"Watergate. I must talk to you."

I was pleased he recognized me.

After the reception, I joined one of the diplomatic groups and went with the entourage to the Watergate. I spoke to him that evening and told him I intended to return home to Nigeria and participate in the next election, to be held in 1981.

I said, "I am hoping to run for a seat in congress for my district."

He said, "Great, it's about time. You've served the country very well. We are very proud of you. But why don't you come home and join our party? I will make sure you are provided for. We have enough money to do the campaign."

I said, "No, my friend—I want to be an independent congressman. I don't want to attach myself to any political organization. What I would like to do is give you a proposal that I have that you can introduce to the country, for a National Endowment for the Arts. I want to make sure we use culture as the basis for uniting our people. All the groups in Nigeria need to come together to build the country together.

"Great, but look, you could still do that. Join our party."

"No. It would be very advantageous, but you know many of the criticisms of both political parties now. Let me come back with no strings attached and be another voice. The whole program is tailored after a successful American program that has been operating for years now. So it doesn't matter which party wins the election. The money for the National Endowment for the Arts is always included in the budget."

"Do you have the money?"

"I don't need much money to do the campaign. You know I am very well known. I am not going to have any opposition, and if I have your support, I don't want the political party giving me a million *naira*. Your support is your accepting this proposal, giving it to your party. Win or lose, the country will never forget that your political party initiated this bill. This is your idea, I'm giving it to you. You don't even have to mention my name. You can say you discussed it with me. I am giving it to you."

"Well, if that is what you want to do, okay. I will be coming to New York next week. There will be a reception at the Waldorf-Astoria. Why don't you bring some members of your group and do a performance?"

I knew then that he didn't really think much of my idea. If he had, he would have accepted that proposal and not just tried to make it public right there in New York. He would have accepted it from me and then held onto it until he got back to Nigeria and discussed it with the president or members of the ruling cabinet. So I had my doubts.

Anyway, I went to the reception given for him at the Waldorf and made a short speech there and presented him with the proposal for a National Endowment for the Arts for Nigeria.

When the time came, I announced that I was returning home. I organized a concert at Avery Fisher Hall, which included performances by Billy Taylor,

Gil Noble of the television show *Like It Is*, and the entire cast of Drums of Passion. I was able to raise about $20,000.

With this money, I traveled to Nigeria to check out the situation there. I called a few friends and told them my intentions. Just as we started spending money for flyers, I read an article in the paper about how much the other candidates were spending. They were spending more for one tea party—just one tea party for their campaign workers—than I had budgeted for my entire campaign. Candidates were spending money to have their names written in the sky. That's when I knew what he was talking about when he said, "Come home, the party will give you a million naira just to start."

I understood now that my country had really gone astray. Where did they get all this campaign money? This was a *developing* country, yet we were spending money on campaigns just like the Americans after two hundred years of practice.

Three weeks after I got home, it was announced on the radio and in the newspapers that Congress had passed a law that no independent candidates would be allowed to run for Congress or for the House of Representatives; in other words, all candidates would have to belong to an existing political party. Because this law was unconstitutional, they changed the Constitution. They amended the Constitution just like that.

But now, the money I had brought back to Nigeria was almost gone. It was so expensive there, with inflation running high. I had no funds to compete. So I came back to the United States.

How would I be able to deal with the situation in New York? The landlord had just raised our rent by 20 percent. He had also put our building up for sale but was refusing us the first option to bid on it. What would we do for money? I was so frustrated. The group was still together, but the Center no longer existed.

I began to think about things from a whole different angle. If there were ever going to be peace and justice in the world, it would come after we achieved equality, after we returned to our spiritual essence and found a new way to deal with one another.

We must recognize again that we are created in the image of God and that we are all of us God's children, wherever we live, whatever the color of our skin or our ethnic background. If we don't, in this coming century man will destroy all that he has worked so hard to gain, and be reduced to the level of the beasts. That is quite an indictment, isn't it? But that is how I feel. And it is beginning to happen.

After all is said and done, I cannot take it with me, I must leave everything here. So why should I bother to accumulate things when I know that, when the time comes, I won't be able to use them? When will man come to that realization so that he can change? We have created monsters, we have put into power people who have lost their sense of fairness, who have become drunk with power and will do whatever they must to keep it.

So, there must be a rebirth in our way of thinking. There must be a rebirth in our beliefs. We must tap into our spirit and begin to think thoughts that will hasten the dawn of a new day during which the son of man will become more gracious and more abiding and very, very truthful and honest in all ways.

8 | World Music Comes of Age

Here I was, back in the United States in the early 1980s, where I had not expected to be, with no Center and no prospects. I had to look for avenues for a comeback. So I said, "Let me try Washington."

I went to Washington, and with the help of friends, I reestablished the Olatunji Center of African Culture.

Through the grapevine, I heard there were many unused school buildings in the city. I approached the city council through the mayor's office, but nothing happened. Then I found a loft owned by a group of African Americans doing programs for children. I joined them, asking them to give me a chance to teach classes. I started bringing members of my group there as teachers, twice a week. Meanwhile, I kept renting studios in New York. I started teaching drumming again. That's how the program for teaching drumming was maintained.

The popularity of *Drums of Passion* enabled me to explore a vision. I have always followed my own mind. I have always been that kind of person. I have always believed that once I made up my mind to do something, I would always succeed. That's because before I started, I always considered the pros and cons and asked myself, "Are you ready for this task? Are you ready to face the challenges? Do you know what the effects of your actions will be? And if you know what they are, are you ready to deal with them, to handle them?"

If I could say, "Yes, I am ready for it, I can handle it, I am prepared to deal with all the unforeseen results surrounding what I plan to achieve," I went ahead with it.

The release of *Drums of Passion* inspired many other recording artists, like Herbie Mann, Max Roach, Randy Weston, and Horace Silver, to start using African materials and African styles of drumming in their recordings.

I respected Herbie Mann in particular. He was a different kind of band leader—a man for all seasons. Whatever direction the music was going, he was right there with it. He was ready to adapt what he did to whatever was going on at any particular time. I really admire him for that. When the African thing was going, he was right there. I became one of his featured artists.

Herbie the Man was one leader who had no fear about anybody outshining him on stage. He had no ego. He said, "Okay, yeah—Herbie Mann featuring Babatunde Olatunji. Write a song for me."

He included me and a couple of Latin American drummers as featured artists in his jazz group. After his return from Africa, where he toured under the sponsorship of the U.S. Information Agency and the State Department, he put together the album *Common Ground*, in which I contributed a piece called "Uhuru" (which means *freedom*), written for the saxophone. Not many people know that Herbie Mann was a saxophonist before became famous as a flautist. Saxophone was one of his main instruments, but he gained fame by playing the flute with so much passion.

He was different, too, in that he was a law-abiding citizen. In the 1960s, during our tour stops, the police would often make a point of tracking down musicians who were smoking marijuana. Herbie would call all of us and say, "Fellas, whatever you do, make sure you do it in your room. You cannot do it when we get on the job." In other words, he was saying, "Keep your business to yourself. Don't bring it on the job, because I will have no hand in it. I want to make this clear."

Sure enough, one night in Philadelphia, about ten minutes before we were set to play, the vice squad came in and told management that we could not go on. They had to check everyone in the dressing room one by one. They did that, and they found nothing. If they'd found anything on one of us, they would have locked us all up. That would have messed up the band's reputation, not just Herbie's, so that we couldn't get jobs anymore. That was the early 1960s.

They did the same thing to my group at Birdland at four in the morning. We'd finished performing. My bass player was going upstairs. The police told him to face the wall, and then they searched him. Then they called me. I was changing from my native clothes into my street clothes. I went to them, and they said, "Turn around."

I said, "Who are you? You have to identify yourselves. What do you mean I should face the wall?" I challenged them. I didn't smoke. I wasn't even smoking cigarettes.

The police weren't going after the drug importers. They were just harassing the small offenders. Why didn't they go after the bankers or the people who brought drugs in? That's what Malcolm X used to talk about: "Stop it downtown and it won't come uptown." Instead they were harassing musicians in the different nightclubs.

Herbie gave a lot of Latin American musicians an opportunity to be heard, to learn. And a lot of African musicians, like me, learned a lot from him. He was more than a musician, he was a businessman, too. I learned so much from him about this whole business, how to demand respect from club owners by being there on time, by rehearsing, by doing your job and then leaving. Whatever you do, you have to make sure you do it with dignity.

Herbie was the one who showed us how the business side of things worked. He would talk to us at length about what to do. At the time, most musicians thought, "If you just play your music, you don't have to know anything about the business."

Herbie would say, "Oh no. You have to know what is happening to you. You have to know what is happening to your music. You have to know how your music is selling. You have to know who is buying it, and who is not buying it. You have to know what the record company is doing to your record. You have to know what your agent is doing for you. You have to know what the promoter is doing. You have to keep tabs on it all. You have to know how to save yourself from parasites."

Our relationship became a little tighter because we had the same agent: Monte Kay, the husband of Diane Carroll. Monte had four acts: Herbie Mann, me, Chris Connor (a wonderful singer), and the Modern Jazz Quartet. Being associated with Monte Kay, we were able to do a lot of jazz festivals. Whenever we did jazz festivals, I was always associated with Herbie.

In the 1950s and early 1960s, jazz festivals really grew, especially the Newport Jazz Festival, where I played with Herbie. The promoter there was George Wein of New York. George was a musician before he became an impresario, and he did a lot of festivals in Newport. I always played the jazz festivals with Herbie, until I put my own group together. Herbie made sure I linked up with Newport. It was very successful. That was where the rebirth of jazz began.

We also played the festival in Central Park. Young promoters could make a splash back then by holding events in the park. The Central Park shows were sponsored by Schaefer Beer, and tickets were only a dollar. So you could have 250,000 people in the park during the summer festival. Robert Wagner was mayor of New York at the time. He contributed so much to the development of culture in the city by supporting cultural organizations and cultural performances in the park and in the schools.

During those years we appeared at many of the other jazz festivals along the East Coast, like the Island Jazz Festival and the festivals in Philadelphia, Boston, and Washington.

Since the release of *Drums of Passion* in 1959, the African style of drumming had become accepted, and percussion was often being used on important albums. This brought me into close contact with all the great jazz musicians, especially in the New York area—people like like Miles Davis, Count Basie, Duke Ellington, Lionel Hampton, and Zoot Simms.

Duke Ellington once described jazz as a phenomenon that borrowed from all sources. What Africa contributed to jazz was rhythm. Rhythm is the soul of life. Everything we do is in rhythm. I must confess that one of the things I'm most proud of is that Duke Ellington admired me. He was living in the same building as I was, at 400 Central Park West, a new development in the 1960s. He was always telling me, "One day we'll have to do something with you." Wherever they were performing, I was always welcome there, especially at Birdland. I got ideas from listening to his band.

I also toured with Lionel Hampton's band, and was invited to participate in recording sessions with Randy Weston, Horace Silver, Cannonball Adderley, and Max Roach. The first cultural group to visit

Nigeria after independence in 1960, through the American Society for African Culture (AMSAC), was the Lionel Hampton Band, Nina Simone, Randy Weston, and Jeffrey Holder. We went there to open a cultural exchange.

Lionel called me once and said, "Babatunde, I've got a job for you. He's only paying a hundred dollars, but this is a campaign." This was when Nixon was running for election. Lionel, through his Republican contacts, put together some deal to get musicians to campaign for Nixon in Harlem. I was one of the musicians he approached. We got our hundred. He said, "That's all we can pay. But we're campaigning for somebody who will be a good president and will do so much for black people."

Randy Weston is a giant of jazz and one of my favorites. For many years, he couldn't get the jobs he deserved because of his fight with Local 802. He claimed it was collecting musicians' membership fees but wasn't getting African Americans enough jobs. He became very upset with them and tried very hard to change that. He worked in Morocco for a while, then came back to the States to perform, but he couldn't ever get a decent job in many of the clubs. Randy was a great pianist. He recorded "Uhuru" with me, for Herbie Mann.

I recorded an album with Cannonball Adderley, an African piece. I recorded with Horace Silver. I used to live next door to Quincy Jones on Western Avenue before he moved to California. One musician I deeply respect, from the day I met him in the early 1960s, is Max Roach. He was another musician who was not well received by club managers. They wouldn't give him a break because of an antisegregation album we did, *We Insist*. Max was highly outspoken, more so than any other artist except Randy Weston. Because of *We Insist*, Max did not get that much support from club owners in those days. He was someone who went about his work and stuck to what he believed in.

My work with John Coltrane enabled me to establish, as a side project from the dance company, a jazz group of my own, the Afro Jazz Sextet. Yusef Lateef became its musical director. He was like 'Trane in many ways—diligent, serious, soft spoken, highly respected. He always told the truth. He always told you exactly how he felt about any situation. He would make his point, and that would be it. He had so much confidence in his abilities that there was no question about his integrity and his knowledge. I wondered why this man wasn't getting any bookings.

Well, nobody was hiring Yusef at the time because of his affiliation with the Muslims. Prejudice against the Muslims was running high in those days. It was difficult for so many African Americans in the 1960s, especially for anyone associated with the Muslims, who were completely ostracized. So nobody wanted to hire Yusef, except me, and that's how he became my musical director. He was a giant of a musician, a master on the saxophone and flute. With him, and another great musician, Chris White, a bass player, I was able to put a group together that was given twelve weeks every year at Birdland to open and close shows for the great bands. That is how the band took off.

I have been lucky to work with so many of the great ones, at the Apollo Theater, the Palladium, the Village Gate. With so many of the great Latin bands like Mongo Santamaria, Eddie Palmieri, Tito Puente. That's how I established the African connection with jazz. Because I played in the New York clubs so late in the evening, I ended up playing for people from Europe who had flown in late and who wanted to check out the clubs before they went to bed. As a result, I was very well known in Europe before I ever visited there.

I wasn't experimenting with jazz simply because it was the thing to do. My environment has always affected me—I can't deny that. But at the same time, I knew the *source*. Being in New York, where everybody was from everywhere, I could put things together, I could write a piece that would reveal the influence of Indian music, or the bossa nova. The edge I had was that I knew the source was *African*—it just had an Indian flavor, or a Bossanova flavor, or a jazz flavor. I put it all together in many different ways, but I never detached it from the source.

What they call world music now, I've been experimenting with it since the 1960s. A part can never be equal to the whole. Yoruba culture is African culture. The Latin tradition is African culture. The jazz tradition is African culture. "Call and response" is traditionally African, but it is also universal.

While I was enjoying the success of *Drums of Passion*, and thanking the Creator for answering my prayers, I was also telling myself, "Why don't you show people how much Africa has contributed to world culture? Why don't you see if you can connect African music with jazz? You could even develop an African classical music." African music, taken to the greatest extent, could even be written for a symphony orchestra. Which is precisely what I did in developing and performing a twelve-minute overture with the sixty-six-piece orchestra at Radio City Music Hall. Wasn't that classical music?

What I really wanted to do was merge musical styles, musical traditions, to form something new. After all, most of these instruments had their beginnings in Africa. All music is one, anyway, when you go back to the source. Rhythm is the source of all music, the rhythm we find in nature, in the universe. There are many variations on this, but the source of all music is the natural rhythm of the universe, in the sounds we hear all the time all around us. My vision was to find the perfect marriage for all the many variations. I envisioned a symphony of many different instruments, of many styles and traditions, in which there would be harmony.

That's why the album we recorded after *Drums of Passion* was not more of the same. Instead, we featured the oboe, the trumpet, the guitar, and the bass with African compositions. *Zungo! Afro-Percussion* was an experiment—we used a fourteen-piece band with brass and woodwinds, along with prominent jazzmen like Clark Terry, Yusef Lateef, and George Duvivier. But it was also a traditional album in the sense that the songs were telling stories, about events that happened in the villages and about the great people who played significant roles in them.

Our third album, *Flaming Drums*, released in 1962 and produced by John Hammond, was another experiment in African music. That one had jazz greats like Snooky Young, Clark Terry, and Bill Lee (Spike Lee's father), along with eight drummers and eight vocalists. *Flaming Drums* also had many traditional elements, including a true African call-and-response piece.

After that one came *High Life*, a very danceable album. *Dance Magazine* even illustrated all the dance steps to the title piece. We borrowed the "high life" beat from an old Yoruba rhythm known as the ashiko, which was the origin for many Latin American rhythms. African slaves had carried that rhythm with them to Brazil and the Caribbean. In Latin America, this beat became a mixture of the samba, the mambo, and the bossa nova. We called the beat the "high life" beat because it was considered music for African high society. It was like *juju* music except that it used Western wind instruments. I was the first one to record African "high life" music with the popular dance steps. People like Sunny Ade and Ebenezer Obey later popularized *juju* music, but they did not come out of a vacuum. I had already prepared the way for them, and for the acceptance of their music when it came out in the 1970s and 1980s.

High Life featured Clark Terry and Snooky Young again. For saxophone we had Jerome Richardson, who had played with Charlie Mingus. This was the album that I recorded my song of tribute to the First Lady, Jackie Kennedy. That whole album became a dance sensation.

"High Life" was released as a single to generate sales, but for some reason the record company didn't promote it much. It started getting some airplay not only here in America, but overseas as well. This music has gone far beyond where I will probably ever visit.

Three years later, I released my next album, my last one for Columbia, *More Drums of Passion*. This was going back to the roots. In it I was trying to offer a small part of Africa's glorious musical heritage, which should never be ignored or forgotten. It featured some of the songs, dances, and rituals that have been passed down through many generations. It really captured the essence of my mission in all my music.

In 1966 my contract with Columbia expired, and they refused to renew it. I was without a recording contract for the next two decades, although I continued to perform and tour, mostly on college campuses. I must have logged over two thousand appearances over that time.

I did arrange to record an album with Roulette Records, which at the time was run by Maurice Levy. Roulette was recording the best-known Latin bands in New York, including Tito Puente, Pacheco, and the big Latin bands.

I called the album *Drums, Drums, Drums*. Then I found out that the album was licensed to three other companies within the company. So *Drums, Drums, Drums* had three different covers. I never collected any royalties from it even though the contract entitled me to 10 percent. I never collected anything from it.

Every time I tried to say, "Give me some money," I was threatened, and told not to come to the office, that the album hadn't sold enough. I would tell them, "Give me the report, let me see if it has sold any. The FCC law requires that you tell the artist."

Finally they would say, "Okay—*you*, give him a check for three hundred dollars."

So I concentrated on performing instead of recording. I kept writing and rehearsing material, hoping that one day I would have an opportunity to record it. Then there would be no problem about having to write material for a new album. I would simply be ready to go into the studio and record.

In the meantime, the group traveled all over the country, performing in theaters from New York to the West Coast, becoming very well known in many big cities like Chicago, Atlanta, Miami, all the way to Vancouver. Then, later, we began making inroads in Europe.

The publicity we received by appearing in different cities all over the country, and the world, was so great that museums would ask us to come and help open exhibits about Africa. So we performed at important museums all over the country, in Chicago, in Washington, in Dallas, in Houston, in Philadelphia.

Maya Angelou was performing with us as a singer, standing right behind me. She doesn't remember doing anything like that with us. She is a very versatile person, and at the time she was trying to find a medium for expressing herself. Before she became a writer, she was a singer and dancer. So she performed with us at African Holiday at the Apollo Theater. When we opened for James Brown at the Apollo, she used to always be with us.

When we played the Howard Theater in Washington, and the Regal Theater in Chicago, these performances did not bring in much money. We had about twenty people in the group, and usually at the Apollo we got $2,500 for the whole group for a week. And from this, the agent kept 10 or 15 percent.

So in those days our people usually got paid a hundred a week. Many people who saw or read about me in those days thought, for good reason, that I was making big money, but I wasn't. Nobody was compensating us or paying us what we deserved. They were only saying, "We appreciate what you do, but this is all we can offer you."

Ben Barks was the owner of Universal Attractions as well as James Brown's agent and manager. He would say, "If we make X amount of dollars over the week, we will add $500 to your $2,500 to make it $3,000."

But even with that, he never paid us more than $2,500 for a whole week. So we were not making any money.

Of course, when we went to Washington they would pay our hotel bill and transportation. The same thing at the Regal in Chicago.

But we were performing really just to be seen, just for the opportunity to show people how beautiful, how wonderful, how important the African heritage is. That is the sacrifice that the pioneer is always called upon to make. I am proud that today, a lot of African performers are making more for one show more than I used to make in one week.

We went around the country doing that, promoting and exposing all the good things about the culture through performances, through lectures, through television appearances.

A woman named Betty Dietz, a professor at Brooklyn College who collected folk songs, happened to be at the African Holiday production and heard me give the chant to Shango, the God of Thunder. She came backstage and said, "I would like to talk to you. I visited Africa as a child with my parents for two weeks. I became interested in African folk songs. Can you can give me a few songs that I can publish in a book of mine on folk songs?"

I made an appointment with her, and after the festival we met.

I said, "Look, I'm collecting material to write a book on African musical instruments, like the drums that I have, and the different kinds of instruments, and how they are made."

She said, "Good. Do you have a publisher?"

I said, "No, but I have the materials."

She said, "Well, why don't you let me be your partner? I'll find a publisher for the book, you write the material, and I'll help you put the material together."

She came to the apartment. With my wife, we sat down and made an agreement. The book that came out of that, *Musical Instruments of Africa: Their Nature, Use and Place in the Life of a Deeply Musical People*, was published in 1965. It is an educational book, and talks about all the major instruments of Africa, how they developed from simpler ones like the upright flute, and how man started entertaining himself by doing body percussion—clapping hands and stomping feet. All of this is illustrated in the book.

Some of my students modeled some of these instruments. One of them became a very important performer of African music. His name is Chuck Davis, from Washington, D.C. We brought him to New York in 1963, and paid his rent for three years while he was studying at the Olatunji Center of African Culture on 19th Street in Manhattan. Now he is one of the leading exponents of African dance, specializing in dances from Senegal and Guinea. His picture is in that book, as well as a picture of one of the dancers, and another one of my late son Kwame Olatunji.

That book is the first book written by an African about musical instruments. I am trying to have it reprinted now.

Our music went on, even though we had no recording contract. We were still being heard and seen all over. We participated in the 1967 World's Fair in Montreal, and we were involved in many international shows. We did everything that groups representing Africa would do. We were chosen to represent Africa at an annual concert for the UN General Assembly. That particular year four other groups played, representing Spain, India, and two other countries. That was when U Thant was secretary general.

At the UN event I met Manitos DePlatas, one of Spain's greatest folk guitarists. Around the same time, I performed the first international percussion festival in India. Drummers from twenty-one countries converged on Bombay to perform. This was during the time of Prime Minister Nehru.

We hadn't been recording recently, but even so, we were right there, in the public eye, performing all over. We were going to colleges, trying to use our music to educate people. We were the first to introduce African dancing and drumming to American campuses. We traveled all over the country, and visited more than a thousand colleges and universities over twenty years.

Wherever we performed, I'd always ask, "Do you have a community hall? Let me give a lecture there." That was very important, because we became more than just people coming and doing a concert for students. I'd give workshops on drumming and dance. These were opportunities to sell the act, but they were also a means to educate people about what we were doing—to bring people a little closer so that they could see, experience, and feel what we were doing, what we were part of, and to show them they could be part of it, too.

Perhaps all of this inspired some people to go back to their roots. Human beings started with body percussion, with the clapping of hands and the stamping of feet. That's how we first entertained ourselves. Then we learned to imitate the sounds of birds and all kinds of things we heard around us. Then we figured out how to make different instruments. That's how it all started, and now we are rediscovering ourselves. We are trying to put together the great things of the past with those of the present, for the future.

We worked extensively at Kent State University. I was on the faculty there when the Kent State Massacre took place and shook the whole world, when the Ohio National Guard shot and killed four students during a demonstration.

I was in Jamaica when Bob Marley died, and was asked to announce it on the radio. I attended his funeral. Because I was a close friend, I was asked to perform the traditional rites, for just his immediate family—his mother and wife and children.

We hadn't recorded anything since 1965, so I went back to my old recording company to see if I could change that. I couldn't—by then, all the people I knew had left. The man who ran it now didn't care much for my music, even though he was African American.

I said, "Well, you're not the one who is going to buy it. I'm still working."

"Well, you were a legend in your own time, but I just don't care for your music."

"I can come up with traditional as well as contemporary. I've shown that."

"Well, I'm sorry. I can't sign you up and renew your contract."

"Even for one album? Just give me a chance."

He refused. I wasn't too happy about it. So I never got another contract with Columbia.

But I always believed in the words of a very wonderful mystic writer, Ella Wilcox: "There is no chance, no destiny, no fate that can circumvent, hinder, or control the firm resolve of a determined soul. Gifts count for nothing. The will alone is great and everything will give before it."

I repeated that over and over again to myself. He couldn't stop me. There were plenty other ways to succeed. So I went about my work and reorganized the band and started all over. I maintained the dance company at the same time. I continued to present the dance company, which found more work than the band. To keep a band together, you have to keep it working steady. If you don't, the members look for work somewhere else.

The only way to have a steady band is to put the members under contract. That was a big problem for big bands. John Coltrane's band did not perform the last few years of his life because he wasn't satisfied with what it was getting paid, which was less than it deserved. He wasn't satisfied with paying a union scale to his musicians.

I know what he was going through, because I was going through it, too. You had to be lucky to find steady bookings. If you wanted a steady band, you had to have an agent who could find you steady work. That is really difficult. I realized that. The dance company was able to perform three or four times a month and generate a little income. Not so with the band.

World music really started way back in the 1960s, right after *Drums of Passion* was released. I liked it that our kind of music enabled us to travel all over the world, and not just to Africa. I toured Japan with the Bossa Nova '76 All-Star Show, which featured Herbie Mann as well as Kenny Burrell on guitar. It was George Wein who put the Japan tour together. He was an amazing promoter. That was a wonderful tour. The three traditional drums that I took with me to Japan are still there. I never brought them home, and they were never sent back.

Before the trip to Japan, George had set things up for me to go to Berlin to play with a symphony orchestra, and to do drum performances throughout Germany. But the morning I was supposed to leave New York, it was snowing, sleeting, and raining. I don't like to fly—I'll do it, but I'm never comfortable with it. In those days, it was worse than it is now.

Because of the weather that day, I told George that my spirit was telling me not to travel.

"Your what? What did you say?"

"You see, I'm all packed, but I still have one day. Why can't I wait until tomorrow? This weather's so bad—it's raining, it's snowing, it's sleeting. I've never seen anything like this."

"Look, if you don't travel today, I'll never book you again."

"Sir, I don't go against my mind. I follow my mind."

"What? You're not going?"

"I won't travel today."

"Then don't travel tomorrow either."

And George never booked me again, after Japan. He refused, even though they asked for me for years at all the jazz festivals. When people asked him about me, he'd say, "Well, he doesn't play jazz."

But I played the festivals with Herbie Mann, and with my own group. I did the festival in New Orleans, where I received the key to the city because it was the city through which I entered the United States back in 1950.

When the Japan tour was coming together, Herbie said, "Babatunde, we're going to play two tunes and then we'll bring you out."

"Fine. It's okay with me, you're the boss."

So Herbie played two tunes and then introduced me. As I walked on stage to stand behind my three drums, the crowd stood and applauded.

I don't know why. Maybe it was the way I looked, the way I raised my hand, maybe I was just so full of life. But they stood and applauded for more than five minutes before I even touched the drums.

So Herbie said, "Look, you're going to close the show from now on. We're not going to bring you on after two tunes, we're going to bring you on toward the end of the show. We're going to play three numbers that involve you, and those will be the last three numbers."

"Okay, you're the boss."

It was such a fantastic reception.

The Japanese were the most enthusiastic, most appreciative, most spontaneous audiences I ever performed in front of. When you're good, they really respond to you, you feel it. They know what's good, they know what art is, they know what an artist can do, and they show you they know all that. I'd never been anywhere where my picture was blown so big as it was in Japan. They did a mammoth production.

And at the end of each concert, every member of the group was handed a bouquet of flowers. After three days, your room would be smelling like a flower shop.

Most interesting of all, the promoters had two people standing at each performer's dressing room, a male and a female.

I asked, "What is this?"

"They're protecting their interests. They don't want just anybody walking into the artist's dressing room, they don't want anyone coming to disturb the artist."

It made me feel appreciated, to be thought so well of, to be treated like a national treasure. In this part of the world, artists don't get that kind of recognition. In Japan, an artist who gives all of himself or herself is regarded as a national treasure. We could learn from that.

By the early 1980s, world music had come of age. But the interesting thing is, I had always been playing world music. And from the start, I was telling Columbia about African musicians I thought would become internationally popular if the company would only sign them and develop them.

I wrote a report to Columbia after my visit to Africa in 1963. I mentioned Sunny Ade, I mentioned Fela Anikulapo Kuti, I mentioned Ebenezer Obey, I mentioned a group from Ghana. The international division frowned on that report. In 1965 the company contributed three hundred dollars toward my travel expenses for another trip to West Africa. I came back with another report. They still didn't pay any attention. I kept trying to show them that the music had a global appeal and was going to be accepted around the world, that they could jump on the bandwagon right then and become the first company to promote African music and cash in on it. But the people running the place in those days lacked vision, or were afraid to stick their necks out and try new things.

So I reorganized the band, and then in the 1980s I started giving drumming workshops at places like the Omega Institute in New York, the Esalen Institute in Big Sur, California, and Hollyhock in Vancouver. This approach reignited an interest in African drumming. For many people, it was a new thing.

And it came to pass that People Express was founded. This is a wonderful story. Suddenly you could fly to California for $199. So now, when people asked my band to come perform in California, I could easily fly seven or eight or even ten of us there for what it used to cost to fly only two. So I started booking the band in California, which is where people had been calling me from. For years, the dance company hadn't been able to perform there, except at workshops at Esalen with two or three people. Then came People Express . . . God works in mysterious ways.

One evening I was appearing in California, at Wolfgang's, the theater owned by the manager of the Grateful Dead. Right after the show a man came backstage with a couple of his friends from the Boston Celtics, including Larry Bird. The man was Mickey Hart.

Mickey said, "Mr. Olatunji, I enjoyed the show very much. You don't know me, but I can never forget you. Twenty-one years ago, when I was in school on Long Island, you brought your drums there to do an assembly program, and when you asked people to stay and play the drums, I was one of them. And you put my hand up and said, 'Well, he's good, give him a hand!' And then I listened to *Drums of Passion*. That album meant so much to me that I became a drummer. I'm with the Grateful Dead. What are you doing tomorrow? Can we have lunch?"

"Lunch? Yes."

"Good. Are you recording with anybody now?"

"No."

"You don't have a contract with anybody?"

"No," I said. "I'm not committed to anybody, we can talk."

I couldn't sleep that night.

I went to lunch with him, and he asked, "How long will it take you to get ready to record?"

"Tomorrow."

"*Tomorrow?*"

"I have enough material in my head to put it together with this group right here."

"Are you kidding?"

"Well, if you can arrange it."

He said, "I want your entire group to open for the Grateful Dead New Year's Eve. Bring all the members of your group, and right after that, we will go into the studio. Figure how many people you are going to bring, let me know."

That's how Mickey Hart became a friend and a benefactor. He wanted to do the right thing. And that was the beginning of our relationship, which was not only musical, but included my being the godfather of his daughter.

New Year's Eve 1985, I brought together twenty-two people from New York and all over the country to open for the Grateful Dead at Oakland Coliseum in front of 22,000 people. The performance was videotaped by KQED. Mickey told them, "You've got one of the greatest drummers in the world here. Just roll the tape, I'll mix it."

KQED kept the broadcast rights, and it was aired on public television. Mickey, who owned the tape, gave the original to me and we used it for promotional purposes.

As promised, that led to the recording of two albums, *Drums of Passion: The Invocation* (I wanted to call it "Invocation to the Gods," but the record company was afraid, they didn't want any controversy) and *Drums of Passion: The Beat*, on the Rykodisc label.

And very uniquely, Mickey Hart and some friends of his and mine— Airto Moreira, the brilliant Brazilian percussionist, and my very good friend, Carlos Santana—agreed to perform on the recording.

Carlos had to be careful, though, because of his contract with CBS. He, by the way, was the first one to record one of my tunes, "Jin-Go-Lo-Ba." It helped his first album sell a million copies. He has now recorded that same tune three times. So I can say that more than anybody else, Carlos Santana has helped me make a little money with a song that I have written.

He and Mickey Hart are in the same class—they have done me a good turn, a great deal of good in return for whatever I might have done for them. They have come out and compensated me for whatever I have done for them.

World music grew to the extent that is today from where it was in 1961 when I started experimenting. Whatever people call it today, I believe that we contributed to a large degree to its popularity.

The relationship with Mickey Hart did not end with recording those two albums. It grew, became more intimate, and led to discussions about projects, some of which I suggested. Mickey Hart, myself, and another musician from Nigeria, Siriku Adepoju, a talking drum player in my band, plus two musicians from India, Zakir Hussain and Vikkui Vinayakram, two from Brazil, Airto Moreira and Flora Purim, and another young Puerto Rican, a real standout whom we added at the last minute, Giovanni Hidalgo, all represented what we considered the planet, so we called ourselves Planet Drum and planned a CD with that title.

The idea was that if I start a rhythmic pattern, you listen to it, you add something to it, each and every one of us adds something to it to make it a complete tune. And what does that become? It becomes a unity of purpose. It makes us equal collaborators. It is telling people that we believe in the power of rhythm, that we are not in competition, that different cultures can come together in unity, and that different ideas can come together as one. It is reminding all of us that we are about the same thing, expressing the same idea, putting into the ether the sound that can rejuvenate, the sound that can be tantalizing, the sound that can be stimulating, the sound that would bring joy, the sound that would gladden the heart. Planet Drum was really about all people coming together in music. It was a model for the world, and an antidote for hate.

Mickey was in a much better financial position than any one of us involved in the group, so the burden of looking for the recording company and the money to develop the idea became his.

We said we were ready to make it happen by contributing our part, because you can have the money but if you don't have the idea it will not be realized, and vice versa. You can have the idea but if you don't have the money to make that idea become a reality, the idea will just be dormant. It would just be there and nothing would be done about it.

Mickey found a record company. He sold the idea to them and it gave birth to *Planet Drum*. Each one of us contributed to each number that was performed on the CD. Then a two-week tour was organized. It took us from Berkeley, to Los Angeles, to Colorado, to Chicago, to St. Louis, to Washington, D.C., to Philadelphia, to Albany, to Boston, to New York, and back to California.

We made that tour at a time when I had a serious eye condition that required an operation. So all the while I was performing for those two weeks, I was blind. To this day, none of the others can understand how I managed it.

I told them nothing was wrong with me except my eyesight. All they had to do was have somebody set up my four drums. I could play them with my eyes closed, and that is exactly what I did. After the operation, I could see as well as I ever could. So for me, that tour was like a miracle—a healing tour.

I am happy to tell you that *Planet Drum* won the Grammy for world music. Mickey accepted the award on our behalf. That was quite an achievement. All of us who were involved were now seen as important contributors to the development of world music. All of us had known from the start that world music was out there. We were happy to have drawn the world's attention to it, and legitimized it, but for us it had always been there.

World music is one of the most important things we have to bring people together, to unite people. It is an irresistible force against any immovable object. We can use it to unify nations, family, community, and the world at large.

All of a sudden, with the popularity of many holistic centers throughout the United States—places like Omega, Esalen, and Hollyhock—I became a featured presenter of drumming programs that included meditation, dance, and chanting.

I make very sure that my presentations at those places are geared toward the message of togetherness and love, and that everyone is allowed to feel important. I think hard about what I say. I understand that my actions speak louder than my words, so I try to practice what I preach.

The effects of the drumming workshops have been amazing. I am now considered one of the leading exponents of this movement, which has coincided with the women's and men's movements. Today, both women and men are participating in my drumming workshops. Actually, I started teaching women many years ago, in Boston. One of them, Layne Redmond, now has her own group. She began coming to me as a sixth-grader in Roxbury. My groups have always encouraged women to join in the art and practice of drumming. Their interest started very slowly and then grew and grew.

In Santa Cruz, out of a class of 200, 150 may be women. At Omega, out of 100 people in my class, 75 may be women. At Esalen, more women than men take my classes.

Our workshop program has been developed to present the African experience. That includes not only drumming and dancing, but chanting as well. The resurgence of interest in African drumming and dancing began at holistic centers and has since spread across the country. Wherever you go, you hear about drumming and dancing classes and workshops, and similar gatherings.

Many entrepreneurial men and women are now making and selling African drums, like the djembe, which is very popular in French-speaking nations like Senegal and Guinea. Nowadays, you can earn a good living making drums.

Men and women are forming their own dance companies. Some people in New Jersey have named their dance company the Gun Go Do Pata Dance and Drum Company. They are now a nonprofit organization that receives funding from the city, state, and federal governments to teach in schools. And this sort of work started years ago, we went to places to perform or give workshops, and I asked, "Do you have a center where people go? Let me go and give a lecture there."

That was very important because it became more than just us coming and giving a concert for the students. I'd give them a workshop in drumming and dance. It was an opportunity for people to gain more of an understanding of what we were doing. It was important to let people get a little closer so that they could see and feel and experience what we were all about and make it something that they could become part of. It's okay for someone to perform and for people to clap their hands at the end, and then leave. But it is much better when the people know they can really be a part of it. People of all ages and all colors respond to drumming. We are all discovering that we need to come back down to earth, back to where we started. It's as if we are just trying to balance things, to get back to the reality of the earth that supports us.

It was the earth that gave birth to us in the first place. It's there to replenish us. We are learning that now. We are rediscovering the simple things that people can do together. All people from all walks of life, all colors, we have things that we can do together, and it's the simplest thing to make music and sing together.

I believe that all of our touring over the past forty years has paid off. It really is gratifying to see so many drumming communities everywhere we go. The resurgence of interest is amazing. I predict that within the next ten or fifteen years, there will be drums in at least two homes out of five in the United States.

9 | Voices of Africa

I remember very well the kind of love and affection that was showered on me as a child. It was so much that when I grew into adulthood, I was ashamed of it in a way. So much admiration and love was tantamount to spoiling a child. I took action about it, as I remember; after I graduated from high school, I asked to be transferred away from home. I was still being pampered—nobody could disagree with me, and even my close associates were likely to be spoiled. Anyone who criticized or antagonized me, my elders were ready to wage war against that person, no matter who that person was.

I knew from the songs that had been sung to me, lullabies, that people were expecting great things from me. That is why I have always thought more than twice before I do anything—I dare not risk ruining the family name. This even affected my marriage; I was always asking myself, "What would they say, what would my people think of me? We don't divorce women, we don't do this, no matter what it is."

I knew I was not getting the kind of support from my wife that I needed in order to do what I was doing. Amy and I loved each other, but she wanted me to do something I didn't want to do. She thought I was wasting my time.

She felt sorry for me. She saw me struggling on my own, trying to tell people about Africa, and people just putting my work down. She listened to Africans telling me, "Stop playing those jungle drums. You're perpetuating Hollywood stereotypes about Africans, playing those big drums." Africans who were students were telling me, "Don't try to present these kinds of dances."

But I was always being asked to put shows together, when student organizations met. At the end of every conference, I would gather students from different parts of Africa to see if they remembered any of their songs and dances, and then I would put those together. This was always popular. Yet some of the students would say, "Don't do such and such a dance. Don't do those dances that are so vigorous, so energetic, so acrobatic."

So my wife was telling me, "You're not going to get anywhere, you're doing it for nothing. You aren't making any money. You have nothing to show for it. You've been doing this for ten years, and we can't even buy a car. And look at So-and-So, your colleague. So-and-So isn't as bright as you are. He's just been appointed ambassador to the United States and you're here knocking your brains out, getting up every day, running to the Center, running to Boston to teach at somebody's school, running to Ohio."

My work—my love for what I do—was the main reason my wife and I separated. In her view, I needed to consider a complete career change, to become a diplomat or at least hold down a nine-to-five job like my colleagues were doing. She didn't exactly say those words; that is how I interpreted her actions. In a way, she was happy when the Center was forced to close.

Because of my tours, and the time I spent at the Center, and the time I spent commuting to Boston and Kent State, I had very little time to spend with my family. I knew she didn't like to travel. It would have been much easier if she had; she could have become more of a part of what I was doing.

Every year after the Center was established, I would send the faculty on an unpaid vacation to Africa. Transportation and their room and board were taken care of. They would be gone for a whole month, which was plenty of time for them to see things for themselves. Since we were not making any money, many of them took advantage of the opportunity. Some of our dancers went to my village and saw my mother and the elders perform some of the dances I had taught them. They heard the women singing to welcome me to the village.

Every time I visited Ajido I announced my arrival the day before so that people could take the day off. It was a big event when I came back to the village. The car we were in had to stop a couple of miles before the village. We had to get out of the car because drummers and children were coming to welcome us to the village, giving us the royal treatment.

Once again I would hear familiar songs. I remember very well one of the songs the women were singing, *ko I dele ariwo nta.'* The words went, "He has not even gotten home yet and the word is around. It has been heralded that he is coming back to take his place, to obtain chieftaincy. He is coming back. He is not here yet, but people already know. Well, he is coming back and he is going to become the chief of this village. Finally, he is coming back!"

I said to myself, "No! I don't want to come back to become chief here. I don't want to go through what I saw, what my grandfather went through to become chief."

Then I said to myself, "What am I really saying? I am saying that my mission is now bigger than the village—my mission has to be global. I have to serve the world and not just this village. My mission is to be of service now to the entire world."

The people would ask me why I wanted to do that. I'd tell them, "I've seen the world. The village is part of it. My forbears have served this place. I am a product of this place. I have received certain training that prepared me to launch a program, a career that will help me serve the world."

I was thinking like that. It was probably something I had gathered from the way my grandmother always gave me a special place in the household, always made sure I was well dressed and got the most nourishing foods to eat.

When I was a child, I was always given the best clothing and ornaments. This was probably because of the love the family had for my father. It made me believe that I was probably my father reincarnated.

It is often said that you can see the adult in what the child does, by how he or she does things. The seed of virtue sown in youth will germinate into good deeds and eventually ripen into good habits.

What a child in the village learned above all was respect for elders. That meant anybody who was older than you, not just in the immediate family but in the entire village. You had to listen to them. Not necessarily accept what they said, but listen. After all, they had lived longer than you, so they knew life better than you. It was considered a virtue to listen to them.

The next thing you learned was sharing. You must share what you have. In whatever you do, think of the person next to you. If you are jumping around and being happy and the person next to you is not, you have to respond to that. Why is that person not as happy as you are? You must make the effort to understand why that person is in that kind of mood.

Above all, you must show reverence for life. The fear of God was instilled in me through the stories I was told about people who failed to show that reverence. Wherever you turn, God is there. As I have gone through changes in my life, I have tried to see the workings of God. I have never doubted He is there. Try to look for Him in your life and you will be successful. And always believe in yourself. When you make up your mind to do something, stick with it. I always knew that great things were expected of me.

My vision of the world changed suddenly after my initiation, when I was inducted into the circle of the community. I was thirteen. That is when I was taught the spiritual principles of the Yoruba people that I have been referring to. My world view can be summed up in an old Yoruba saying: *Afi olorun, afi enia*. "God first and man second."

I would sum up the purpose of life in one word: service. This is the greatest word. If what you are doing does not serve other people, it is not worth doing, it is not meaningful. That is probably the most important knowledge that one can learn. When you know that, you will be happy with your life, you will find fulfillment. I discovered this as I continued to grow. When trying to achieve your goals, ask yourself: "Does it involve other people?" "Who will it benefit?" Unless it is benefits others, it will not be meaningful, it will not be very satisfying.

I could not have survived without a deep immersion in traditional village life. Having experienced and participated in that life, I was thrown into the amphitheater of the world. I was looking at the world from inside Africa and seeing Africa's connections with the rest of the world. Then, as a city boy, I observed that the world is the same everywhere. I wanted to be of consequence in that world.

My wife did not work after our first child was born. She had worked as a librarian in the New York Public Library system. We agreed that our children should be at least two years old before she went back to work, which I believe was the right thing to do. But two years after the birth of our first child, Kwame, came two girls, Folasade and Modupe. So she never went back to work. There was no reason why she couldn't come on those trips with me. I interpreted her refusal as meaning that she wasn't really interested in traveling.

At that time, to maintain the Center and the group, I had to go around performing and touring, and teaching at colleges and institutes besides my own school. On Saturdays I was in the office at least half an hour before the start of the children's program, which brought about two hundred children to the Center every Saturday.

My wife and I tried to raise our children in such a way that they would be able to function in society. We did not send them to private schools, but to public schools.

My two girls finished high school in Nigeria. One was in the tenth grade and the other in the eighth grade when we sent them to a boarding high school in Nigeria. This school was attended by all the children of expatriates in Nigeria. The teachers were university professors. I was trying to give my children an opportunity to enjoy all facets of their heritage, both American and African.

Our children were asked to come back to the United States every summer after the boarding school closed. They should have spent their summers in Africa as well—for them to taste the real Africa, they should have done that. Disagreements over things like this didn't make our marriage gel.

The most important thing for me was my life's work. My wife did not agree with me that I should be sacrificing my life to promote African culture. In the end, because of this disagreement, we decided to separate.

After I returned from Nigeria, having failed to launch a political career, the Center having being closed, and my marriage in trouble, you can imagine how bleak I felt about the future.

I knew I would have to choose between my career and my marriage. I chose my career. That was a difficult and deeply painful decision, but I'm glad I made it. I told her, "I'm sorry, but at this stage in my life I have to be married to my drums. We can still be friends." That is how the situation stands today. We are still separated, and I'm still single.

A month after I made the decision, things began to happen again for me. I am still trying to understand why. Maybe some questions don't have answers, or maybe the answers wouldn't matter anyway. So I leave it be.

But I do know that no one can own anyone else. That is another universal thing.

The children have been wonderful. Kwame turned into a brilliant scholar and a strong athlete. He was offered scholarships to five Ivy League universities: Harvard, Yale, Princeton, Columbia, and Cornell—both athletic and academic scholarships. All we had to do was pay a thousand dollars a year.

He chose Harvard. I wanted him to go to Morehouse, my alma mater, like Spike Lee did. Kwame was a very close friend of Spike, whose father had been at Morehouse with me, besides being my best player on some of my recordings. But we couldn't just disregard Kwame's scholarships to all these wonderful schools. He went to Harvard when he was sixteen and graduated four years later.

Because he had done so well, I gave him a ticket to take a whole year off, to travel to Africa and just do whatever he wanted to do. But he wouldn't do that. I asked him to take a year off and go back to Harvard and get a master's degree; that way he could become an outstanding member of that club of Harvard men. But he had his own ideas. He wanted to start his own company. He said he didn't have to go for his master's to become what he wanted to become. He was very interested in so many things, in making things, just like Spike Lee. It was Kwame who advised Spike to go to NYU film school.

Kwame started his own company called Kato, putting gem buyers and gem sellers together at an international level. He was thinking big, just like his father. To my regret, he had decided to pursue his own course, make his own decisions, without consulting me or listening to whatever advice I had. His business of representing buyers and sellers of precious gems was one of the most dangerous jobs anybody could take on.

On a business trip to Sierra Leone, he went swimming with the son of the secretary to the president. While he was trying to save the life of this ten-year-old, he himself drowned. Nobody helped him. That's how we lost Kwame. He had a wife and two children. That was another painful turning point in my life, the unexpected passing of my son.

My two girls are doing very well. Both of them graduated from college. Folasade, the older one, attended law school after having four children. Modupe, who has a daughter, is a member of the dance company. So now the company has six college graduates.

As I look into the future, the third generation is the one I pin my hopes on, that they will do what their parents didn't do. It was very difficult to get my own children to become involved whole-heartedly in what I was doing. My grandchildren have already appeared with me on stage. So there is a bright future for the third generation.

Asiko. Time. What is time? "Time," Lincoln said, "what an empty vapor it is. And days how swift they are, swift like an Indian arrow, fly on like a shooting star. The present moment just is here and flies away in haste, that we may never see the hours but only see their past." Time moves on and life with it and each loved one is beloved for this eternal movement, like passengers on the express train of time. They move with us and we move with them until either they or we are no more.

Here I am, after forty some years, still dreaming about changing the ugly image of Africa in the minds of millions not only in America, but all over the world, including in Africa itself. Here I am, looking inside Africa as an African living outside Africa, experiencing and dealing with all the external forces coming to bear on the entire continent, observing how the rape of the continent continues, not only by those outside Africa but also by those within the continent itself, those who have assumed power, or those who have replaced their colonial masters to become even worse exploiters of their own people.

I am still trying to comprehend how all the wrongs can be righted. I still believe that somehow, there is a cultural basis for our unity, that the myths and stereotypes about Africa that have remained in the minds of millions of people probably will remain in the minds of generations yet to be born if something is not done right now to stop it from happening.

I am still trying to take all my frustrations out on the drum instead of on people. There are people I know very well from childhood who demonstrated their intentions long ago to bring about positive change that would help eliminate illiteracy, improve health care, and contribute to the well-being of their own people. Instead they have become exploiters of their own people.

Here I am, at center stage, in the middle of a situation where one cannot help but feel the sufferings of those who have been so horribly mistreated and exploited.

So I ask, "Why does God allow this to happen, not only in Africa but on other continents? Why do so many women, through their actions or inactions, show so little respect for others, so little reverence for life?"

Then I remember that God has nothing to do with it. The Creator, in His majesty, laid down the ground rules but has nothing to do with how we treat one another. The Creator will sometimes answer the prayers of a thief, but will also remind him that one day he will be caught. One day all of us are going to be judged by our actions or inactions. That is one of the reasons why I feel compelled to keep forging ahead in what I do— I well realize that one day I will be judged by my actions or inactions.

This kind of thinking has always motivated me. In 1985, after the Ethiopian famine broke out, Bob Geldof, a young Irish musician, organized a benefit concert called Live Aid for Africa. He recruited some of the most famous musicians in the West. Within weeks, Live Aid had raised more than $20 million. And this was by European musicians—no African performers were included. Geldof was knighted for this work by the Queen of England.

The interest on that money was used to help African farmers, to dig wells, and to buy medicines. Many people criticized Geldof: "Why did he put that money in a British bank?" But at least he did something. When I read about it I was very grateful, and I commended him for his efforts.

Then I asked myself, "What are we Africans doing to help our own situation, to help ourselves?"

This, and all the other events in Africa around Pan-Africanism, led to the formation in 1987 of Voices of Africa, an organization for bringing together internationally known African performers.

I put together a proposal. Voices of Africa would be a cooperative effort by African musicians, singers, dancers, writers, poets, and other performers to raise millions of dollars in order to alleviate some of the human suffering in Africa. It would be a statement of mutual respect from the musicians of Africa to the musicians of the world. Through the international language of music, the people of the world would hear about these needs and respond to them.

Voices of Africa has become a nonprofit organization. It brings together internationally known musical artists from Africa, the United States, the West Indies, and South America. They perform together to raise funds to fight illiteracy in Africa and to help alleviate the health crisis there. It is the beginning of a dialogue between the musicians and performers of the world who share an awareness of and commitment to African culture.

My view of the "global village" has led me to a life of social and political action in the struggle for world peace. Voices of Africa is designed to address health issues, education, technological development, and awareness. Imagine a concert stage on which appear, one after the other, musicians from Senegal, Nigeria, Ghana, Gambia, South Africa, and other African countries. Imagine the joyous sounds, the exotic instruments, and the colorful native dress, all for the purpose of raising funds to reduce hunger and disease in Africa. We have a distinguished board of directors from all over the world. Other organizations have lent their help to us, and so will many talented artists and performers.

The idea is that these performers will take a month off out of the year. They will tell their managers or agents that they must get together with their peers and perform all over the world to raise money. Then they will all sit down at the roundtable and decide how to use this money to do what the politicians have not done since the independence of more than forty African countries, beginning with Ghana in 1957. This will be something similar to the Marshall Plan that the United States put together to rebuild Western Europe after the Second World War.

Voices of Africa will help solve African illiteracy, and African health problems, of which there are many, including the AIDS virus, which is killing millions there now. It will help stop other countries from dumping atomic wastes on the continent, and stop them from selling obsolete weapons to African nations. It will provide education, and commit Africans to the well-being of their own people. It will raise Africa and Africans to the same level as the rest of the world.

For three years I traveled to Africa, to Nigeria, making a video, explaining why it was necessary for Africans to come together, how this program could be put together, how this program would empower every African to make a contribution and have a voice in how the money that was raised would be spent, how that money would be a means to introduce and develop new talents for the rest of the world, and how it would stop the exploitation of the talent coming from Africa—exploitation that has been going on since colonial times. Hundreds of artists have never been compensated for their work, have never received royalties.

For five years I made a concerted effort to enlist the help of international artists. Some heard me out, some didn't even respond. At one point I got letters from twelve Nigerian artists who agreed to participate, but when the time came to put the show together, nobody showed up.

I made arrangements with well-known artists in 1986 to do a fundraising concert at Madison Square Garden. I made a deposit for the venue— $10,000 that I had borrowed from a friend. But at the last minute, a big-name band backed out and I had to cancel the show. I lost the deposit, plus another very large loan from a friend that I had borrowed for other costs. It took me four years to pay back the people I owed.

It was not easy to get Voices of Africa set up as a nonprofit organization. Officials in Washington raised a conflict of interest point about me being the director of Drums of Passion. After nine months of legal pleas and filings, I convinced them that those people who loaned the money for the production would get their money back, and that the nonprofit status was necessary for me to be able to pay back whoever loaned me money, so that my person wouldn't be sued. After that, we contacted many organizations in Africa that were raising millions of dollars to help the African situation. But none of these groups would join forces with me—they could not see how they would benefit.

I appealed to them that we could do this together, that there were many African artists who were known all over the world and who would help us stage this first show and then we would be on our own. "You have all the tools, the contacts," I told them. "Help us set it up. You need to empower us—why should we always depend on outside promoters? We want to learn. Give us the opportunity to learn to be producers, promoters ourselves."

I'd been in the business for more than thirty years. I needed to graduate from a performing artist to a producer. I wrote to friends, or those whom I considered friends, people I knew who had the money to underwrite this project, and I got no response. I couldn't believe this could happen to me. I couldn't understand why support wasn't coming from those who over the years had indicated to me in conversation and by their participation in similar events—for which they received my support and participation— how they could turn me down. I cannot tell you how hurt I was and how disappointed in people I became. But I never lost my faith in humanity.

I thought about the many wonderful causes that had called on me to contribute my talents and to which I had always responded with enthusiasm. But for almost four years, I could find no support for my own project. I was forced to sit down and analyze this failure. Were there some things I had forgotten to do? Was I not expressing my plan clearly enough?

I confided in some close friends, and one or two told me, "You know, Baba, you think so big. Maybe you should scale down your approach to this project about raising funds. Maybe you should start with mini-fundraising projects instead of doing it in places like Madison Square Garden."

Yes, it is true that I always think big. And I will continue to think big, because when you think about the enormous problems facing Africa and its people, you have no choice. Africa is three times the size of the United States, yet it is almost five hundred years behind the world's developed countries. Almost nothing has been done to accelerate the pace of development so that Africa and Africans will one day be able to rub shoulders with the rest of the world. The UN cannot solve Africa's problems. Charity begins at home. When you think about Africa, you have to think big.

It is always easy to point a finger at the other person without noticing or realizing that you have four fingers pointing back at yourself. Africans need to stop pointing their fingers at one another. We should begin, in Africa, to take a look at the four fingers pointing toward ourselves, asking, "What can we do? What have we done? What have we done wrong? What are we doing right?"

These are the questions that African leaders who are enjoying political power without economic emancipation need to ask themselves. They need to consider what Kennedy said: "Ask not what your country can do for you, but what you can do for your country." So I *have* to think big. That was my answer to questions raised by friends.

There is sense in scaling down the approach. But we have to be able to produce fundraising programs that will bring in millions of dollars, because that is what it will take to solve some of the problems facing Africa. We have to come together and remind the people who are benefiting from Africa, the companies that are doing business in Africa, the nations that are exploiting African resources, to replenish the source. More than that, they must help Africans become self-sufficient so that Africans will be able to run their own businesses.

For more than one hundred years, the Firestone Rubber Company has been leasing thousands of acres of land in Liberia for rubber plantations. It employs 2,500 rubber tappers there, but those workers have never been taught how to turn the sap into tires. Most of them don't even know that after they have tapped the rubber trees, the sap is shipped from Monrovia to Akron, Ohio, where Firestone has its factory, which turns the raw product into the wheels that keep America rolling. It would be very profitable in the long run if such a factory were built in Africa, if rubber tires were produced in Africa, where the raw materials actually come from.

Many, many raw materials leave Africa every day for other parts of the world on ships bearing the Liberian flag. That flag, though, is just a legal dodge—it has no financial value to the people of Liberia except perhaps to one or two of the nation's leaders.

Voices of Africa was going to use the talents of musicians who had no political power but who nevertheless were loved and respected by people all over the world. This would have raised a tremendous amount of money to do what African political leaders were not doing.

It took me about two months to regroup after the first concert was cancelled. I decided to make this project a life's work. One way or another, I would find a way to make it work. If the present group of internationally known musicians were so tied up with their agents, I would discover new talents over the next few years to start the project all over again.

I have great hope in the younger generation. There are always new talents out there, and they will have the opportunity to know that it is their responsibility to help alleviate suffering and lift Africa's burden of dependency. I rely on Psalm 91, my article of faith: "He that dwelleth in the secret place of the most High shall abide under the shadow of the Almighty."

This program will need a Center of African Performing Arts, where all the strengths of African culture will come into focus, where people will be able to learn more about Africa, and how Africans came to be who they are, and how Africans relate to everybody else in the universe.

Voices of Africa will also be teaching artists about the business side of their work. This is important. Those who really want to learn how to market and promote themselves, and how to value what they offer and negotiate for that value, will be able to get what they deserve.

Participating artists in Voices of Africa will have a chance to sit down at the conference table and say, "Look, I am part of the decision-making process of how to use what we have for a worthy cause."

Somebody asked me, "How will the artists benefit?"

The artist is going to benefit in so many ways. First of all, knowing that you are doing something worthwhile for your country is a joy that words cannot describe.

Second, artists will be able to benefit from their work through sales of smaller things, like T-shirts and posters. At the same time, their transportation and living expenses will be taken care of. The artists will receive honoraria, not salaries. And if they make recordings, which they will, every artist who contributes will get royalties.

Many African artists have never collected royalties. They never did for many of the years they recorded for Decca in London. What almost always happened at Decca was that the artist would visit the headquarters and say, "I need five hundred dollars."

They'd hear, "Okay, give him three hundred."

Until very recently, African countries had no copyright laws. Here in the United States, companies must report sales figures to their artists, every three months or six months—it's the law. So the law is on the side of the artist. Even in African countries that have set up copyright laws, those laws are never really enforced. Usually, producers find ways to violate those laws or bribe government officials to overlook the laws.

It has always been my vision to establish an African cultural center in every big city in the United States. That was my dream, my vision, in 1958. It happened for a while in New York and Washington, and it almost happened in Atlanta.

I have suffered many setbacks along the road of my life. But I have also enjoyed many spiritual epiphanies—or spiritual upliftments, I will call them.

I can almost always tell whether I am going to succeed in any project I take on. That's because I think so hard about it that I can almost see its future. Also, I can sense how difficult it will be, and knowing that, can answer this question: "Are you ready for the consequences?"

Usually I have said, "Yes," and then I have gone ahead.

So when I have encountered disappointment, delays, or moments of failure, I have known they are temporary. Some friends have always maintained: "When Baba looks like he's finished, that's when he's about to shine again."

That is about nothing more than keeping the faith in yourself, and in what you believe you can accomplish. You learn not to allow anything to turn you from your goal. You also remember that one thing is certain—that the shortest road has a turn and the longest journey has an end. I remember that every day. It has given me great spiritual encouragement to know that I can help change the course of events myself, for me, so that it will affect others around me.

I am able to heal myself physically, mentally, and spiritually. When I'm really in the dumps, I know how to raise my own spirits.

I have always had the attitude that I must never let problems into in my life. I never have any problems, I only have situations. That way, I can pull myself up. I never let a situation become a problem; I immediately get rid of that situation *before* it becomes a problem. It doesn't matter whether it involves my mother, my father, my daughters, my son, or my wife.

With my intensity and passion, problems would be the death of me. So I never allow problems to get to me. I don't let anyone create problems for me. Nobody.

I'll give you an example. I've never bought a car, except for a station wagon to carry my drums. That tells you I have never made any money. People always think I'm a multimillionaire. Even some members of my family think I'm hiding millions somewhere. I always told my children that when I pass into the spirit world, they will have nothing to fight over because I am not saving anything for anyone to fight about. I don't possess anything, so I will do for you right now what I can do for you.

If I have money, you can always take it, because I'm going to give you some—right away I'm going to give you some. I didn't bring anything here, and I'm not taking anything with me. I'm a firm believer in that.

So I had this old station wagon that we used for our work. I took it to a mechanic and asked him what was wrong.

He said, "We have to change this, we have to change that."

"How much is it going to cost?"

"$344."

"Fine."

A few hours later he called me.

"Mr. Olatunji, I just found out something is wrong with the valve. It will cost you another $50."

"Do anything that you need. Let me know before you do anything if you have to buy something, not after the bill. When will the car be ready?"

He said the next day. I went to collect the car.

He said, "By the way, when I was changing the oil, I found the oil filter and other things needed replacing. That's another $39 that had to be added to your bill."

I said, "No sir, I'm not paying that. You didn't get my okay. I have a budget, that's all I have. You didn't call me to add to it, so this is what I brought you."

"Well, then you aren't going to get your car."

"Really? Okay. I'm going to leave the car with you."

"What?"

"I said I am going to leave the car with you. You said I am not going to get it. You've got the car."

So I turned to leave.

He said, "Are you crazy? You're not going to give me $39, you're going to leave the car?"

"That's right. You knew what to do, but you didn't call me. I'm not going to court with you. I'll leave the car with you. If you want to sell the car, get your money and give me the balance."

He said, "Wait a minute, are you kidding?"

"I'm not. I'm leaving it right here with you now. We are using a car tomorrow morning, we are going to Ohio, Kent State. I am going to rent a car because I am not going to pay the extra money. I'm not going to pay, and I'm not going to sue you, because I don't believe in going to court with anybody."

He looked at me and I left! I didn't say anything.

My wife asked me, "Where's the car?"

I said, "It's still with the mechanic, he's working on it."

"I thought you said it was finished."

"Well he found a lot of things wrong with it."

I didn't tell her what happened because I knew she would react so differently from my way.

So I didn't let the man get to me. I'm not the kind of person who lets other people do that. So I left the car with him, and left the next day for Ohio.

Guess who came to my house and asked my wife to please beg me to take the car back? He said he had never, never met anybody like me.

She said, "Oh, you don't know who you are dealing with, do you?"

"Does he really mean he's going to leave the car with me?"

"He left it with you, you can take it. He's not going to ask you."

I came back from tour, and the man called me and said, "Can I be your friend?" We became very good friends.

So I don't entertain problems. I have all kinds of stories like that.

You have to give thanks that the Creator puts you in positions like that. I acknowledge it and give thanks. It all goes back to the way you were brought up. I also give thanks to the unbelievable support I have received from so many other people, people who never knew my mother or my father, people who, of their own volition, gave me a helping hand when I asked for it. The good health, support, and protection that I have enjoyed over the years is all through the grace of God.

Voices of Africa will go way beyond what I have been able to do so far. Through its participating artists, many African governments will become known, recognized, and admired.

Over the past few years, my drummers and dancers have become known in many parts of the world through our workshops and performances in Europe and South America. Since Mandela's release from prison, and the death of apartheid, we have visited South Africa along with celebrated artists like Hugh Masekela, Miriam Makeba, Dorothy Nsuku, and Dollar Brand. We have discussed the Voices of Africa program and how we can raise millions of dollars together to help fight the spread of AIDS and to treat the millions of people who are now its victims. We want to guarantee every child in Africa an education. Countries in West Africa like Nigeria, Senegal, Ghana, and Cameroon—which has produced more than a dozen internationally known artists—will support Voices of Africa.

For the past sixty-five years of my life I have never been in a hospital. I've always been the get-up-and-go fellow, one who has always believed there is nothing I cannot accomplish. That was until I developed diabetes, which has damaged my kidneys so much that I can only survive by having dialysis. I made up my mind I would continue the fight.

If we persist though often we may fail, in time our efforts shall prevail. With this clearer understanding I pursue relentlessly and continue the struggle. I wake up every morning, sit with my feet on the ground, and ask for that which is of the highest good to come to me that day. It is important to think very seriously about supporting Voices of Africa and to visualize the contribution that such an organization will make toward changing the image and the perceptions of Africa and Africans in the minds of people. In recent months I have received word from organizations and from friends who are willing to help raise money.

This effort will bring a lot of people closer together. It will improve global communication. It will provide better opportunities for people beyond the borders of their respective countries. It will enable people from different parts of the world to see for themselves what Africa really is, and to unravel the mysteries of Africa.

The Africa that has been painted for so long in such lurid colors will evaporate from people's minds, and they will see my homeland more clearly than they ever have. They will learn, finally, to respect Africa and Africans. And they will begin to understand that all of us are created in His image.

Once a Center of African Performing Arts has been established, it will offer programs that bring together people from all levels. These programs will help unify Africans themselves, who speak so many different languages yet are also similar in ways they have yet to discover. This will enable Africans themselves to understand their own spirituality—a spirituality they share with all other people. Once that happens, we will one day all become that one spirit which rules the whole universe, that one spirit which makes the sun rise in the east and set in the west.

This realization that all of us are one will mark a new beginning in the twenty-first century. For that is when we shall know that the past and the present are inevitably linked together. It is from the past that we must put together things in the present to make a wonderful tomorrow.

I believe that everything is already in perfect order. The only thing I would change is human institutions. Everything else is in divine order, governed by the law of opposites. The Creator has given us the gift of choice. But remember, whatever you choose, you pay for it. The law of reciprocity prevails. All religions share certain things. Every religion has a rule of conduct, a way to live. All religions lead to one thing, a common practice of reverence for life.

Life is a gift. So is death, which is a necessary thing. I look around me now, and see the leaves changing; before spring, a time of rebirth, we must go through winter. Life is everlasting. The physical body dies, but not the spirit. The spirit becomes what we call *Ajaja*, the higher spirit, the energy that makes our universe function the way it does. You are now part of that spirit. I want to become part of that spirit which is responsible for the dawn of the day, nightfall, and the changing of the seasons. It never fails because there is no obstacle that can stay its mighty force. A river is meant to empty itself into the great ocean, nothing can stop it. So it is with the human spirit.

What is most important to me now is peace, peace of mind, consideration of others, trying not to step on other people's toes, sharing my joy, my laughter, my enthusiasm, my talent, and trying to live up to the greatest law, love of my neighbor as I love myself. I believe that my needs will be met, and that I must go beyond that while being careful not to overstep my bounds. I am happiest when I have the opportunity to express myself, be it for one person or ten million.

What saddens me most is man's inhumanity to man, when we deny one another our inalienable rights, when we demonstrate disrespect and irreverence for human life. One thing I know is that I am a child of the universe. As I said in one of my songs, when the world hears the beat of my drums, the spirits of the gods will descend on all of the people who are there and those who hear it. They will be able to tell this in their hearts, feel it in their souls, see it in their eyes, and feel it in their feet, when they dance to the beat of the drum. The world is the same everywhere you go because the sun and the rain, the moon and the stars, the ocean and the waves, the beasts and the birds all dance to the beat of the drum. I discovered that, and I know that it is true.

The most important thing I have learned in life is that there are good people everywhere—you just have to pray, and wait for them to come your way. Even in the places where people have been labeled as treacherous, there are still good people. If this wasn't true, there is no way I could have survived. There are good people who are doing God's work who do not really look for recognition, compensation, or accolades. Like Kendall Weisiger; he didn't know anything about me and my cousin Akiwowo or our families, he just read a letter we wrote asking if we could study in America. He didn't even see our pictures, he just read the letter. At no time was that man's picture in any of the big magazines, *Time*, *Newsweek*, *Life*. But he was responsible for bringing a lot of people here, including me.

Spirituality plays a very big role in my life. I take a spiritual perspective in everything I do. I resolved long ago to constantly try to improve myself on the spiritual level. If I do that, I will succeed in my life's work. I have concluded that the only reason the Creator endowed me with long life and an able body was so that I would be able to serve others. I ask in my prayers that I can be as old as I can get and not stop being of service.

To give you an idea of how the spirit works in my life, recently I developed an ailment that affected my sight. It was my fault—I'd neglected to take care of my eyes. My ophthalmologist told me maybe twenty-five years ago that I should really take better care of my eyes, that

I should be using eye drops. I didn't pay him any attention. He had just graduated from medical school and was trying to specialize in ophthalmology. We happened to be living in the same building. Well, he has never given me a bill when I go to have my eyes checked. The same secretary who has been with him for twenty-five years asked me, "Why does the doctor not charge you?"

I said, "I don't know. He won't charge me or any member of my family. Ask him." He doesn't give me a bill, even today.

She asked him. He said that I did him and his family a favor years ago when we were living in the same building. He said he would be forever grateful.

I don't know what I did, because I didn't have any money to give him; he was in a much better financial position than I was when we were living in the same building. His children grew up with my children. He still doesn't charge me any money. And it's not just me going there once or twice a year. That's a blessing. That's why I believe we reap what we sow. Whatever it is I did, he never forgot, he's paying me back.

So I finally had this operation on my eyes at the time of the release of the *Planet Drum* CD. I collaborated with Mickey Hart and six other musicians and we all shared in the success of it. Being able to play four drums on a tour of twelve cities without being able to see was, to me, a spiritual experience.

Many times when I felt that I was in a hopeless situation, others have guided and helped me. At the last minute, the way is opened and the problem is solved. For example, in 1990 I was planning to take a giant step and become a promoter, someone who introduced new acts. I loved performing, but I was asking myself, "How much longer will I have the strength?" So I wrote a proposal and took it to the Nigerian government. In it I said that I had had marvelous experiences over the years presenting groups—for example, in 1959 I was a consultant to the First African Ballet. Now I wanted to do something for Nigeria. At my suggestion, the National Company was put together, but I was excluded once again. I was not called upon to help put it together. I said, "Give me the chance to use my years of experience for you." To my great surprise, senior government officials gave some else the opportunity to produce the show—someone with no knowledge of show business. So of course, the show was a failure. They never consulted me.

But I didn't give up. I turned to another country, and in an unbelievable turn of events, without any expectations, I was given the opportunity to produce, which I am pursuing now. This tells me that if you don't succeed at first, try, try, try again. The door will be opened for you if you knock, though many times it will not be in the way you expect. When things like that happen, I know that some force is working in my favor. Stay focused and concentrate all your energies on what you do and what you know you can do best. The results can be astonishing.

When I possibly can, I rise at 5:30 or 6:00. Every morning when I wake up, wherever I am, I sit on the edge of the bed for a few minutes and just tell myself how glad I am to be awake. Then I stand up and do my meditation. Usually this takes an hour and a half. I ask for that which is of the highest good to come to me that day. The next thing I do, because of my medical condition, is have a grapefruit and an orange before I go out to breakfast. I don't cook.

Then, if I have no appointments, the spirit leads me to my drums, and I pound out some rhythms that have come to me during the night. This has happened many times—I just repeat the rhythm over and over so that I will remember it when day breaks. This is a daily routine. And I read Psalm 91 every day, seven times. I read it as the Psalm of Protection.

This practice goes back to my childhood. I was brought up to understand how power can be used to help people and how it can corrupt as well. I learned what responsibility means when you are a leader—that your life is never your own again. I grew up watching the chief of the village totally involve himself in the lives of every villager. I observed how he delegated duties to others. This helped him manage village affairs. I saw him rise from bed sometimes three or four times in one night. Unless he was out of town on a pilgrimage or a visit to another village, he was required to greet the drummers every morning when they came to salute him and to ask after him. He had to peek through the window, wave to the drummers, and order them to be fed before they continued on to the market. I saw him get so caught up in the village's affairs that he had no time for anything else. All of this showed me what it meant to be of service to others. Nowadays, I cannot help but remember all of that in doing what I do. When anybody calls me, I know they need help, and you can bet your bottom dollar that I'm going to help out.

We have enough to take care of everybody on this planet; there is no doubt in my mind about that. We can be of tremendous help to one another, but we are behind in learning how to cope with the technology we have developed. If we are not careful, our so-called leaders will lead us into spiritual bankruptcy as human values gradually deteriorate and people continue to lose their reverence for life. My only fear is of that which paralyzes the soul, that which leads certain people to destroy others or make war against society, like in Waco or Oklahoma City. There are ways you can tell when people are not happy with their lives. We should learn to read those signs, and help them solve their spiritual problems while there is still time.

What makes me uneasy about the future is that we are not electing the right people to govern. Most places in the world are run by people consumed with political and material greed. And those people are training future generations to undermine one another, teaching them to compete unfairly, to be so "smart" enough to disregard one another's needs so that they can "possess" more than they can ever use. I'm afraid that unless we go back to the driving energy that helped the founding fathers write a body of laws that placed limits on our selfishness, most people won't be able to handle the future.

But I also believe that the powers that run the universe will not allow its total destruction. The Creator will not allow that to happen, will not permit us to destroy ourselves. There have been so many real achievements just within my own lifetime, that something will happen for the best. So I believe. This is a demonstration of hope; I keep the faith that good shall triumph over evil. The Creator has made us for a purpose, and that purpose is to be of service, and to improve the world we see around us, and to develop to a much higher level of consciousness.

What is broken in our lives is the connection that makes us feel like we are one. That thread has been snapped. It is not easy to spin that thread again, to recover that insight. It is a lifetime job. It is a labor I need to carry out all over the world. We must change our educational system so that young people will be able to learn how to use their tools, their hands, especially through hand drumming. Because whatever we put in the most reliable computer, our brain, the hand delivers it. The hand is a very important tool.

Destruction is easier than construction. That is why we tell young people, "Drums, not guns." Let them use their hands to beat on the drum instead of taking their frustrations out on one another. By the time they play the drum for an hour, they're going to be calm.

If schools would only teach drumming to all the children in their community, they would soon develop a community action group. They will have developed a community that can come together during crisis and find solutions. They will have developed young men and women who can use the power of the drum to mobilize people. And those young people will grow into good parents because they have a sense of belonging to a community that is pulling in one direction, a direction they all know. They will all know from experience with drumming that unless you act *together*, there will be discord. They will feel discord when they are not living their lives together.

There is no doubt in my mind that if we taught all our children drumming, within a generation or two, we would be able to identify what is going wrong in our society, and come together and solve those problems. Drums will help our young people develop a unity of purpose. Once they have that, they will be able to develop positive programs of action.

Unless children feel committed to their community, how can they help that community? They can learn to commit themselves through drumming. By coming together to drum, to chant, to dance, to sing, they will produce a community that knows how to take action to resolve problems between members of the community or between communities.

And beyond that, they will learn that rhythm is the soul of life. Everything we do, we do in rhythm—there is no escape from it. And this is true of everyone. Stand on a street corner and watch people walking, and you will notice they are all walking in rhythm, even though their styles are different. Some will be keeping the left arm to the side and swinging the right arm constantly. Others will be swinging both arms and swaying at the hips. Everybody is in rhythm, and when we get out of rhythm, that is when we become diseased. So the earlier we start young people understanding what can come out of drumming together, the more likely it is we will achieve great results, universal results. If we can accomplish that, we will be able to solve other problems that are not only local but also global.

The greatest gift I have been given is the gift of my voice. It's unbelievable what people have written to me in letters. I have loads and loads of letters that people have sent me, telling me what it has done to them to hear my voice, or listen to my words, and how their contact with me has profoundly changed the way they feel and how they think. Even little children—and I do a lot of work with children. Without fail, I children tell me, "Would you like to be my other dad?"

I say, "Go and ask your father."

He says, "Yeah, Babatunde can be your other father, your African father."

Around the country, in Canada, everywhere I go, I have kids like that coming to me: "I want you to be my other father."

"Sure—now I am your African father."

They're amazing, these boys and girls. They draw what I look like on stage. One of them came to me on stage one time and said, "I didn't know you weren't six feet tall."

I said, "It's the way I stand behind my drums and raise my hand to play." They think I'm six feet tall. I'm only five foot seven.

They say, "That's all right. From where I see you on the stage, I'll draw you so big." Fascinating things like that happen.

It's time this kind of activity began, especially with the young, because unless we start them early, they're likely to become stubborn enough to reject community action. Start them early enough, and they'll know the importance and significance of drumming together and using what they learn from it to enhance community programs. They'll be able to understand why those programs are necessary. These young people will become responsible members of the community. People who *want* to serve to their community will be helping the entire world.

I'm so grateful that interest in Africa has revived as a result of exchanges between different performing groups from Africa and from the United States and South America in the past twenty years. Our group is proud we were the first ones bold enough to teach women how to play the drums and to explore the healing aspect of the drum.

Day after day, I come across people who are newcomers in drum making, people who are interested in starting their own programs to work with children in this field. As we move around the country, touring colleges and universities, we are presenting programs that bring people at all levels together, programs that bring all the members of families, people of all ethnic backgrounds, and people of all religious faiths and affiliations together in a group that becomes nonsectarian, a group that becomes unified instantaneously as they play the drums. This gives me the unshakable faith that drumming, singing, dancing, and chanting will become one of the most powerful phenomena to help right the wrongs, heal the wounds, bridge the gaps that have existed between people all over the world.

Whatever we do from now on will determine how we will survive. I believe that His eye is on the sparrow and will continue to be. God is watching everything. Ajaja is the great spirit that we all shall one day become. That is the spirit through which the sun rises in the east and sets in the west. *Ajaja emi lo*—I am that spirit, you are that spirit, we are that spirit.

Afterword

Robert Atkinson

On April 6, 2003, we lost a global village elder. Tradition says that when this happens, we lose a vast library. We do have Baba's story in his own words here, but there is much more that we don't have. Baba's seventy-six years were intertwined with those of world leaders, civil rights leaders, and musicians of many genres. The vision he shared is rooted in the rich Yoruba culture and is expressed in his words, "the brotherhood of mankind, of men, women, and children, young and old." His life taught him that "if this were something that was promoted, encouraged, introduced into our educational system beginning from kindergarten, this would be a wonderful world to live in. People would be able to realize their inner strengths and fulfill the purposes for which we were created."

Wherever he went, his drumming, his words, and his own spirit touched and influenced countless people. I am fortunate to have had the opportunity to listen to Baba's inspiring life story in its entirety in his presence, and to have recorded it for others to experience. How this came about is part of the central thread of his story as well as mine.

I was just beginning high school out on eastern Long Island when Drums of Passion, a totally new, different, and unique sound, burst onto the music scene. I was already into folk music and doo wop, but Baba was my introduction to music from Africa. It was so vibrant and powerful that it never left my awareness or my interest.

Long after I had earned a master's degree in American folk culture, and a doctorate in cross-cultural human development, and after I had expanded my world view—in part through my own travels to Africa and other parts of the world—I ran into Baba at a conference in 1992 I was attending and where he was performing. I was extremely pleased to see him, hear his music again, and witness his spirit as well as his special message.

Recognizing that he was approaching seventy, that he had a fascinating and unusual life to tell about, and that he had a vital message to share with the world, I went up to him afterwards, introduced myself, and asked him if he had thought about writing his autobiography. I mentioned that I was director of the Center for the Study of Lives at the University of Southern Maine, that I had written several books on life storytelling, that the center's archive had about four hundred life stories in it, and that I could help him tell his story, if he would be interested in that.

I must have said or done something right, because to my surprise and delight, he took me up on my offer, with very few questions asked and with total confidence in me—something for which I will be forever grateful.

Between April 1993 and June 1998, I had the distinct and unique honor of listening to and recording Baba's entire life story, from his traditional Yoruba upbringing to his vision for Voices of Africa. Literally at the feet of the master, I heard a story that no one else in this world today could tell, totally transfixed and visualizing his vivid images.

My intent was to help him tell and write his autobiography in his own voice and words. We would meet in Portland, Maine, where I lived, or in Providence, Rhode Island, halfway between us, and spend a few days recording his life story, bit by bit. I would transcribe what I had, and then we would meet again for more of his story. After amassing more than forty hours of tapes, and after a long process of transcribing his words—entirely his own words—and putting them in narrative form, the first draft was given to the publishers. They wanted some additions and revisions. It took us nearly three more years to complete these, because of Baba's health problems, his trips to Africa, his performances, and scheduling problems. We got the revised manuscript back to the publisher in August 2002, just before I took off on a Semester at Sea voyage around the world for three months. When I got back, we both were eager to get the book out. The publisher told us in January that it would have a publication schedule by the end of April. Baba didn't quite make it that long.

He spent his final months at the Esalen Institute in Big Sur, California, a setting where he had presented dozens of workshops and performances over the years. The administration, including the Board of Trustees, wanted to ensure that Baba had a supportive and caring home there. He became the elder "teacher in residence"—a title that meant a great deal to him, because he knew it came with respect. Esalen was a place where he could recuperate and rest, but also honor those who honored him. David Price, the institute's general manager, exemplified the truly reciprocal relationship that the Esalen family shared with Baba, who played a key role in the christening of David's son.

Many people at Esalen took an interest in caring for Baba, especially Maryann Will, a staff member who is also a nurse. Other volunteers were always available to help Baba meet his many health needs, which included twice-weekly dialysis treatments. Notable among those who helped him were Leon Ryan, son of Gordy Ryan, one of Baba's drummers, Nora Arjuna, and Stefan Gunter, a chiropractor, who closed his practice for a month to assist Baba in a number of ways. Stefan remembers Baba's last weeks, even up to his last days, as a time when, with multiple health issues draining him, Baba always tried to push forward with his projects. Although his body was weak, his spirit shone forth with enthusiasm and vitality. He spoke in March about playing for the annual Esalen Fourth of July event, as he had done previously. Baba was happy to be at Esalen; everyone who provided for him there must have reminded him of the community he knew as a child in Ajido.

There were three Memorial Services for Baba: one in Marin Country, organized by Mickey Hart; one at Esalen, put together by his adopted family there; and one organized by his immediate family, at the Riverside Church in New York City.

At the Riverside Church, to an overflowing audience of family, friends, associates, and others touched by his life, the third generation of Olatunji children offered their tribute to their grandfather: "You became the glue that held us together. We have grown to carry on the rich tradition."

The Reverend Dr. James A. Forbes, Jr., of the Riverside Church, presided, and in his eulogy offered an inspired and insightful overview of

Baba's life. He said, in part: "His spirit has escaped to become a member of the Council of Òrìsàs. As you think of Baba, think of these four things: ministry, music, movement, and message. Whether one resonates with his music is a way to tell if one is dead or alive. People who are touched by his drums and his voice will come to know that all of life is sacred . . . We are all one tribe . . . We must love all the children of the world."

From his memorial service, it was clear that Baba's legacy is about peace, love, and unity. In his last published interview, two months before his passing, when asked if he had one message to give to the world, he said: "Love one another, this is the greatest of all laws. The world will forever be without peace if it is without love, indiscriminate love. Coltrane calls it 'Love Supreme.' You don't wait until things get good to come closer. Love is not a possession, it is not about what you get. Love is a lifetime process. Love is the most important thing."

Baba's story as we have it here is his story, told from his perspective, in his voice. Other people might tell his story differently, from their own perspectives. But their stories would not be Baba's story. This natural, normal phenomenon of different people seeing—and telling—the same things differently is both the bane and the benefit of autobiography. Some of these differences might be considered differences of opinion or interpretation by some, or even errors of fact by others. We have been very careful in trying to identify what may have been factual errors, but this is, after all, Baba's story as he sees it and remembers it. Since Baba is no longer able to have a say in this matter of differences, his account of how events in his life unfolded, and his interpretations of those events, remains intact. And this is as it needs to be. If there are what some might see as exaggerations in his story, these are not only part of his voice, part of his perspective, but also essential ingredients in his storytelling, *and* what make Baba who he is, while solidifying his personal myth. Dr. Akiwowo has been especially helpful in navigating this delicate process of editing Baba's life story, as well as in many other ways.

Others I would like to thank for their role in supporting this project, not already mentioned here, are: Shelley Roth, Paul Skiff, Bill Krasilovsky, Randy Armstrong, Folasade Olatunji Olusekun, Modupe Olatunji Anuku, Della Flack, Elizabeth Lesser, John Werner, Bob Henriques, Ken Friedman, Jay Blakesberg, Daniel Bianchetta, Bill Weaver, Skip Mason, Phuong Baum, Eric Charry, Mickey Hart, Joan Baez, Mark Spector, Bernice Reagon, and Cynthia Atkinson.

Baba's place in history, his role as a legitimate elder tradition bearer for a very large diaspora of people of African heritage, is secure. Yet some may criticize him for a lack of authenticity, for not being born into the lineage of drummers from his village. (There have actually been many elder tradition bearers who not only were not born into the tradition they chose to carry on, but who also picked that tradition up later in life.) Baba was born into a lineage of chiefs, and sacrificed his political position of honor in his community for one of promoting his people's cultural heritage. Tradition is more a commitment than a lineage. Baba's lifelong commitment to learning and carrying on traditional drumming began at a very young age.

There have also been many tradition bearers who were innovators. Baba's commitment to being an ambassador of his own cultural heritage was always coupled with his vision that his village was more global than local. As his fishing village in coastal Nigeria became too small for him, the world became his village. The foundation of his strong and rich Yoruba tradition and the innovations he built on this, are both essential to, and what made possible, his unique and significant contribution to world music. He carried on his own tradition while innovating and developing his music for the benefit of all.

What was perhaps even more important in all of this was his heart. He took in everything, and he made everything part of him. He saw everything—and everyone—as part of one whole, each part as important as any other. He had the greatest respect for the collective, as well as for the individual. I felt this every moment I was with him. Baba's greatest commitment was an all-embracing love for people. With every step he took beyond the village, humanity became his family. This may have been to the detriment of those closest to him, but this is who he was, this is what he lived for.

His vision will long outlive his life, as well as ours. Baba will be remembered by many, for many things, beyond his drumming, beyond his role as Africa's pioneer cultural ambassador. As much as for anything else, he deserves to be remembered for his role as a political activist in the Civil Rights Movement before it even was a movement. Three years before Rosa Parks sat for integration on her Montgomery bus, Baba, as a student leader at Morehouse College, with a few other students, challenged the Jim Crow laws by refusing to sit in the back of the bus. This contribution to the struggle for freedom and civil rights was as significant to the movement as any other nonviolent civil disobedience.

Less than a decade later, Baba and his music were in great demand by everyone from all parts of the movement. One of his proudest moments was when he carried the placard at the UN protest after the Sharpeville massacre in 1960. That placard read: "We insist that South Africa be ousted from the UN."

His mission—cultural understanding, human rights, civil rights, and social justice—and his message—one Spirit, unity of purpose—were his life. Voices of Africa, his most ambitious effort to help heal the sick and lessen the gap between the rich and poor, is yet to be fulfilled. Baba was as much a visionary as Dr. Martin Luther King, Jr.

In concert halls all over America, and the world, Babatunde Olatunji and his Drums of Passion singers and dancers have led their procession toward the stage as the audience gives their warm, cheering approval in time with the rhythm of the drums. The long invocation comes to an end, and Baba speaks from the stage: "Let us give thanks for this beautiful day. That was Ajaja, the only spirit, the highest spirit that you and I can become, and we struggle so hard, we work so hard, without even realizing that there is only one spirit that rules the whole universe of ours. Can you imagine? The spirit that allows the sun to rise in the east, and set in the west. We are that One Spirit! That realization can become true to every one of us . . ."

Will his performing group continue to spread the music and culture of the Yoruba and African people? There will be thousands of musicians, drummers, friends, and appreciative fans who will carry on his spirit, and the spirit of the drum. Yet his importance and influence goes well beyond the vast drumming circle that emerged around him, and around the world.

Who will carry on his Voices of Africa work, to bring African artists together to help alleviate illiteracy, poverty, and poor health in Africa? Humanitarian aid to Africa is still a critical need, and may be for many more generations. The efforts of individuals can make a significant difference, but greatest in meeting these essential needs is a unified global effort.

Will there be an African Cultural Center in every major city in the country? With thousands of African refugees and immigrants resettling in many American cities, this vision, this effort that Baba pioneered, may one day be realized as more people of African heritage discover the importance of preserving and carrying on their culture here. This is already beginning to happen; many are acting on this need, and in their own ways fulfilling Baba's dream.

Index

Riverside Church (New York City), 239
Roach, Max, 2, 7, 8, 194, 196–97
Robbins, Warren, 185
Robinson, Jackie, 179
Rockefeller Foundation, 172–73
Rollins, Sonny, 5
Roosevelt, Eleanor, 9
Rotary Education Foundation, of Atlanta,
  Georgia, 84–85, 103–4; and Rotary
  Club, 91
Roulette Records, 200
Ryan, Gordy, 14, 239
Ryan, Leon, 239

Sakara, 87–88
Sanders, Pharoah, 11
Sanders, Roger "Montego Joe," 4, 12, 16, 140
Santamaria, Mongo, 5, 198
Santana, 8; and Santana, Carlos, 208–9
Sapele, Nigeria, 82–83, 85
Sarnoff, Morton, 188
Seeger, Pete, 188
Senghor, Léopold, 18
Shakespeare, 36
Shakur, Tupac, 4
Shango (God of Thunder and Lightning), 33,
  132, 148, 149, 202. See also Yoruba
Sharpeville massacre (South Africa),
  167, 241
Silver, Horace, 194, 196–97
Simms, Zoot, 196
Simone, Nina, 197
Southern Baptist Convention, 78
Southern Christian Leadership Conference,
  130, 176, 180
Soyinka, Wole, 18
Spelman College, 92–93, 109, 112, 115, 117,
  118, 121, 178
Spirit possession. See Possession, spirit
Student Nonviolent Coordinating Committee
  (SNCC), 130, 157, 165, 166, 176, 177
Sullivan, Ed, 133, 137, 149
Sullivan, Louis W., 119
Sun Ra, 5

Tanglewood Music Festival, 117
Taylor, Billy, 190
Taylor, Elizabeth, 133
Terry, Clark, 199, 200
Thant, U, 203
Tutu, Desmond, 167

Twain, Mark, 93

UNICEF, 131–32
United Jewish Appeal, 167, 176
Unity, cultural basis for, 42, 138, 190, 235

Village Gate, 3
Village Vanguard, 7
Vinayakram, Vikkui, 209
Vismeel, Calvin and Mary, 125–26, 139
Voices of Africa, 17, 220–22, 224, 228, 238, 242

Wagner, Robert, 196
Walker, Helena, 140
Warren, Guy, 4, 5
Washington (Aug. 1963), March on, 179–80
Wein, George, 196, 205
Weisiger, Kendall, 93, 95, 103–4, 106, 230
West African Pilot, 80, 164
Westerfield, Dr. Samuel, 171
Weston, Randy, 5, 7, 8, 11–12, 194, 196–97
Whalum, Dr. Wendell, 111, 118
Wilcox, Ella, 204
Wiles, Olukose, 13
Wilkins, Roy, 130, 166
Will, Maryann, 239
Williams, Andy, 154
Williams, G. Mennen, 185
Wilson, Sule Greg, 11, 13
Winding, Kai, 7
Wolfson, Michael, 189
Woodstock, N.Y., 34
World Saxophone Quartet, 11
Wright, Herb, 166
Wright, Ray, 132–33

YMCA, 91, 99–100, 108
Yoruba, 3, 4, 6, 16–17; culture and tradition,
  30, 32, 43, 45–46, 50–51, 55, 57, 64, 67,
  147, 148, 198–99, 216, 232, 238, 241–42;
  language, 44, 81, 151, 187; musicians,
  categories of, 39; names of God, 45–46, 59;
  opican (historian), 39; religion, 45–46, 48,
  59, 77–79; rhythms, 33, 38, 199; ritual,
  37–38, 66–67; songs and stories, 39, 46–50,
  117, 132, 213; spirits of the ancestors
  (Òrìsà), 33, 240; village life, 50–58
Young, Snooky, 199–200

Zannu, father of Babatunde, 53
Zikist youth movement, 164